critical essays

T0351433

THE FRENCH LIST

critical essays

(Situations I)

JEAN-PAUL SARTRE

TRANSLATED BY CHRIS TURNER

LONDON NEW YORK CALCUTTA

Seagull Books 2010

Situations I. Essais critiques.
© Editions GALLIMARD, Paris, 1947

English translation © Chris Turner 2010

First published in English by Seagull Books, 2010

ISBN-13   978 1 9064 9 760 6

British Library Cataloguing-in-Publication Data
A catalogue record for this book is available
from the British Library

Typeset by Seagull Books, Calcutta, India
Printed and bound Hyam Enterprises, Calcutta, India

contents

Sartoris *by* *William Faulkner*

Once a certain time has elapsed, good novels come to seem almost like natural phenomena. We forget that they have authors; we accept them like stones or trees, because they are there, because they exist. *Light in August* was a hermetic object of this kind, a mineral substance. We do not accept *Sartoris* and that is what makes it so precious. It is a book in which Faulkner shows himself; we see throughout the evidence of his handiwork, his artifice. I understand now the mainspring of his art: underhandedness. Admittedly, all art is underhanded. A painting lies about perspective. Yet there are paintings that are true and there are *trompe-l'oeil* paintings.

I had accepted the 'man' of *Light in August* uncritically (I thought of him as Faulknerian man, the way one says Dostoevskian or Meredithian man)—that great, divine, godless animal, doomed from birth and bent eagerly on his own destruction; cruel, moral even in murder, and redeemed not by death or in death, but by the last moments before death; and great even in torment and in the most abject humiliations of the flesh. I had not forgotten his lofty, threatening tyrant's face, nor his unseeing eyes. I found him again in *Sartoris*; I recognized the 'gloomy arrogance' of Bayard. And yet I can no longer accept Faulknerian man: he is the stuff of *trompe-l'oeil*. It is all done with lighting. There is a formula, and it consists in not saying, in keeping secret, underhandedly secret—in saying *a little*. We are told, stealthily, that old Bayard is shattered by the unexpected return of his grandson. Stealthily, in a half-sentence that might well pass unnoticed, and which the author hopes will pass *almost* unnoticed. After which, when we are expecting storms, we are instead shown banal little actions, at length and in minute detail. Faulkner isn't unaware of our impatience; he is relying on it, but he goes on with his innocent chatter about insignificant action. There have been other chatterers: the Realists or Dreiser.[1] But Dreiser's descriptions are pedagogical in intent; they have documentary value. Here the actions (putting on boots, climbing a staircase, jumping on a horse) are intended not to depict, but to conceal. We are on the lookout for the one that will betray Bayard's distress, but the Sartorises never get carried away; they never betray themselves through actions. Yet these idols, whose actions seem like threatening rituals, also possess consciousness. They speak, they have their own thoughts, they feel emotion. Faulkner knows this. From time to time, he carelessly reveals a consciousness to us. But this is like a conjuror showing us his box when it is empty. What do we see? No more than we could see from the outside: actions. Or we catch off-guard consciousnesses sliding towards sleep. And then, once again, there are actions—tennis, piano-playing, whisky, conversation. And here is what I cannot accept: the entire intention is to persuade us that these consciousnesses are still as empty, still as elusive.

Why? Because consciousness is a too-human thing. The Aztec gods do not engage in pleasant little conversations among themselves. But Faulkner knows perfectly well that consciousnesses are not and *cannot* be empty. He knows it well enough to write: '. . . she again held her consciousness submerged deliberately, as you hold a puppy underwater until its struggles cease.'[2]

But what there is *in* this consciousness that needs to be drowned he doesn't tell us. It is not exactly that he wants to hide it from us: he would like us to divine it, because divination makes whatever it touches magical. And the actions begin once again. We would like to say 'Too many actions', the way they said 'too many notes' to Mozart. Too many words too. Faulkner's volubility, his abstract, haughty, anthropomorphic preacher's style—these too are all optical illusions. The style paints the daily gestures too thickly, weighs them down, overwhelms them with an epic magnificence and sinks them like lead weights. Deliberately so. It is precisely this sickening, solemn monotony, this ritual of the everyday that Faulkner has in his sights; actions are the world of boredom. These rich people, respectable and uneducated, having neither work nor leisure, captive on their own lands and simultaneously masters and slaves to their negroes, are bored; they try to fill up the time with their actions. But this boredom (has Faulkner always managed to differentiate that of his heroes from that of his readers?), is merely an appearance; it is Faulkner's defence against us, and the Sartorises' against themselves. The boredom is the social order; it is the monotonous languor of all that can be seen, heard, touched: Faulkner's landscapes are as bored as his characters. The real drama lies *behind*— behind the boredom, behind the actions, behind the characters' consciousness. Suddenly, from the depths of this drama, the Deed wells up, like a meteorite. A Deed—at last something that *happens*, a message. But Faulkner disappoints us again. He rarely describes Deeds. This is because he comes up against an old problem of novelistic technique and sidesteps it: Deeds are the real stuff of the novel; they are prepared for with care and then, when they occur, they are bare and polished as bronze. They are infinitely simple and slip between our fingers. There is nothing more to be said about them; it is enough, one might say, simply to name them. Faulkner doesn't name them, doesn't speak of them and hence suggests they are unnameable, beyond language. He will show only their results: an old man dead in his chair, a car overturned in the river and two feet sticking out of the water. These still, violent consequences, as solid and compact as the Deed is elusive, appear and display themselves, definitive and inexplicable amid the fine, steady rain of daily actions. Later, these unfathomable instances of violence will change into 'stories': they will be named, explained, recounted. All these people, all these families have their stories. The Sartorises carry the heavy burden of two wars, of two sets of stories: the Civil War, in which old Bayard died, and the 1914 War, in which John Sartoris was killed. The stories appear and disappear, passing from mouth to mouth, lingering on alongside the daily actions. They do not belong entirely to the past, but are, rather, a super-present:

> As usual, old man Falls had brought John Sartoris into the room with him . . . Freed as he was of time and flesh, he was a far more palpable presence than either of the other two old men who sat shouting periodically into one another's deafness.[3]

6

They make up the poetry of the present and its fatedness: 'fatal immortality and immortal fatality'. It is with stories that Faulkner's heroes forge their destinies: by way of these fine, carefully polished tales, sometimes embellished by many generations, an unnameable, long-buried Deed signals to other Deeds, charming and attracting them as a sharp point attracts lightning. Such is the insidious power of words and stories; and yet Faulkner doesn't believe in these incantations:

> What had been a hare-brained prank of two heedless and reckless boys wild with their own youth had become a gallant and finely tragical focal point to which the history of the race had been raised . . . by two angels valiantly fallen and strayed, altering the course of human events . . .[4]

He is never entirely taken in. He knows what these tales are worth since he is the one telling them, since he is, like Sherwood Anderson, 'a storyteller and a liar'. Only he dreams of a world in which stories would be believed, where they would really have effects on people: and his novels depict the world he dreams of. We are familiar with the 'technique of disorder' of *The Sound and the Fury* and *Light in August*, those inextricable tangles of past and present. I think I have found the twofold origin of this in *Sartoris*: it is, on the one hand, the irresistible need to tell a tale, to stop the most urgent action in order to bring in a story—this seems to me a characteristic feature of many lyrical novelists—and, on the other, the semi-sincere, semi-imagined faith in the magical power of stories. But when he writes *Sartoris* he has not yet perfected his technique. He shifts between past and present, between action and stories with a great deal of clumsiness.

Here, then, is the human being Faulkner presents us with, and wants us to accept. He is wholly elusive; one can grasp him neither in his actions, which are a facade, nor in his stories, which are false, nor in his Deeds, which are indescribable flashes of lightning. And yet beyond behaviour and words, beyond empty consciousness, the human being exists: we sense a genuine drama about him, a sort of intelligible quality that explains everything. But what is this quality? A taint of breeding or family flaw, an Adlerian inferiority complex or repressed libido? At times it is one, at times another: it depends on the stories and the characters. Often, Faulkner doesn't tell us. And besides, he isn't much concerned with this: what matters to him is, rather, the *nature* of this new creature, a nature that is, first and foremost, *poetic* and magical, the contradictions of which are manifold, but veiled. Grasped through psychical manifestations, this 'nature' (for what else can we call it?) is part of psychical existence; it is not, in fact, entirely of the order of the unconscious, since it often seems the human beings impelled by it can turn around and contemplate it. But, on the other hand, it is fixed and changeless, like a curse. Faulkner's heroes carry it with them from birth; it is as stubborn as stone or rock; it is *a thing*. A spirit-thing, a solidified, opaque spirit behind consciousness, shadows whose essence is, nonetheless, light. This is the supreme magical object. Faulkner's creatures are bewitched, a stifling atmosphere of sorcery surrounds them. And this is what I referred to as underhandedness: these bewitchments are not possible. Nor even conceivable. And so Faulkner is at pains not to let us conceive them. But his whole method consists in suggesting them.

Is he entirely underhanded? I don't believe so. Or if he lies, he does so to himself. A curious passage in

Sartoris provides us with the key to his lies and to his sincerity:

> 'Your Arlens and Sabatinis talk a lot, and nobody ever had more to say and more trouble saying it than old Dreiser.'

> 'But they have secrets,' she explained. 'Shakespeare doesn't have any secrets. He tells everything.'

> 'I see. Shakespeare had no sense of discrimination and no instinct for reticence. In other words, he wasn't a gentleman,' he suggested.

> 'Yes . . . that's what I mean.'

> 'And so, to be a gentleman, you must have secrets.'

> 'Oh, you make me tired.'

This is an ambiguous and, no doubt, ironic dialogue. Narcissa is not very clever and, besides, Michael Arlen and Sabatini are bad writers. Yet it seems to me Faulkner reveals much of himself here. If Narcissa is, perhaps, somewhat lacking in literary taste, her instinct is sound when it causes her to opt for Bayard, a man with secrets. Horace Benbow is perhaps right to like Shakespeare, but he is weak and garrulous; he says everything, he is not a man. The men Faulkner likes, the negro in *Light in August*, Bayard Sartoris and the father in *Absolom* have secrets; they remain silent.

I dare say Faulkner's humanism is the only acceptable sort: he hates our well-adjusted, babbling, engineers' minds. But does he not know that his great, dark figures are mere exteriors? Is he fooled by his own art? To him, it would probably not be enough for our secrets to be repressed into the unconscious; he yearns for a total darkness at the heart of consciousness, a total darkness we would ourselves fashion within ourselves. Silence. Silence outside us, silence within—this is the impossible dream of a Puritan ultra-Stoicism. Is he lying to us? What does he do when he is on his own? Does he put up with the endless babbling of his all-too-human consciousness? To have an answer, we should have to know him.

February 1938

Notes

1 Theodore Dreiser (1871–1945): perhaps the most prominent novelist of the American 'Naturalist' school. [Trans.]

2 William Faulkner, *Sartoris* (New York: The New American Library, 1963), p. 133. Sartre gives few references to the material he cites. Where possible, I have added these myself and they appear simply as endnotes. Where I have added *explanatory* notes, these are marked '[Trans.]'.

3 Ibid., p. 1.

4 Ibid., p. 33.

On John Dos Passos and **1919**

A novel is a mirror. Everyone says so. But what is it to *read* a novel? I believe that it is to jump into the mirror. Suddenly, you find yourself through the looking-glass, among people and objects that seem familiar. But this is simply an appearance; in fact we have never seen them before. And the things in our world are now external in their turn and have become mere reflections. You close the book, climb back over the rim of the mirror and re-enter *this* honest-to-goodness world, and you are back with furniture, gardens and people who have nothing to say to you. The mirror that has reconsituted itself behind you reflects them peacefully. After which you would swear that art is a reflection. And the cleverest will go so far as to speak of distorting mirrors. Dos Passos uses this absurd, obstinate illusion very consciously to prick us into revolt. He has done the needful for his novel to appear a mere reflection; he has even donned the dowdy garb of populism. But the fact is that his art is not gratuitous; he has something to prove. Yet consider what a curious enterprise this is: the aim is to show us *this* world, our world. To *show* it only, with no explanation or commentary. No revelations about the police's double-dealings, the oil barons' imperialism or the Ku Klux Klan. And no cruel depictions of poverty. Everything he wants to show us is something we have already seen—and seen, as it initially seems, in just the way he wants to make us see it. We immediately recognize the sad abundance of these untragic lives. They are our lives, these thousand adventures sketched out, botched, immediately forgotten, but constantly begun again, which slide by without a trace, without ever connecting with anything, until the day when suddenly one of them, just like all the others, as though out of clumsiness and trickery, sickens a man forever and carelessly throws a machinery out of kilter. It is by depicting—as we ourselves could depict them—these all too well-known phenomena, which everyone normally accepts, that Dos Passos renders them unbearable. He infuriates those who have never been infuriated before, he frightens those who are frightened of nothing. Has there not perhaps been some sleight of hand here? I look around me and see people, cities, ships, warfare. But they aren't the real thing: they are discreetly suspect and sinister, as in nightmares. My indignation against that world also seems suspect. It merely *resembles* that other indignation, the indignation a little story in the newspaper can arouse—and it does so rather remotely. I am on the other side of the mirror.

Dos Passos' hatred, despair and lofty contempt are genuine. But for just that reason, his world is not: it is a creation. I know of none, not even those of Faulkner or Kafka, in which the art is greater or better concealed. I know of none closer to us, more precious, more affecting. This is because he takes his material from our world. And yet there is no world further removed from our own or stranger. Dos Passos has invented only one thing: an art of storytelling. But that is enough to create a whole universe.

We live in time and it is in time that we count. The novel unfolds in the present, the way that life does. Only in appearance is the past preterite the tense of the novel; we have to see it as a present *with aesthetic distance*, a staging device. In a novel, matters are not settled once and for all, for human beings in novels are free. They create themselves before our eyes; our impatience, our ignorance and our expectation are the same as the hero's. By contrast, Fernandez[1] has shown that pure *narrative* is situated in the past. But narrative explains: there, chronological order, the order of life, barely conceals the causal order, the order of the understanding. Events in narrative do not move us; they are located mid-way between fact and law. Dos Passos' time is his own creation: it is neither novel, nor narrative. It is rather, if you will, historical time. The past tenses are not employed to conform to the rules: the *reality* of Joe's or Eveline's adventures is that they are now past. The whole is narrated as if someone were remembering:

> *The years Dick was little*, he never heard anything about his Dad . . .[2] All Eveline thought

16

about *that winter* was going to the Art Insti-
tute . . .[3] They waited two weeks in Vigo
while the official quarrelled about their status
and they got pretty fed up with it.[4]

The event in a novel is an unnamed presence: you
cannot say anything about it because it is unfolding;
we can be shown two men looking all around a city
for their mistresses, but we are not told that they
'don't find them', because that is not how it is: so long
as there is still a street, a cafe or a house to explore,
that is not how it is *yet*. With Dos Passos, we begin
with the event being named. The die is cast, as in our
memories:

Glen and Joe only got ashore for a few hours
and couldn't find Marcelline and Loulou.[5]

The facts have a clear outline to them; they are
just ripe for *thinking about*. But Dos Passos never
thinks about them. Not for a moment do we catch
the order of causes beneath the order of dates. This
is not narrative: it is the jerky unwinding of a raw
memory full of holes, which sums up a period of several years in a few words, then lingers languidly over
some tiny fact. In this it is just like our real memories,
a jumble of frescoes and miniatures. There is no lack

of relief, but it is artfully distributed at random. One step further and we would be back at the famous idiot's monologue in *The Sound and the Fury*. But that would still be to intellectualize, to suggest an explanation in terms of the irrational, to hint at a Freudian order behind this disorder. Dos Passos halts himself in time. As a result of which, past facts retain a savour of the present. They remain, in their exile, what they once were for a day, a single day: inexplicable tumults of colour, noise and passion. Each event is a—gleaming, solitary—*thing* that doesn't ensue from any other, but emerges suddenly and adds itself to other things. It is irreducible. For Dos Passos, storytelling is an act of addition. Hence this loose air to his style: 'and . . . and . . . and . . .' The great tumultous phenomena—war, love, a political movement or a strike—fade and crumble into an infinity of little trifles that one can just place side by side. Here is the Armistice:

> In early November rumours of an armistice began to fly around and then suddenly one afternoon Major Wood ran into the office that Eleanor and Eveline shared and dragged them both away from their desks and kissed them both and shouted, 'At last it's come.'

Before she knew it, Eveline found herself kissing Major Moorehouse right on the mouth. The Red Cross office turned into a college dormitory on the night of a football victory: It was the Armistice.

Everybody seemed suddenly to have bottles of cognac and to be singing. *There's a long long trail awinding* or *La Madel-lon pour nous n'est pas sévère.*[6]

These Americans see war the way Fabrice del Dongo saw the battle of Waterloo.[7] And the intention, like the method, is clear when one thinks about it. But one must first close the book and reflect.

Passions and actions are also things. Proust analysed them, connected them to previous states and, as a consequence, rendered them necessary. Dos Passos wants to preserve their *factual* character. We can only say, 'At that time Richard was like this, and at another time he was different.' Love and decisions are great self-contained spheres. At best we can grasp a kind of *match-up* between psychological state and external situation: something like a colour harmony. Perhaps, too, we will suspect that explanations are *possible*. But they seem frivolous and futile, like a spider's web lying on heavy red flowers. Nowhere, however, do we have the sense of novelistic freedom. Rather Dos Passos forces on us the unpleasant impression of an indeterminacy of detail. Acts, emotions and ideas settle suddenly upon a character, make their nests and then fly off, without the character himself having much to do with it. We should not say that he *undergoes* these things; he registers them, and no one can say what law governs their appearance.

Yet they did exist. This lawless past is irremediable. In his storytelling Dos Passos deliberately chose the perspective of history: he wants to make us feel that the die is cast. In *Man's Hope*, Malraux says, more or less, that the tragic thing about death is that it 'transforms life into fate'.[8] From the first lines of his book, Dos Passos has settled into death. All the existences he retraces have closed upon themselves. They are like those Bergsonian memories that float around, after the death of the body, full of shouts and smells and light, in some sort of limbo. We have a constant sense of these vague, humble lives as Destinies. Our own pasts are not like this: there is not one of our past acts whose value and meaning we could not still transform today. But, beneath their violent hues, these fine, gaily coloured objects Dos Passos presents us with have something petrified about them. Their meaning is fixed. Close your eyes and try to remember your own life. Try to remember it like this. You will suffocate. It is this unrelieved suffocation Dos Passos has tried to express. In capitalist society, people do not have lives; they have only destinies. He doesn't say this anywhere, but he implies it everywhere. Discreetly and cautiously, he presses the point till he fills us with a desire to shatter our destinies. We are rebels now and his goal is achieved.

Rebels *behind the mirror*. For this isn't what the this-worldly rebel wants to change. He wants to change the *present* condition of human beings, the condition that evolves day by day. To relate the present in the past tense is to employ artifice, to create a strange and beautiful world, a world as rigid as one of those Mardi-Gras masks that become terrifying when real, live human beings wear them on their faces.

But what are these memories that are unreeled in this way throughout the novel? At first sight, it seems as though they are the memories of the heroes—of Joe, Dick, Daughter and Eveline. And, on more than one occasion, this is true. It is true as a general rule,

21

each time a character is sincere, each time he has a fullness in him of some sort or another:

> When he went off duty he'd walk home achingly tired through the strawberry-scented early Parisian morning, thinking of the faces and the eyes and the sweat-drenched hair and the clenched fingers clotted with blood and dirt . . .[9]

But often the narrator doesn't coincide entirely with the hero. The hero couldn't precisely have said what he says, but one feels a discreet complicity between the two; the narrator recounts things from outside in the way the hero would like them to have been recounted. Under cover of this complicity, without alerting us to the fact, Dos Passos has us make the transition he was trying for: we suddenly find ourselves inside a horrible memory, and every recollection in it makes us ill at ease. It is a memory in which we lose our bearings, being neither that of the characters nor of the author. It is like a chorus remembering—a sententious, yet complicit chorus:

> All the same he got along very well at school and the teachers liked him, particularly Miss Teazle, the English teacher, because he had

nice manners and said little things that weren't fresh, but that made them laugh. Miss Teazle said he showed a real feeling for English composition. One Christmas he sent her a little rhyme he made up about the Christ Child and the three Kings and she declared he had a gift.[10]

The narrative becomes a little stilted and everything we are told about the hero assumes the air of solemn, publicity-style information. 'She declared he had a gift.' There is no commentary on the sentence, but it acquires a kind of collective resonance. It is a *declaration.* And indeed, when we would like to know the thoughts of his characters, Dos Passos most often provides us, with respectful objectivity, with their declarations:

Fred . . . said the last night before they left he was going to tear loose. When they got to the front he might get killed and then what? Dick said he liked talking to the girls but that the whole business was too commercial and turned his stomach. Ed Shuyler, who'd been nicknamed Frenchie and was getting very continental in his ways, said that the street girls were too naïve.[11]

I open *Paris-Soir* and read: 'From our special correspondent: Charlie Chaplin says he has killed off the little tramp.' Now I have it: Dos Passos reports all his characters' words in the style of press statements. They are, as a result, immediately cut off from thought; they are pure words, simple reactions to be registered as such, after the fashion of the behaviourists, from whom Dos Passos takes occasional inspiration. But at the same time utterances assume a social importance: they are sacred, they become maxims. No matter what Dick had in his mind when he pronounced this sentence, thinks the satisfied chorus; all that matters is that it was pronounced. Besides, it came from way beyond him; it didn't form inside him. Even before he spoke, it was a high-sounding, ritualized noise; he merely lent it his power of assertion. It seems there is a celestial store of utterances and commonplaces from which each of us plucks the words appropriate to the situation. And a store of actions too. Dos Passos pretends to present us with actions as pure events, as mere *exteriors*, the free movements of an animal. But this is only a semblance: in relating them he actually adopts the standpoint of a chorus, of public opinion. Every one of Dick or Eleanor's actions is a public manifestation, accompanied by a low murmur of flattery:

> At Chantilly they went through the chateau and fed the big carp in the moat. They ate their lunch in the woods, sitting on rubber cushions. J. W. kept everybody laughing explaining how he hated picnics, asking everybody what it was that got into even the most intelligent women that they were always trying to make people go on picnics. After lunch they drove out to Senlis to see the houses that the Uhlans had destroyed there in the battle of the Marne.[12]

Isn't this like the account of a veterans' dinner reported in a local newspaper? At the same time as the action dwindles merely to a thin film, we suddenly realize that it *counts*, in the sense both that it commits the characters and is sacred. Sacred for whom? For the vile consciousness of 'everyone', for what Heidegger calls 'das Man'. But who brings this consciousness to life? Who represents it as I read? Why, I do. To understand the words, to give a meaning to the paragraphs, I first have to adopt the point of view of everyone's consciousness. I have to become the obliging chorus. That consciousness exists only through me; without me there would merely be black flecks on white sheets of paper. But at the very moment when I *am* this collective consciousness, I also want to wrench myself away from it, to assume the viewpoint of the judge—that is to say, to wrench myself away from myself. Hence this shame and unease Dos Passos is so good at imparting to his readers. I am complicit despite myself—though I am not so sure that it is despite myself—creating and rejecting taboos at one and the same time. I am, once again, to my very core—and against myself—revolutionary.

On the other hand, how I hate Dos Passos' people! Their minds are revealed to me for a second, just to show me that they are living beasts, and then there they are, interminably unfurling their tissue of ritual declarations and sacred acts. Not for them the divide between exterior and interior, between consciousness and the body, but one between the stammerings of an individual, timid, intermittent, inarticulate thinking and the viscous world of collective representations. What a simple procedure this is, and how effective! You have only to relate a life using the techniques of American journalism and life, like Stendhal's '*rameau*

de Salzbourg', crystallizes into something social.[13] By
the same token, the problem of the transition to 'the
typical'—that stumbling block of the social novel—
is solved. There is no need to present us with a typical
worker, to put together, as Nizan does in *Antoine Bloyé*,
an existence that is the precise average of thousands
of existences. Dos Passos can devote all his attention
to portraying the singularity of a life. Each of his
characters is unique; what happens to them could happen only to them. And what matter, since social life
has marked them more deeply than any particular cir-
cumstance could, since *they are* that social life? Beyond
the chance workings of destiny and the contingency
of details, we glimpse in this way an order more flex-
ible than Zola's physiological necessity or Proust's psychological mechanism. It is a gentle, wheedling form
of constraint that seems to let go of its victims, only
to take hold of them again later without their suspect-
ing it. It is, in short, a statistical determinism. They
live as they are able, these people submerged in their
own lives; they pursue their various struggles and what
happens to them wasn't determined beforehand. And
yet neither their crimes, their efforts nor their worst
acts of violence can disrupt the regularity of births,

marriages and suicides. The pressure a gas exerts on the walls of its containing vessel doesn't depend on the individual history of the molecules that make it up.

We are still on the other side of the mirror. Yesterday you saw your best friend and told him of your passionate hatred of war. Now try to tell yourself that story in the style of Dos Passos. 'And they ordered two beers and said that war was appalling. Paul stated he'd rather do anything than fight and John said he concurred and both were moved and said they were happy to agree. As he was going home, Paul decided to see more of John.' You will immediately hate yourself. But it won't take you long to see that you *can't* speak of yourself in this tone. However insincere you might have been, at least you lived out your insincerity; you played it out on your own, you extended its existence at every moment in a process of continued creation. And even if you let yourself be dragged down into collective representations, you had first to live these out as an individual abdication. We are neither mechanisms nor possessed souls, but something worse: we are free. Entirely *outside* or entirely *inside*. Dos Passos' human is a hybrid, internal-external creature. We are with him and in him. We live with his vacillating individual consciousness and, suddenly, it falters, weakens and flows off into the collective consciousness. We follow him and suddenly, here we are, outside, without having noticed it. This is the creature beyond the looking-glass—strange, contemptible and fascinating. Dos Passos knows how to achieve some marvellous effects with this perpetual slippage. I know of nothing more striking than the death of Joe:

> Joe laid out a couple of frogs and was backing off towards the door, when he saw in the mirror that a big guy in a blouse was bringing down a bottle on his head held with both hands. He tried to swing around but he didn't have time. The bottle crashed his skull and he was out.[14]

We are inside, with him, until the impact of the bottle on his head. Immediately afterwards, we are outside, with the chorus: '. . . and he was out.' Nothing conveys the sense of annihilation more clearly. And every page you turn after that, speaking of other minds and a world that carries on without Joe, is like a spadeful of earth on his corpse. But this is a behind-the-looking-glass death. What we apprehend is, in fact, merely the fine *semblance* of nothingness. True nothingness can neither be felt nor thought. Of our real deaths neither we nor anyone after us will ever have anything to say.

Dos Passos' world, like Faulkner's, Kafka's or Stendhal's, is impossible, because it is contradictory. But therein lies its beauty. Beauty is a veiled contradiction. I regard Dos Passos as the greatest writer of our time.

August 1938

Notes

1   The reference is to Ramon Fernandez (1894–1944): novelist and literary critic. [Trans.]

2   John Dos Passos, '1919', in *U.S.A.* (Harmondsworth: Penguin, 1978), p. 400.

3   Ibid., p. 433.

4   Ibid., p. 470.

5   Ibid., p. 469.

6   Ibid., p. 578. Other editions of this work show that the hyphen in '*La Madel-lon*' is intended by Dos Passos. [Trans.]

7   Fabrice del Dongo is the central character of Stendhal's *La Chartreuse de Parme* (1839). [Trans.]

8   André Malraux (1901–76): a French novelist and adventurer and, in his latter years, de Gaulle's minister of culture (1959–69). His novel *L'Espoir*, translated into English as *Man's Hope*, was published in 1937. [Trans.]

9   Dos Passos, *U.S.A.*, p. 509.

10 Ibid., p. 401.

11 Ibid., p. 420.

12 Ibid., p. 659.

13 Sartre is referring to the branches which the miners at Hallein near Salzburg throw down into the abandoned depths of the salt mine in winter. These are recovered two or three months later covered in sparkling crystals. [Trans.]

14 Dos Passos, *U.S.A.*, p. 238.

The Conspiracy *by Paul Nizan*

Nizan speaks of youth. But a Marxist has too much
of a sense of history to describe an age of life in general, such as Youth or Maturity, the way these parade
before us in Strasbourg Cathedral when the clock
strikes noon.[1] His young people are assigned historical
dates and ascribed to class backgrounds. They, like
Nizan himself, were twenty years old in 1929, in the
'boom years' of that post-war period that has just
ended. They are bourgeois; the sons, mostly, of that

32

upper middle class that entertains 'anxious doubts about its future', of those 'rich tradespeople who brought up their children admirably', but who had ended up respecting only the things of the mind,

> without thinking that this ludicrous venera-
> tion for the most disinterested activities of
> life ruined everything, and that it was merely
> the mark of their commercial decadence and
> of a bourgeois bad conscience of which as
> yet they had no suspicion.[2]

Wayward sons, who had been diverted 'out of the paths of commerce' towards the careers of 'creators of alibis'. But there is in Marx a phenomenology of economic essences: I have in mind particularly his admirable analyses of commodity fetishism. In this sense, we can find a phenomenology in Nizan. In other words, he identifies and describes, on the basis of social and historical data, that essence-in-motion that is youth—a faked, fetishized age. It is in this complex proportioning of history and analysis that the great value of his book lies.

Nizan lived his youth to the full. When he was immersed in it, when it limited his horizons on every side, he wrote, in *Aden, Arabie*, 'I was twenty. I won't let anyone tell me it's the best time of life.'[3] It seemed to him then that youth was a *natural* age, like childhood, though much unhappier; and that responsibility for his woes had to be laid at the door of capitalist society. Today, he looks back over it and judges it with brutal frankness. It is an artificial age, an age that has been constructed and that one constructs, an age whose very structure and existence depend on society. It is the age of inauthenticity *par excellence*. The twenty-year-old workers, who 'already have mistresses or wives, children, a profession . . . in short a life',[4] are protected from it by their misfortunes, their cares and their struggles to make a living—these young workers who, when their adolescence comes to an end, become young men, without ever having been 'young people'. But Lafforgue[5] and Rosenthal, students and scions of the bourgeoisie, live this great period of bloodless *ennui* to the full. Their grim frivolity and aggressive futility derive from the fact that they have no calls upon them and are by nature irresponsible. They 'are improvising' and nothing can claim their commitment, not even their membership of extremist parties: 'these diversions . . . had no great consequences for the sons of bankers and industrialists who could always return to the embrace of their class.'[6] They are wise, perhaps, if these improvisations were merely the product of a rapid contact with reality. Their actions lead nowhere and they forget them immediately. Their initiatives are entirely insubstantial; they know this and it is what gives them the courage to take action, even though they feign ignorance on that score. What else could their ventures be called, serious and frivolous as they are, but 'conspiracies'? But Lafforgue and Rosenthal are not *Camelots du roi*:[7] young bourgeois can come and make their conspiracies at the other end of the political spectrum, even in the parties of grown men. We can appreciate all that this fine word 'conspire' implies in the way of whisperings, little mysteries, hollow pretensions and fictitious perils—flimsy intrigues that are, in the end, mere play. And the great 'Dostoevskian' plot hatched by Rosenthal is mere play; all it will leave behind are two incomplete and entirely uninteresting files at the bottom of a drawer; and the manufactured love Rosenthal feels for his sister-in-law, itself an aborted conspiracy, is also fevered, angry play. And from play, it is a short leap to play-acting: they are lying to themselves because they know they are running no risk; they are trying in vain to frighten themselves; in vain—or almost—to deceive themselves. I think I can sense what great, mute sincerity of effort, physical suffering and hunger Nizan would set against their idle chatter. In fact, Bernard Rosenthal, who has, out of anger and idleness, gone through the irreparable motions of suicide, will know no other reality but his own death throes. They alone will show him—though too late—that he has 'missed love . . . that he no longer even loved Catherine and he was going to die cheated'. Yet these young people show the external signs of goodwill: they want to live, love, rebuild a crumbling world. But at the heart of this goodwill is that abstract, self-assured frivolity that cuts them off from the world and from themselves: 'their politics is still based only upon metaphors and shouts.'[8] This is because youth is the age of resentment. Not the age of the great anger of suffering humanity: these young people define themselves in relation to their families; they '[tend] to confuse capitalism with grown-ups'; they think they are moving towards a 'world destined for great metamorphoses',[9] but above all they want to give their parents some trouble. The young man is a product of the bourgeois family, his economic situation and worldview are exclusively family-centred.

These young people will not all make evil men. But Nizan shows that from this age, which Comte termed 'metaphysical', one exits only by revolution. Youth doesn't carry its solution within it: it has to crumble and wither; either the young man dies, like Rosenthal, or he is, like Pluvinage, condemned by his inferiority complex within the family to drag out an eternal, miserable adolescence. Nizan sees things going as badly awry in youth as they do for Freud in childhood; the pages in which he shows us Lafforgue's painful transition to adulthood are among the finest in the book.

I don't think Nizan wanted to write a novel. His young people are not novelistic: they don't do very much and aren't greatly differentiated from one another. At times they seem mere expressions, among so many others, of their families or their class. At other times, they are the tenuous thread linking events. But this is deliberate. In Nizan's eyes, they deserve no better; later he will make them human beings. Can a Communist write a novel? I am not convinced that he can: he doesn't have the right to become his characters' accomplice. But to find this a good and beautiful book, it is enough that we encounter on every page the haunting evocation of this unhappy, guilty age of life; it is enough for it to be a harsh, true testimony to the time when 'the Young' group together and feel good about themselves, when young men believe they have *rights* because they are young, the way taxpayers believe they have because they pay their taxes or fathers because they have children. It is a joy to rediscover, behind these derisory heroes, the bitter, gloomy personality of Nizan, the man who has not forgiven his youth: to rediscover, too, his beautiful, terse, carefree style; his long Cartesian sentences that collapse in the middle as though unable to support themselves, then take off again suddenly and finish up in the air; and those oratorical flights that suddenly stop short and give way to a curt, frosty judgement. Not a novelist's sly, concealed style, but a combative style, a weapon.

November 1938

Notes

1   The Cathedral's famous astronomical clock incorporates figures representing the different ages of

life which, at various different times of day, pass before the figure of Death. [Trans.]

2 Paul Nizan, *The Conspiracy* (London: Verso, 1988), p. 68.

3 Paul Nizan, *Aden, Arabie* (New York: Columbia University Press, 1986), p. 59 (translation modified).

4 Nizan, *The Conspiracy*, p. 71.

5 Sartre misspells the name of the character Laforgue. [Trans.]

6 Nizan, *The Conspiracy*, p. 228.

7 The Camelots du roi were a violent grouping of the extreme Right within the monarchist Action française movement. [Trans.]

8 Nizan, *The Conspiracy*, p. 48.

9 Ibid., p. 49 (translation modified).

A Fundamental Idea
of Husserl's Phenomenology:
Intentionality

'He devoured her with his eyes.' This phrase and many other indications point up to some extent the illusion, common to both realism and idealism, that to know is to eat. After a hundred years of academicism, French philosophy is still at this point. We have all read Brunschvicg, Lalande and Meyerson;[1] we all once believed that the Spider-Mind attracted things into its web, covered them with a white spittle and slowly ingested them, reducing them to its own substance.

What is a table, a rock or a house? A certain assemblage of 'contents of consciousness', an ordering of those contents. Oh alimentary philosophy! Yet nothing seemed more obvious: isn't the table the current content of my perception? Isn't perception the present state of my consciousness? Nutrition, assimilation. The assimilation, as Lalande said, of things to ideas, of ideas among themselves and of minds between themselves. The powerful bones of the world were picked apart by these painstaking diastases: assimilation, unification and identification. In vain did the simplest and coarsest of us search for something solid, something that was not, ultimately, mere mind. But they encountered everywhere an insubstantial, though very distinguished, mist: themselves.

Against the digestive philosophy of empirio-criticism and neo-Kantianism and all forms of 'psychologism', Husserl never tires of asserting that one cannot dissolve things in consciousness. Admittedly, you see this tree here. But you see it at the place where it is: beside the road, amid the dust, standing alone and distorted in the heat, twenty leagues from the Mediterranean coast. It cannot enter your consciousness, because it is not of the same nature as consciousness. You think you recognize Bergson's position in the first chapter of *Matter and Memory* here. But Husserl isn't in any way a realist: he doesn't make this tree, standing on its bit of cracked earth, an absolute that would subsequently enter into communication with us. Consciousness and the world are given at a single stroke: the world, external by its essence to consciousness is, by its essence, relative to consciousness. This is because Husserl sees consciousness as an irreducible fact, which no physical image can render. Except, perhaps, the rapid, obscure image of bursting. To know is to 'burst out towards', to wrest oneself from moist, gastric intimacy and fly out over there, beyond oneself, to what is not oneself. To fly over there, to the tree, and yet outside the tree, because it eludes and repels me and I can no more lose myself in it than it can dissolve itself into me: outside it, outside myself. Don't you recognize your own exigencies and sense of things in this description? You knew very well that the tree wasn't you, that you couldn't take it inside your dark stomach, and that knowledge couldn't, without dishonesty, be compared to possession. And, in this same process, consciousness is purified and becomes clear as a great gust of wind.

There is nothing in it any more, except an impulse to flee itself, a sliding outside of itself. If, impossibly, you were to 'enter' a consciousness, you would be picked up by a whirlwind and thrown back outside to where the tree is and all the dust, for consciousness has no 'inside'. It is merely the exterior of itself and it is this absolute flight, this refusal to be substance, that constitute it as a consciousness. Imagine now a linked series of bursts that wrest us from ourselves, that do not even leave an 'ourself' the time to form behind them, but rather hurl us out beyond them into the dry dust of the world, on to the rough earth, among things. Imagine we are thrown out in this way, abandoned by our very natures in an indifferent, hostile, resistant world. If you do so, you will have grasped the profound meaning of the discovery Husserl expresses in this famous phrase: 'All consciousness is consciousness *of* something.' This is all it takes to put an end to the cosy philosophy of immanence, in which everything works by compromise, by protoplasmic exchanges, by a tepid cellular chemistry. The philosophy of transcendence throws us out on to the high road, amid threats and under a blinding light. Being, says Heidegger, is being-in-the-world. This 'being-in' is to be understood in the sense of movement. To be is to burst forth into the world. It is to start out from a nothingness-of-world-and-consciousness and suddenly to burst-out-as-consciousness-in-the-world. If consciousness attempts to regain control of itself, to coincide, at long last, with itself, in a nice warm room with the shutters closed, it annihilates itself. Husserl calls this need on the part of consciousness to exist as consciousness of something other than itself 'intentionality'.

If I have spoken, first, of knowledge, I have done so to gain a better hearing: the French philosophy that shaped us is almost totally confined now to epistemology. But, for Husserl and the phenomenologists, the consciousness we have of things is not in any way limited to mere knowledge of them. Knowledge or 'pure' representation is only one of the possible forms of my consciousness *of* this tree. I may also love it, fear it, hate it, and this surpassing of consciousness by itself that we call intentionality turns up again in fear, hatred and love. To hate another person is one more way of bursting out towards him; it is to find oneself suddenly faced with a stranger whose objective 'hateful' quality one experiences or, rather, first

suffers. Suddenly, then, these famous 'subjective' reactions of love and loathing, fear and liking, which
were floating around in the foul-smelling brine of the
Mind, tear themselves away from it; they are merely
ways of discovering the world. It is things that suddenly disclose themselves to us as hateful, pleasant,
horrible or lovable. Fearsomeness is a *property* of this
Japanese mask, an inexhaustible, irreducible property
that constitutes its very nature—not the sum of our
subjective reactions to a piece of carved wood.
Husserl has put horror and charm back into things.
He has given us back the world of artists and
prophets: terrifying, hostile and dangerous, with
havens of grace and love. He has cleared the way for
a new Treatise of Passions that would take its inspiration from this very simple truth that is so poorly understood by our finest minds: if we love a woman, it
is because she is lovable. We can leave Proust behind
now. And, with him, the 'inner life': in vain would we
seek, like Amiel,[2] or like a child kissing her own shoul-
der, the caresses and fondlings of a private intimacy,
since, at long last, everything is outside. Everything,
including ourselves. It is outside, in the world, among
others. It is not in some lonely refuge that we shall

discover ourselves, but on the road, in the town, in the crowd, as a thing among things and a human being among human beings.

January 1939

Notes

1   Léon Brunschvicg (1869–1944), André Lalande (1867–1963) and Émile Meyerson (1859–1933): prominent academic philosophers whose work had largely passed out of vogue by Sartre's day. [Trans.]

2   Henri-Frédéric Amiel (1821–81): Swiss philosopher and diarist. [Trans.]

Monsieur François Mauriac and Freedom

The novel doesn't present things, but their signs.[1] How, with these mere signs—words—which are *indications* in a void, can we make a world that holds up? How is it that Stavrogin is alive? We would be wrong to believe he draws his life from my imagination: words give rise to images when we muse on them, but when I read, I am not musing: I am deciphering. No, I do not imagine Stavrogin. I await him, I await his acts and the end of his adventure. This dense matter

I stir around when I read Dostoevsky's *Demons* is my own expectancy, my time.[2] For a book is either merely a little pile of dry leaves or, alternatively, a great form in movement: the act of reading. The novelist seizes upon this movement, guides and inflects it; he makes it the substance of his characters. A novel, a succession of acts of reading, of little parasitic lives, each of them no more than the length of a dance, swells with, and feeds on, its readers' time. But, for my periods of impatience and ignorance to be caught, shaped and, ultimately, presented to me as the flesh of these invented creatures, the novelist has to know how to draw them into his trap. He has to hollow out in his book, by means of the signs available to him, a time similar to mine, in which the future is not decided. If I suspect the future actions of the hero are determined in advance by heredity, social influences or some other mechanism, my own time ebbs back to me and I am left there alone, reading and persisting in the face of a motionless book. Do you want your characters to live? Make them free. The thing is not to define, nor even less to explain, unforeseeable acts and passions (in a novel, the best psychological analyses reek of death), but merely to *present* them. What

Rogogine is going to do, neither he nor I know. I know he is going to see his guilty mistress again, and yet I cannot guess whether he will control himself or whether excess of anger will drive him to murder: he is free. I slip into him and there he is, awaiting his own self with my expectancy. *Inside me*, he is afraid of himself; he is alive.

As I was about to begin reading *The End of the Night*,[3] it occurred to me that Christian authors are, by the nature of their belief, the best placed to write novels. The man of religion is free. The supreme forebearance of Catholics may irritate us, because it is something learned, but if they are novelists, it plays in their favour. Figures in a novel and Christians, being centres of indeterminacy, both have characters, but they have them in order to escape them. They are free above and beyond their natures and, if they give in to those natures, they do so once more out of freedom. They may get caught up in psychical mechanisms, but they will never be mechanical. Even the Christian notion of sin is strictly in keeping with the principles of the genre. The Christian sins and the hero of the novel also must transgress. The novel's duration, dense as it is, would lack the urgency that confers necessity and cruelty on the work of art, if the existence of the transgression—which cannot be wiped away and must be redeemed—didn't reveal to the reader the irreversibility of time. Dostoevsky too was a Christian novelist. Not a novelist *and* a Christian, in the way that Pasteur was a Christian *and* a scientist, but a novelist in the service of Christ.

Monsieur Mauriac is a Christian novelist too. And his book *La Fin de la Nuit* aims to plumb the depths of a woman's freedom. He tells us in his preface that what he is trying to depict is 'that power, granted to all human beings—no matter how much they may seem to be the slaves of a hostile fate—of saying "No" to the law which beats them down'.[4] We are at the heart of the art of the novel here, at the heart of faith. However, when I finish reading, I confess to feeling disappointed. Not for a moment was I sucked in; not for a moment did I forget *my* time. I existed and could feel myself living. I yawned a little, and at times said, 'Well played!' I thought more of François Mauriac than of Thérèse Desqueyroux.[5] Of Mauriac, refined, sensitive and narrow, with his unabashed discretion, his intermittent goodwill, his pathos that is a product of his nerves, his sour, stumbling poetry, his awkward style and sudden vulgarity. Why was I not able to forget him or myself? And what had become of this Christian predisposition towards novel-writing? We have to come back, here, to freedom. By what procedures does M. Mauriac reveal to us that freedom he has bestowed upon his heroine?

Thérèse Desqueyroux struggles against her destiny. So far, so good. She is, then, a twofold creature. One part of her is wholly encompassed by Nature; we can say of her that she is like this or like that, as we can of a pebble or a log. A whole other part escapes description and definition, because it is merely an absence. When freedom accepts Nature, then fate alone rules. When it rejects it and battles back against the grain, then Thérèse Desqueyroux *is free*. She has the freedom to say 'no'—or, at the very least, not to say 'yes' ('All that is asked of them is that they should not resign themselves to night's darkness').[6] A Cartesian, infinite, formless, nameless, fateless freedom, 'forever re-begun', whose only power is to assent, but which is sovereign because it can withhold that assent. This at least is how we glimpse that freedom in the preface. But will we find it in the novel?

We must say, to begin with, that this suspensive will seems more tragic than novelistic. Thérèse's vacillations between following the impulses of her nature and recovering her will are reminiscent of Rotrou's stanzas;[7] the true novelistic conflict is, rather, the battle freedom fights with itself. In Dostoevsky, freedom is poisoned at its very sources; it gets entangled at the very point where it seeks to unfurl itself. The pride and irascibility of Dmitri Karamazov are as free as Aliosha's profound peace. The nature that stifles him and with which he wrestles is not how God made him, but how he has made himself. It is what he has sworn to be, which has become fixed and frozen by the irreversibility of time. Thinking along these same lines, Alain[8] says that a character is a solemn oath. Reading M. Mauriac—and perhaps this is to his credit—we muse on the possibility of another Thérèse, who would have been a more capable, greater character. But, ultimately, what commends this battle of freedom against nature to us is its venerable antiquity and orthodoxy. It is reason battling against the passions; it is the Christian soul, united to the body through the imagination, rebelling against the appetites of the body. Let us accept this theme provisionally, even if

it doesn't seem true: its beauty might be thought a sufficient justification.

However, is this 'fatality' against which Thérèse
must struggle really, solely, the determinism of her
natural tendencies? M. Mauriac calls it destiny. But let
us not confuse destiny and character. Character is still
us; it is the set of mild forces that insinuates itself into
our intentions, imperceptibly deflecting our efforts
from them—always in the same direction. When
Thérèse is angry with Mondoux, who has humiliated
her, M. Mauriac writes: 'This time it really was she
who was speaking, that Thérèse who was quite prepared to bite.'[9] This clearly concerns Thérèse's character. But a little later, as she is leaving, having
managed to find a wounding riposte,[10] we read: 'The
blow which she had delivered with so sure a hand had
helped her to measure the extent of her power and
take cognizance of her mission.'[11] What mission?
Then I recall these words from the preface: 'the power
she exercises to poison and corrupt'.[12] And here we
have Destiny, encompassing and exceeding character,
and representing within Nature, and in the—at times
so basely psychological—*oeuvre* of M. Mauriac, the
power of the Supernatural. As soon as Thérèse's acts

escape her grasp, they are governed by a certain law, independent of Thérèse's will, a law that brings doom-laden consequences down on all of them, even the most well-intentioned. This reminds us of the punishment meted out by the fairy in the tale: 'Every time you open your mouth, toads will jump out.'[13] If you don't believe, then this sorcery will mean nothing to you. But the believer understands it very well: what is it, ultimately, but the expression of that other sorcery, original sin? I accept, then, that M. Mauriac is in earnest when he speaks, as a Christian, of Destiny. But when he speaks of it as a novelist, I can no longer follow him. Thérèse Desqueyroux's destiny is the product, in part, of a flaw in her character and, in part, of a curse afflicting her actions. These two factors are not compatible: the one may be discerned from within by the heroine herself, the other would require an infinite series of observations made from outside by a witness bent on following all of Thérèse's undertakings through to their final consequences. So well does M. Mauriac knows this himself that, when he wants to have us see Thérèse as predestined, he resorts to artifice: he shows her to us as she appears *to others*: 'It was not surprising that people turned to look as she passed. An animal can be detected by its smell even before it is seen.'[14] This, then, is the great hybrid phenomenon revealed to us throughout the novel: Thérèse—but not limited to her pure freedom—, Thérèse, as she eludes her own grasp and moves, in a baleful fog, towards her earthly destruction. But, in the end, how could Thérèse know she had a destiny, except by already having consented to it? And how does M. Mauriac know it? The idea of destiny is poetic and contemplative. But the novel is action and the novelist has no right to leave the field and ensconce himself comfortably on some hillock to assess the battle and muse on the Fortunes of War.

We shouldn't think M. Mauriac succumbed just the once, by chance, to the temptations of poetry: this way of first identifying with his character, then suddenly abandoning her and contemplating her from the outside, like a judge, is characteristic of his art. He led us to believe, from the very first page, that he was going to tell the story by adopting Thérèse's standpoint; and, indeed, between our eyes and Thérèse's room, her servant and the rumours rising from the street, we immediately sense the translucent density of another consciousness. But a few pages further on, when we believe we are still inside that consciousness, we have already left it; we are outside, with M. Mauriac, taking a hard look at Thérèse. The fact is that, in order to pull off this illusion, M. Mauriac uses the novelistic ambiguity of the 'third person'. In a novel, the pronoun 'she' may refer to another person, that is to say, an opaque object, someone whom we only ever see from the outside. As, for example, when I write, 'I noticed *she* was trembling.' But it also happens that this pronoun takes us into an intimacy that should logically be expressed in the first person: 'She was astounded to hear her own words resonating.' This is something I can actually only know if *I* am *she* or, in other words, if I am able to write, 'I could hear my own words resonating.' Novelists actually use this entirely conventional mode of expression out of a sort of discretion, so as not to ask an unreserved complicity of the reader and to cover the dizzying intimacy of the 'I' with a kind of glaze. The heroine's consciousness represents the lens through which the reader can cast an eye on the world of the novel, and the word 'she' gives the illusion of a lens situated at some distance from the action; it reminds us that this revealing consciousness is also a novelistic creation, representing an alternative viewpoint on the favoured point of view and fulfilling for the reader that heart-felt desire of those in love: to be, at one and the same time, oneself and someone else. Thus the same word has two opposing functions: as 'she-subject' or 'she-object'. M. Mauriac exploits this indeterminacy to have us shift imperceptibly from the one aspect of Thérèse to the other: 'Thérèse was ashamed of what she felt.' Right. This Thérèse is a subject, she is an *I* kept at a certain distance from myself and I know this shame *in Thérèse* because Thérèse herself knows that she feels it. But in this case, since it is with *her* eyes that I read her, I can never know any more of her than what she herself knows: I know all that she knows, but *only* what she knows. To understand who Thérèse is in reality, I would have to close the book and shatter this complicity. At that point, all that would be left to me would be a memory of this consciousness that was still clear, but had, like all past things, become hermetic, and I would attempt to interpret it as though it were a fragment of my own past life. But here we have M. Mauriac, while I am still in this absolute proximity to his characters—their dupe when they deceive themselves, their accomplice when they lie to themselves—suddenly striking them—though they suspect nothing of this—with dazzling lightning-bolts that plumb, for me alone, the depths of their souls, of which they themselves know nothing, but which bear the stamp of their character as might a medal: 'Never once had she associated the mysterious adventure of Thérèse Desqueyroux with crime—at least not consciously.'[15] This leaves me in a strange situation: I *am* Thérèse, and she is myself with a degree of aesthetic distance. Her thoughts are my thoughts, and I form them as she does. And yet I have revelations about her that she doesn't have. Or, alternatively, I am located within the heart of her consciousness and help her to lie to herself, while, at the same time, I judge her, condemn her and put myself inside her as *another person*: 'She couldn't *not* have realized the lie she was acting: but now she nestled into it, seeking rest.'[16] This sentence is ample evidence of the constant betrayal M. Mauriac demands of me. Lying to herself, uncovering her lie and yet attempting to conceal it from herself—this is Thérèse's attitude, an attitude I can only know from her alone. But in the very way this attitude is revealed to me, there is a witness' merciless judgement. Moreover, this uneasy position doesn't last for long: under cover of that 'third person', the ambiguity of which I have noted, M. Mauriac suddenly slips outside his character, dragging me along with him: '"How well that make-up suits you, dear . . ." Those were the first words that Thérèse spoke—the words of one woman to another.'[17] The lights of Thérèse's consciousness have gone out; no longer illuminated from within, she has reassumed her compact opacity. But neither the noun nor the pronoun that refer to her have changed. Nor has the cast of the narrative. M. Mauriac even finds this to-ing and fro-ing so natural that he shifts from Thérèse-as-subject to Thérèse-as-object in the course of a single sentence: 'She heard nine o'clock strike. She must still find some way of killing time, for it was too early as yet to swallow the cachet which would assure her a few hours of sleep; *not that such was the habit of this cautious and desperate woman,* but tonight she could not resist its promise of help.'[18] Who is adjudging Thérèse a 'cautious and desperate woman' in this way? It cannot be she. No, it is M. Mauriac. It is myself. We have the Desqueyroux file before us and we are pronouncing judgement.

M. Mauriac's games don't end there: he likes to take hold of roofs by a corner and lift them, like

Asmodeus, that prying, harum-scarum devil he is so fond of. When he finds it more convenient, he leaves Thérèse and suddenly goes and instals himself inside another mind—that of Georges, Marie, Bernard Desqueyroux or Anne the servant. He has a little look around, then disappears again the way puppets do.

> Thérèse could read nothing on the averted face. She did not know that her daughter was thinking: 'In the whole of my life, I shall never go half as far as this old woman has gone in the last few days.'[19]

She didn't know? Well, never mind. M. Mauriac suddenly abandons her, leaves her to her ignorance, jumps to Marie and brings back this little snapshot for us. By contrast, on other occasions he generously has one of his creatures share in the novelist's divine lucidity: 'She stretched out her arms, tried to draw him to her, but he broke violently from her touch. It was then she realized that she had lost him.'[20] Signs are uncertain and are binding only on the present, but what matter? M. Mauriac has decided that Georges is lost to Thérèse. He decided it the way the ancient Gods decreed Oedipus' parricide and incest. Then, to impart his decree to us, for a few moments he lends his

creature the divinatory powers of Tiresias: have no
fear, she will soon relapse into her darkness. And here,
indeed, comes the curfew, at which point all consciousnesses are extinguished: a wearying M. Mauriac
suddenly withdraws from all his characters at once
and all that remains is the world's exterior, a few puppets in a cardboard landscape:

> The girl dropped her hand from before her
> eyes.
>
> 'I thought you were asleep.'
>
> Once more a note of supplication came into
> the elder woman's voice:
>
> 'Swear to me that you are happy.'[21]

Gestures and sounds in the shadows. A few feet
away, M. Mauriac is sitting, musing:

> 'What terrible pain you must have been
> through, Mamma!'
>
> 'No, I felt nothing, except the prick when
> you used the hypodermic . . .'
>
> But that rattling in the throat and that con-
> gested face. Is it possible that human beings
> can go through such a hell of agony, yet keep
> no memory of it?

To anyone who knows the character of Marie, there can be no doubt that the young girl wastes no time on such thoughts. No, this is the creator resting on the seventh day and M. Mauriac is worrying, wondering and musing over his creation.

This is where things go wrong for him. He wrote once that the novelist was to his creatures what God was to His, and all the oddities of his technique can be explained by his taking the standpoint of God towards his characters. God sees the inside and the outside; he sees the depth of souls and bodies—the whole universe at a stroke. Similarly, M. Mauriac is omniscient about everything relating to his little world. What he says about his characters is the Gospel truth: he explains them, classifies them, condemns them unreservedly. If you asked him, 'How do you know Thérèse is a cautious and desperate woman?' he would no doubt be amazed and would reply, 'Didn't I create her?'

Well, no, he didn't! The time has come to say that the novelist isn't God. Recall, rather, the precautions Conrad takes when suggesting to us that Lord Jim may perhaps be 'romantic'.[22] He is careful not to assert this himself, putting the word into the mouth of one of his creatures, a fallible human being who pronounces it hesitantly. Clear as it may be, the term 'romantic' is given depth, pathos and a hint of mystery. There is nothing of the sort with M. Mauriac. 'Cautious and desperate woman' isn't a hypothesis; it is a clear statement handed down from on high. Impatient to have us grasp the character of his heroine, the author suddenly provides us with the key. But I am arguing that he doesn't have the right to make these absolute judgements. A novel is an action related from various viewpoints. And M. Mauriac knows this well, writing as he does in *The End of the Night* that, 'one can make the most contrary judgements about the same person, and yet be right—that it is all a question of the way the light falls, and . . . no one form of lighting is more revealing than another.'[23] But each of these interpretations must be in motion; in other words, they must be carried along by the very action they are interpreting. Such an interpretation is, in short, the testimony of a participant, and it must reveal the person testifying as well as the event to which it testifies. It must arouse our impatience (will it be confirmed or refuted by events?) and in that way make us feel the resistance of time. Each point of view, then, is relative and the best will be of such a kind that time offers the reader the greatest resistance. The interpretations and explanations given by the participants will all be conjectural. Beyond these conjectures, the reader may perhaps sense an absolute reality of the event, but it is for him alone to establish this, if it suits him to do so, and, if he tries, he will never get beyond the realm of likelihoods and probabilities. In any event, the introduction of absolute truth or the viewpoint of God into a novel is a twofold technical error. First, it presupposes a narrator who is withdrawn from the action and purely contemplative, which offends against the aesthetic law, formulated by Paul Valéry, that any element of a work of art must always maintain a plurality of relations with the other elements. Second, the absolute is timeless. If you elevate the narrative into an absolute realm, the thread of time is broken and the novel vanishes before your very eyes. All that remains is a listless verity *sub specie aeternitatis*.

But there is something more serious. The definitive assessments M. Mauriac is always ready to slip into the narrative prove that he doesn't conceive his characters as he ought. He forges their essences before he writes; he decrees that they *will be* this or that. The essence of Thérèse, the evil-smelling animal or the cautious and desperate woman, is, I admit, complex, and not to be summed up in a single phrase. But what exactly is it? Her innermost depths? Let us take a close look at this. Conrad correctly saw that the word 'romantic' had meaning if it expressed an aspect of the character *for someone else*. Can we not see that 'cautious and desperate woman', 'evil-smelling animal', 'castaway' and all these neat little formulas are of the same kind as this little word that Conrad puts into the mouth of an inter-island merchant: they are the pithy turns of phrase of the moralist or the historian. And when Thérèse sums up her story ('As often as had been necessary . . . she . . . would drag herself out of the depths and then slip again to the bottom, and so on indefinitely, caught in the same weary process. For years she had not realized that this was to be the rhythm of her destiny, but now she had come through the dark night and could see her way clearly'),[24] she is able to judge her past so easily only because she cannot go back to it. In this way, M. Mauriac, when he believes he is probing into the depths of his characters, remains outside, at the door. There would be no problem if he realized this. In that case, he would gives us novels like Hemingway's, where we barely know the characters except through their actions and words and the vague judgements they pass on each other. But when M. Mauriac, drawing on all his authority as creator, has us take these external views for the inner substance of his creations, he thereby transforms them into *things*. Except that things *are:* they have only exteriors. Minds cannot simply *be*: they *become*. Thus M. Mauriac, in sculpting his Thérèse *sub specie aeternitatis* turns her, first of all, into a thing. After which, he adds in a whole layer of consciousness below. But he does so in vain. Characters in novels have their laws and this is the strictest of them: the novelist may be their witness or their accomplice, but never both at the same time. Outside or inside. In failing to observe these laws, M. Mauriac slays the consciousnesses of his characters.

So we are brought back again to freedom, that other dimension of Thérèse. What becomes of her in this lifeless world? Up to now, Thèrèse was a *thing* for us, an ordered succession of motifs and models, passions, habits and interests—a *story* we could sum up in a few maxims—*a fate*. And now suddenly, this witch, this possessed creature is presented to us as free. M. Mauriac is at pains to tell us what we are to understand by this particular kind of freedom:

> But what really gave me pleasure was that decision I made yesterday to surrender my fortune. When I did that I felt as though I were floating at an incredible height above my *ordinary everyday self*. I climb and climb and climb—and then suddenly I slip back into this frozen nastiness of malevolence—which is my true self when I'm not making an effort, *the self to which I keep on returning*.[25]

So her freedom no more constitutes Thérèse's 'real self' than did her consciousness. This self, 'which . . . I fall back to when I fall back to myself', is given in advance: it is the *thing*. Consciousness and freedom come afterwards, consciousness as a power to deceive oneself about oneself, freedom as a power to escape oneself. This means that, for M. Mauriac, freedom cannot *be constructive*. A human being cannot, with his freedom, create himself or forge his own history. Free will is merely a discontinuous power that enables one to escape from oneself for short periods, but produces nothing, except for a few inconsequential events. Hence, *The End of the Night*, which in M. Mauriac's eyes is supposed to be the novel of a character's freedom, seems to us chiefly to be a novel of bondage—to the point where the author, who initially wanted to show us 'the stages of a spiritual ascension', confesses in his preface that, against his will, Thérèse has dragged him down to Hell. 'Now that the story is finished,' he notes, not without regret, 'it has, to some extent, disappointed the hopes I had when I decided on its title.'[26] But how could it be otherwise? The very fact that the freedom is tacked on over and above the fixed, compact nature of Thérèse means it loses its omnipotence and indeterminacy; it receives a definition and a nature, since we know *what* it is a freedom *against*. More than this, indeed, M. Mauriac subjects it to a law: 'I climb and climb and climb—and then suddenly I slip back.' It is decreed in advance, then, that Thérèse will fall back each time. We are even warned in the preface that it would be indiscreet to ask more of her: 'She belongs to that class of human beings . . . for whom night can end only when life itself ends. All that is asked of them is that they should not resign themselves to night's darkness.'[27] And was it not Thérèse herself who was speaking, a moment ago, of the 'rhythm of her destiny': freedom is one of the phases of that rhythm. Thérèse is predictable even in her freedom. The little independence M. Mauriac grants her he has measured out precisely, as in a doctor's prescription or a recipe. I expect nothing from her; I know everything. Hence her ascents and falls move me little more than those of a cockroach mindlessly persisting in climbing a wall.

The point is that no scope has been left for freedom. Having been measured out with a pipette, Thérèse's freedom no more resembles real freedom than her consciousness resembles a real consciousness. And M. Mauriac, engrossed in describing Thérèse's psychological mechanisms, is suddenly at a loss when he wants to make us feel she is no longer a mechanism. Admittedly, he shows us Thérèse battling with her evil inclinations: 'Thérèse compressed her lips. "I won't tell her about that Garcin creature," she kept saying to herself.'[28] But what is there to suggest that, behind this sudden revolt, a more thorough analysis wouldn't uncover the reasons and solid linkages of determinism? M. Mauriac is so acutely aware of this that, from time to time, he tugs at our sleeves and whispers to us, 'There you are, this time it's for real, she's free.' As in the following passage: 'She broke off in the middle of a sentence (for she was acting in entire good faith).'[29] I know of no cruder device than this parenthetical admonition. But we can understand why the author is bound to resort to it: if we start out from that hybrid being M. Mauriac has engendered and which he calls Thérèse's nature, *no sign could make the distinction between a free action and a passion.* Except perhaps for a kind of evanescent grace playing over the features or within the soul of a character who has just won a victory over him- or herself:

> Her gaze was as lovely as he had ever known it . . .[30]

> She felt no pang . . . Rather was she conscious of a sense of lightness. She seemed to have been freed by some *operation* of she knew not what. It was as though she were no longer walking in a circle, but moving straight ahead towards a goal.[31]

But these moral recompenses are not sufficient to convince us. They show us, rather, that for M. Mauriac freedom differs from bondage in its *value*, not its nature. Any intention directed upwards, towards Good, is free. Any desire for Evil is in bondage. The value of this distinguishing principle is not our concern here. The point is simply that it stifles novelistic freedom and, with it, the immediate *durée* that is the substance of the novel.

How could Thérèse's story *have duration*? We run up here against the old theological conflict between divine omniscience and human freedom: the 'rhythm of [Thérèse's] destiny', that graph of her rises and falls, resembles a temperature curve. We have before us dead time, since the future stretches out like the past, merely repeating it. The reader of the novel doesn't want to be God. For the transfusion of my own time into the veins of Thérèse and Marie Desqueyroux to take place, I would have to be—at least once—ignorant of their destinies and impatient to know about them. But M. Mauriac shows no concern to arouse impatience in me: his only aim is to provide me with as much knowledge as he possesses. He plies me with information, piling it on mercilessly. Barely has my curiosity been piqued than it is satisfied beyond all measure. Dostoevsky would have surrounded Thérèse with dense, secretive constructions, the meaning of which would have been on the point of revealing itself on every page, but would have eluded me. But right away M. Mauriac lodges me in the innermost hearts of his characters. No one has any secrets. An equal light is cast on all. So, even if, at times, I might have some appetite to know what happens next, I couldn't identify my impatience with Thérèse's, since we are not waiting for the same things and I have known the things she wants to know for quite some time. From my point of view, she is like those abstract partners in a 'demonstration hand' of bridge who are kept, hypothetically, in ignorance of their opponents' play and make their plans on the basis of that very ignorance, whereas I can see all the cards and can see that their calculations and hopes are erroneous; she is outside of my time, a fleshless shadow.

It is evident, moreover, that M. Mauriac doesn't at all like time or the Bergsonian necessity to wait 'for the sugar to melt'. His creatures' time is, for him, a dream, an all-too-human illusion. He casts it off and instals himself resolutely in the realm of the eternal. But, in my view, that alone should have deterred him from writing novels. The true novelist is excited by all that resists, by a door because it has to be opened, by an envelope because it has to be unsealed. In Hem-

critical essays

it.'[18] Given that state of affairs, in which I perhaps tell an untruth when I want to be truthful, can I be sure of telling an untruth when I mean to lie? We know of those mental patients suffering from the 'psychosis of influence', who complain that their 'thought is being stolen' or, in other words, that their thought is being deflected from its original meaning before it reaches its conclusion. They are not so mad and this is something that befalls every one of us: words drink our thought before we have the time to recognize it; we had a vague intention, we put it clearly into words and now here we are saying something quite different from what we meant. There are no liars. There are only oppressed individuals getting by as best they can with language. Parain never forgot the story of the banker or other similar stories. He still remembers it when he speaks, twenty years later, of his daughter's lies:

> When my daughter tells me she has done her homework even though she has not, she doesn't do so . . . *with the intention* of misleading me, but to indicate to me that she could have done it, that she wanted to do it, that she should have done it, but that none of

been deprived of my right to witness them. He would, no doubt, describe these sudden stops, followed by equally sudden starts, as 'foreshortenings'. Personally, I would be inclined to term them breakdowns. One has, admittedly, to 'foreshorten' occasionally, but that doesn't mean one should suddenly purge the narrative of its duration. In a novel, one must either remain silent or tell all: one must, above all, not omit or 'skip' anything. A foreshortening is simply a gear-change in the narration. M. Mauriac, for his part, is in a hurry. He has probably vowed that none of his books will ever exceed the dimensions of a novella. I have looked in vain in *The End of the Night* for those long stammering conversations, so common in English novels, in which the protagonists rake over their stories endlessly, without managing to get them forward, those periods of respite that suspend the action only to increase its urgency, those interludes in which, beneath a darkened sky, the characters are engrossed, like ants, in their familiar occupations. M. Mauriac will consent only to handling the essential passages, which he subsequently links together with brief summaries.

It is this taste for concision which explains why his creatures speak as if they are in the theatre. It is

M. Mauriac's aim simply to have them express what they have to say as quickly and clearly as possible. Excluding superfluous detail, repetition and the stumblings of spoken language, he gives his protagonists' remarks their naked force of meaning. And since we have, nonetheless, to sense a difference between what he writes in his own name and what he makes them say, he imparts a kind of torrential speed to these excessively clear speeches that is, precisely, theatrical. This is Thérèse, for example:

> What are you trying to imply?—that I did not do what I say I did! It was evil, but nothing like so evil as my later crimes. They were more cowardly and more secret. With them I took no risks.[33]

This is a passage for recitation rather than for reading. Note the oratorical style of the beginning and the repeated question that swells with the repetition. Doesn't it remind you of the rages of Hermione in Racine's *Andromaque*? I catch myself pronouncing the words *sotto voce*, in the grip of that rhetorical beginning that characterizes all good tragic dialogue. And now read this:

objects, but they had fallen too far behind. What, for example, did 'peace' mean? The Japanese were advancing with guns and tanks into the heart of China; yet they were at peace with the Chinese, since war was not declared. The Japanese and the Russians were fighting on the Manchurian front, yet peace was preserved, since the Japanese ambassador remained in Moscow and the Soviet ambassador in Tokyo. And if two countries are at war and a third keeps out of the operations, can I say it is at peace? Yes, if it remains neutral. But what is neutrality? If it supplies one of the warring parties, is it neutral? If it suffers blockade, is it neutral? Is armed neutrality still neutrality? And what of pre-belligerence? Or intervention? And if we stop defining war as armed conflict, shall we say the inter-war period was wartime or peacetime? Everyone is entitled to their own opinion. Blockades, industrial rivalries, class struggles—aren't these enough for us to speak of war? Yet can I not legitimately look back nostalgically to the peacetime of '39? There are people who say that, since 1914, there has been no end to war—and they provide evidence. But others also prove that the war dates from September 1939. So was there a period of peace between two wars or one single war? Who knows?

© Editions GALLIMARD, Paris, 1947

ISBN-13   978 1 9064 9 760 6

British Library Cataloguing-in-Publication Data
A catalogue record for this book is available
from the British Library

Typeset by Seagull Books, Calcutta, India
Printed and bound Hyam Enterprises, Calcutta, India

contents

Perhaps there was a single period of peace? Who will decide? I am put in mind here of the uncertainties of biology, whose terms were ill able to designate clearly defined species and which suddenly discovered the continuity of living forms. Should we leave words to rot where they stand? 'Our language,' writes Camus, commenting on Parain, 'seems in need of a dictionary.' But Parain would reply that a dictionary presupposes a degree of discontinuity and usefulness of meanings; it is, therefore, impossible to establish one today.

In an age which, like ours, is one of deep social transformations, in which social values disappear without having been replaced yet by others and, by analogy, in any age, since there is no moment that is not undergoing transformation at a greater or lesser rate, no one can know precisely what other people's words mean and what. Even their own. In Faulkner

It is at this point, when all is lost, that Parain believes he has found a solution *in extremis*. There are people who have given up trying to understand the world and merely want to change it. Marx writes:

The question whether objective truth can be attributed to human thinking is not a confrontation. Marie is unaware that her mother is mad; what will she do when she realizes? The problem is clearly formulated; determinism merely has to be left to run its course with its blows and counterblows, its predictable dramatic turnabouts. It will lead us, without fail, to the final catastrophe, with Marie transforming herself into a nursemaid and persuading her mother to come back to the Desqueyroux household. Is this not reminiscent of Sardou and the big scene in *L'Espionne*?[35] Or of Bernstein and the second act of *Le Voleur*?[36] I can quite understand M. Mauriac being tempted by the theatre: time and again, reading *The End of the Night*, I had the impression I was being presented with the plot and main extracts from a four-act play.

Look again now at the pages of *Beauchamp's Career* in which Meredith shows us the last meeting between Beauchamp and Renée: they are still in love and are within an ace of telling each other as much, and yet they separate.[37] When they meet, *everything* is possible between them; the future is not decided. Gradually, their tiny faults, their little misunderstandings and vexations begin to outweigh their goodwill. Their vision is clouded. And yet to the end, even as I am beginning to fear they will break up, I have a sense that *everything can still be different*. This is because they are free and they will themselves be the architects of their final separation. That is a novel.

The End of the Night is not a novel. Are you going to call this angular, frosty work, with its theatrical passages, snippets of analysis and poetic meditations a novel? Can you mistake these jerky starts and equally violent applications of the brakes, these painful resumptions and breakdowns for the majestic course of novelistic time? Will you let your attention be grabbed by this static narrative, whose intellectual armature is visible at first glance, in which the mute figures of the protagonists are inscribed like angles within a circle? If it is the case that a novel is a *thing*, like a picture or an architectural creation, if it is the case that a novel is made with free minds and time, just as a picture is made with oil and pigments, then *The End of the Night* is not a novel. It is, at best, an assemblage of signs and intentions. M. Mauriac is not a novelist.

Why? Why has this serious, diligent author not reached his goal? The sin of pride is, I think, to blame. He has tried to ignore, as most of our authors do, that the theory of relativity applies fully to the universe of you. Parain's adherence to the activist doctrine appears to be as much a product of anger as of resignation. To him, the word remains an intermediary, but its function is now clearer: it interposes itself between the desire and its realization. 'What guides man at every moment, what musters him and orders him is what he says of himself, of his needs, his desires and his means. These are his watchwords.'[25] This is to recognize a primacy of desire and affectivity. Language is an instrument of realization. With this, reason is reduced to a more modest role.

> Reason is nothing but intelligence, which is itself nothing but the power to build a system of signs to be tested, that is to say the power to frame a hypothesis . . . Reason . . . is the endeavour man pursues . . . to present his desires with an exact, effective means of satisfaction . . . Its subservient role is very precise . . . The desires need to control it frequently, the way one takes an idling workman to task.[26]

With this, the scandal of language becomes clearer: if there is pressure to force Parain to adopt the language of the banker, that is because the banker is in

command. For a ~~Sartoris by William Faulkner~~ soldier, the point is
neither to strive to understand a language that is not
made for him—which would lead him into servitude—nor to invent for himself a system of signs that
is valid for him alone—which would lead him straight
to madness. He has to find a community of the oppressed that are eager to take power and impose their
language, a language forged in the silent solidarity of
work and suffering. Parain can now say, modifying
Marx's thesis slightly, 'We do not wish to understand
words, we wish to change them.' But if it comes to
re-inventing a language, you have to opt for a rigorous,
precise one; the wobble in the handle or the 'play' in
the gears has to be eliminated. For the order to be
obeyed, it has to be understood down to its last details.
And conversely, to understand is to act. You have to
tighten the drive belts and the screws. Since you can
not be silent—that is to say, accede directly and immediately to being—you have at least to control the
intermediaries strictly. Parain admits that his youth
was blanched between two dreams. *Sartoris* and that is what
makes it so precious. It is a book in which Faulkner
shows himself: we see throughout the evidence of his
handiwork, his artifice. I understand now the main-

*Once a certain time has elapsed, good novels come
to seem almost like natural phenomena. We forget
that they have authors; we accept them like stones or
trees, because they are there, because they exist. Light
in August was a hermetic object of this kind, a mineral
substance. We do not accept Sartoris.*

*Symbols lead us to believe that by eliminating
all transmissions we can be said to be
eliminating all hitches and to believe too,*

9 Mauriac, *La Fin de la Nuit*, p. 179. This passage is omitted from the edition from which the English translation was made. [Trans.]

10 I know of few scenes more vulgar than this one and the curious thing is that we clearly have to ascribe this vulgarity to M. Mauriac himself.

11 Mauriac, *Thérèse*, p. 275.

12 Ibid., p. 161.

13 This is clearly a reference to Charles Perrault's tale, 'Les Fées' in *Perrault's Popular Tales* (Oxford: Clarendon Press, 1888).

14 Mauriac, *Thérèse*, p. 275

15 Ibid., p. 190.

16 Ibid., p. 229.

17 Ibid., p. 172.

18 Ibid., p. 169 (translation modified; the English translation is based on a different edition from that to which Sartre refers [Trans.]).

19 Ibid., p. 311.

20 Ibid., p. 256.

21 Ibid., p. 311.

22 Joseph Conrad, *Lord Jim* (Edinburgh and London: William Blackwood and Sons, 1900). [Trans.]

23 Mauriac, *Thérèse*, p. 257.

24 Ibid., p. 256.

25 Ibid., p. 218. My emphasis. [J.-P. S.]

26 Ibid., p. 161.

27 Ibid., p. 161.

28 Ibid., p. 217.

29 Ibid., p. 240.

30 Ibid., p. 258.

31 Ibid., p. 199.

32 Ibid., p. 249.

33 Ibid., p. 252.

34 Mauriac, *La Fin de la Nuit*, p. 179. This passage is omitted from the edition used for the English translation. [Trans.]

35 Victorien Sardou (1831–1908): a prominent French dramatist. *L'Espionne* was a revised version of his play *Dora*, which had originally been produced at the Théâtre du Vaudeville in 1877. It was subsequently adapted for the English stage as *Diplomacy*. [Trans.]

36 Henri Bernstein (1876–1953): came to prominence thanks to the success of his play *Le Voleur* in 1906. [Trans.]

interpolates itself between the intuition and its object, must terrorists were rejected, like Bataille himself, from silence and, throughout the postwar period, we can see an attempt to destroy words with words, going on and an attempt to destroy painting with painting, and art with art. There can be no doubt that this Surrealist destruction should be subjected to existential analysis. We need to know, in fact, what it means to *destroy*. But it is certain that this destruction implicates itself, as in Bataille's case, to The Word. This lies *proved* to a great extent by Max Ernst's famous definition. 'She dealises the encounter, on a dissecting table, between a sewing machine and an umbrella.' And indeed just to *effect* this encounter that *Happen is*, nothing to. But to stimulate disappointment an umbrella, a sewing machine Dada dissecting tables are so many natural objects, institutions of human misery that in no sense do they merely after their little trees on a table, neighborhood pile of objects that smack of hospitals and wage labour, it is the are tools that clash, not things—the words within their simplicity and their repercussions. And this leads to the automatic writing and its subsequent variants, sleights made by hawkers to set up the short circuits between and terms. 'Poetry,' said the one Paul Eluard, 'is words that he ends up killing his double and passing himself off as the dead man. Another perfect crime, you will say. True, but this is a crime of a special kind because the resemblance on which it is based may well be an illusion. In the end, when the murder has been carried out, Hermann Karlovich is not entirely sure he hasn't made a mistake. Perhaps he was wrong; perhaps what he had seen was just one of those phantom similarities that we notice, on days when we are tired, in the faces of passers-by. So the crime is undermined from within, as also is the novel.

It seems to me that this zeal in self-criticism and self-destruction is rather characteristic of Mr Nabokov's manner. He is an author with a great deal of talent, but he is the son of old parents. I am ascribing blame here only to his spiritual parents, particularly Dostoevsky. Even more than he resembles his double Felix, Nabokov's hero resembles the characters of *The Raw Youth*, 'The Eternal Husband' or *Notes from Underground*, those stiff, clever obsessives, always worthy and always humiliated, who wrestle in the inferno of reason, are contemptuous of everything and are continually doing their utmost to justify themselves, and who offer a glimpse, through the

holes in their proud, faked confessions, of their hope-
less bewilderment.

But Dostoevsky believed in his characters. Mr
Nabokov no longer believes in his, nor indeed in the
novelist's art. He is open about his borrowing of Dos-
toevskyan techniques, but at the same time he mocks
them; he presents them, in the narrative itself, as indispensable but outdated clichés:

> Did it actually go on like this? . . . There is
> something a shade too literary about that talk
> of ours, smacking of thumb-screw conver-
> sations in those stage taverns where Dosto-
> evski is at home; a little more of it and we
> should hear that sibilant whisper of false
> humility, that catch in the breath, those
> repetitions of incantatory adverbs—and
> then all the rest of it would come, the
> mystical trimming dear to that famous writer
> of Russian thrillers.[1]

As is the case everywhere else, we must, in the
novel, distinguish between a time for making tools
and a time for reflecting on the tools made. Mr
Nabokov is an author of the second period. He lo-
cates himself resolutely on the level of reflection. He

must have felt a little of the stupor experienced by the Pythagoreans at the incommensurability of the sides of a right-angled triangle. If a society philosophizes, this means, there is still, in the 'gears', a place for individual dreams, for each person's fantasy, for questioning and incomprehension. That means, then, ultimately that there is no perfectly rigorous social order, for Parain saw philosophy and literature as the last dream of an imperfect language. However, this is purely external. Experience counts for little in my view, since one can still, in the end, decide to perfect the most imperfect of social orders. Will it *never* be rigorous? Or is it just not rigorous *yet*? The facts do not speak for themselves; it is for everyone to decide. Parain's decision seems rather to have been dictated to him by a deeper, more inward experience, a self-testing that is similar in more than one respect to what Rauh termed 'moral experience'. Parain the peasant had set out upon the paths of pride, the ways of the town, and the proletariat, as a result of a misunderstanding. But what is this quality? A taint of which he had recently subscribed were at odds with his thoroughgoing individualism. And

328

what a lot of fuss over nothing. And then, if Mr Nabokov is so superior to the novels he writes, why does he write them? You would swear it was out of masochism, so as to have the pleasure of catching himself red-handed in an act of fakery. And then, lastly, I'm willing to admit that Mr Nabokov is right to skip the big novelistic set-pieces, but what does he give us in their place? Preparatory chatter (though when we are duly readied, nothing happens), excellent little scenes, charming portraits and literary essays. Where is the novel? It has dissolved into its own venom: this is what I call a literature of the learned. The hero of *Despair* confesses: 'From the end of 1914 to the middle of 1919 I read exactly one thousand and eighteen books.'[3] I fear that Mr Nabokov, like his hero, has read too much.

But I can see another similarity too between the author and his character: both are victims of war and emigration. Admittedly, Dostoevsky has no shortage of cynical descendants today, with less stamina, but more intelligence than their famous forebear. I have in mind, particularly, the Soviet writer Yuri Olesha. Only, for all Olesha's sly individualism, he is still part of Soviet society. He has roots. But at the present

moment there is a curious literature of Russian—
and other—émigrés, who are rootless. Mr Nabokov's
rootlessness, like that of Hermann Karlovich is total.
Neither is concerned with any society, even to rebel
against it, because they belong to no society. As a
result, Karlovich is reduced to committing perfect
crimes and Mr Nabokov to writing, in the English
language, on gratuitous themes.

1939

Notes

1   Vladimir Nabokov, *Despair* (New York: Perigee
    Books, 1979), p. 98.

2   Ibid., p. 106.

3   Ibid., p. 14.

Denis de Rougemont:
L'Amour et l'occident[1]

[*T*]*he passionate love which the myth* [*of Tristan and Iseult*] *celebrates actually became in the twelfth century—the moment when it first came to be cultivated—a religion in the full sense of the word, and in particularly a historically determinate Christian heresy.* Whereupon it may be inferred . . . that the passion which novels and films have now popularized is nothing else than *a lawless invasion and flowing back* into our lives of a spiritual heresy the key to which we have lost.[2]

This is the thesis Monsieur de Rougemont attempts to demonstrate. I must admit that I was not equally convinced by all his arguments. In particular, the attachment of the Tristan myth to the Cathar heresy is more asserted than proved. Elsewhere, M. de Rougemont has need, in support of his cause, to show that the Chinese know nothing of passionate love. He asserts, as a consequence, that this is the case and I am only too willing to believe it. But it occurs to me immediately that China has five thousand years of history and enormous, highly diverse populations. I go immediately to the Appendix in which M. de Rougemont justifies his assertions and I see that he bases the whole of his psychology of the Chinese on a short passage from *Désespoirs*, a posthumous anthology of the writings of Leo Ferrero.[3] Is this really serious? But perhaps he has other unstated reasons for not weighing down his treatise with references: let us grant him the Chinese. It will be more difficult to let pass most of his ideas on contemporary literature. On page 233, for example, our author cites Caldwell, Lawrence, Faulkner and Céline, in no particular order, as representatives of a mystic doctrine of life, which is said moreover to lie at the origins of the 'National-Socialist' movement. Faulkner as a representative of a mystic doctrine of life? Caldwell a cousin of the Nazis! One can only advise M. de Rougement to re-read—or to read—*Light in August* and *God's Little Acre*. But this is the danger of panoramic visions of this kind.

Happily, this is not entirely a work of such casual audacity. The insightfulness of the analyses, the subtlety and originality of certain comparisons (the chapter on love and war is, in my view, excellent) and the deftness of style are certainly worthy of admiration. But the interest of the book, for me, lies primarily in the fact that it reflects a recent, thoroughgoing freeing of historical method under the threefold influence of psychoanalysis, Marxism and sociology. It is to sociology, it seems to me, that M. de Rougemont owes his intention to treat myth as an object of rigorous study. However, his approach will be that of the historian. That is to say, he will not be concerned to compare primitive mythologies so as to extract their common laws: rather, he selects a particular myth, which can be precisely dated, and follows its individual development. The comparison that comes to mind is with Roger Caillois—not the Caillois who explains the myth of the preying mantis, but the Caillois who studies the formation and development in the nineteenth century of the myth of Paris as *great city*—but I am rather afraid that, being so different from each other, the comparison will annoy both authors. They will, however, agree that they have, at least in this particular case, a single approach to myth as both an expression of general affective reactions and the symbolic product of an individual historical situation. Moreover, this idea of myth is itself a product of the age and has been very much in vogue since Sorel.[4] Wasn't it Bloch who called recently for a myth for the twentieth century?[5] And didn't Malraux speak, precisely, of the myths of love in the preface he contributed to a translation of D. H. Lawrence? To the point that we may fear—to speak like these authors—that there is today a myth of the myth, which ought itself to be subjected to sociological investigation.

I don't think either that M. de Rougemont would unreservedly admit the influence of dialectical materialism that I believe I discerned in his book. And I will acknowledge, if he so pleases, that it is not direct: I am not forgetting that our author is a Christian. But, where else, ultimately, does he get the precious idea that there are deep analogies and correspondences between the various superstructures of a civilization? For our author, a society seems to be a signifying totality whose components, each in their own way, express a single meaning. A Marxist wouldn't disagree. And isn't this idea of a sort of logic specific to each superstructure, which seems both to reflect a basic situation and to develop through human consciousnesses in accordance with objective laws of development, a Marxist conception? At this level, and by supposing an objective development of the mind or, if one prefers, of ideologies, we connect up also with psychoanalysis: 'The myth, that is to say, the unconscious . . .' writes M. de Rougemont as a true Freudian; and when he interrogates the troubadours and *trouvères*, he shows little concern for whether or not they were conscious of the esoteric value of their songs. Societies, like human beings, have their secrets; myths are symbols—like our dreams. Hence this new mission for historians: to psychoanalyse texts.

The most fortunate outcome of these divergent influences is, without doubt, its disposing M. de Rougemont to take a *verstehend* approach to the interpretation of historical phenomena. This use of *Verstehen*, the logic of which Raymond Aron has attempted to trace in his *Introduction to the Philosophy of History*, seems to me to mark a genuine advance in historical studies. I should make clear that we shall not find in M. de Rougemont's work either those causal series that can be established by the sociologist (as, for example, the connection made by Simiand[6] between rising wages and the discovery of goldmines in the nineteenth century), the rational deductions of the classical economist or those mere chronological lists of facts we find too often in Lavisse or Seignobos.[7] Our author is attempting to bring to light relations of understanding that relate to the objective spirit of communities, which we shall define briefly here as the revelation of a certain type of finality immanent in cultural phenomena.

Thus, passionate love is not a primal datum of the human condition. We may assign a date to its appearance in Western society and we may imagine its total disappearance: 'The enforced practice of eugenics may succeed where all moral doctrines have failed, resulting in the effective disappearance of any . . . need of passion.'[8] This idea is not perhaps as new as it first seems. In his study of 'the Prohibition of Incest', Durkheim suggested that our modern concenption of love had its origins in primitive man being forbidden to take a wife from within his own clan. If it had been permitted, he said, incest would have made the sexual act an austere, sacred family rite. But in the writings of M. de Rougemont, who is a Christian, this degree of historicism may be surprising. This is because historicism, if taken to its limits, leads automatically to total relativism. On this path, M. de Rougemont stops at a point that suits him: he asserts, in fact, the absolute of faith. This enables us to grasp the ambiguous nature of Christianity, which is the *historical* revelation of the absolute. There is nothing inherently shocking in this paradox, since human beings are such that they experience eternal truths *in time*. But M. de Rougemont will have to be careful. If he takes advantage of the *historicity* of the 'passionate love' phenomenon to assert its relativity, he prompts us to want to do the same with religion. And if he defends his faith with the contention that the absolute may very well appear to us *in time*, then we shall ask in turn: if that is the case, then why couldn't certain essential structures of the human condition realize themselves through determinate historical conditions? What is there to prevent me from supposing that in Greece passionate love was *masked* by paganism, by the religion of the *polis* and by the power of family constraints?

Indeed, I believe I have noticed a slight vacillation on this question in our author's thinking. He seems to believe, at times, that passion is the normal outcome of natural Eros and he even goes so far as to speak of the 'perpetual threat that passion and the death instinct present for the whole of society', and at times he calls it 'the oriental temptation of the West'. But, he will no doubt say, this is the same thing, since the Oriental is natural man. Well, not exactly, since M. de Rougemont himself acknowledges that 'these same beliefs have not produced the same effects among the peoples of the East.' This is because they have not, he says, met with the same obstacles: 'Christian marriage, by becoming a sacrament, imposed an unbearable fidelity on natural man . . . He was ready to welcome, under cover of Catholic forms, all the revivals of pagan mysticism that were capable of liberating him.' Right. But this takes us a long way from that 'perpetual threat' which passion poses for every society. Passionate love is, indeed, a debased myth. And M. de Rougemont is curiously close to the psychoanalysts since, like them, he asserts that human affectivity is originally a *tabula rasa*. It is the circumstances of individual or collective history that inscribe their lessons upon it. All this is not very clear. Nor perhaps is it coherent. And the distinction between the natural man and the man of faith, which the author accepts throughout as though it were self-evident, probably requires some explanation. But no matter. Let us take the argument as presented to us and consider its merits.

For my part, I admire its ingenious nature, but I do not believe it at all. It would first have to be proved that literature expresses *mores* exactly. And also that it influences them. M. de Rougemont confines himself to asserting that influence because, he says, 'passion has its source in that surge of the spirit which, more-over, gives rise to language.' This is true. But language and literary expression are not the same thing. To at-tempt to study a myth solely on the basis of its liter-ary—in other words, its conscious, reflective—forms is like trying to determine the *mores* of a community by looking at its written law. At most, M. de Rouge-mont has shown that literature creates a fixed representation of passion, something like a label of passion, which may perhaps underlie many an amorous adventure. But we knew that already. We have known it since Stendhal. 'If the word love is spoken between them, I am lost,' says Count Mosca, as he watches the coach carrying la Sanseverina and Fabrice recede into the distance. But does *real* passion, the passion that suddenly forms within a soul, also crystallize in these stereotyped forms? Is it true that without them it would be just a dumb, obtuse sexual desire? Would it not, as a psychological phenomenon, have its own dialectic? And are not its eager, hapless efforts aimed at removing obstacles, rather than constantly giving rise to new ones? This is what ought to have been elucidated. I hear M. de Rougemont telling me that the sexual instinct, when left to itself, is incapable of dialectic. If he is referring to that itching of the loins that nineteenth-century psychology describes as sexuality, then I agree with him. But the question remains whether sexual desire is really an itching of the loins.

It seems to me that M. de Rougemont touches on the real problem when he writes, 'The history of passionate love . . . is . . . the account of the more and more desperate attempts Eros makes to replace *mystical Transcendence* with an emotional intensity.'[9] Here we are then: passionate love, like mysticism, raises the question of transcendence. But the author brings to the examination of the problem the immanentist, subjectivist prejudices of a psychology that has had its day. What if transcendence were precisely the 'existential' structure of the human being? Would there still be a narcissism of love? Would we need a courtly myth to explain passion? M. de Rougemont hasn't speculated on this. And yet these questions are essential. If man is 'transcendent', then he can exist only by transcending *himself*, that is to say, by throwing himself out of himself and into the world—what Heidegger calls *Sich-vorweg-sein-bei*. In this case, to love is merely one aspect of transcendence: one loves outside of oneself, beside another; he who loves depends on another to the very heart of his existence. And if M. de Rougemont should find that this word 'love' refers to a sentiment that is already too developed, I shall tell him that sexual desire is, itself, transcendence. One doesn't 'desire' a mere evacuation, like a cow who is going to be milked. Nor even the highly subjective impressions afforded by a fresh contact. One desires a person in her flesh. To desire is to throw oneself into the world, in danger beside the flesh of a woman, in danger in the very flesh of that woman; it is to wish to attain a state of consciousness, through the flesh and *on* the flesh—to attain that 'divine absence' Paul

Valéry speaks of. Is anything more required for desire naturally to entail its own contradiction, its haplessness and its dialectic? Doesn't it seek a union which, by its nature, it rejects? Isn't it desire for the freedom of another which, by its essence, eludes it? Lastly, if it is true that man's authentic being is a 'being-for death', any authentic passion must have a taste of ashes about it. If death is present in love, this is not in any sense the fault of love or of any sort of narcissism; it is the fault of death.

Since it makes no attempt to discuss these problems, M. de Rougemont's book seems merely a fine piece of entertainment. But no matter. Read it. It will give you great pleasure. Perhaps you will catch yourself dreaming of what might have happened if, by some miracle, the Cathars had massacred all the Christians (it was, unfortunately, the opposite that happened) and if their religion had continued into our own day. They were decent people.

Notes

1   Denis de Rougemont, *L'Amour et l'occident* (Paris: Union générale d'éditions, 1939). Translated by

Montgomery Belgion as *Love in the Western World* (Princeton: Princeton University Press, 1983 [1956]).

2   Ibid., p. 137 (translation modified).

3   Leo Ferrero (1903–33): an Italian writer and dramatist. [Trans.]

4   Georges Sorel (1847–1922) argued that myth could play a legitimate mobilizing role in radical social movements. [Trans.]

5   Jean-Richard Bloch (1884–1947): a French novelist, playwright and critic. [Trans.]

6   François Simian (1873–1935), a student of Durkheim and Bergson, was a French economist and sociologist.

7   Ernest Lavisse (1842–1922): a French historian and, famously, an editor of French official school manuals in his subject; Charles Seignobos (1854–1942): an equally renowned positivist historian. [Trans.]

8   De Rougemont, *Love* . . . , p. 291 (translation modified).

9   Ibid., p. 170 (translation modified). My emphasis. [J.-P. S.]

On The Sound and the Fury:
Temporality in Faulkner

When you read *The Sound and the Fury*, what strikes you first are oddities of technique. Why has Faulkner broken up the timeline of his story and scrambled the pieces? Why is the first window that opens on to this fictional world the mind of an idiot? The reader is tempted to search out markers and re-establish the chronology for himself: 'Jason and Caroline Compson have had three sons and a daughter. The daughter, Caddy, has given herself to Dalton Ames and become pregnant by him. Forced to get hold of a husband quickly . . .' Here the reader stops, for he realizes that he is telling a different story. Faulkner didn't first conceive this orderly plot, then shuffle it like a pack of cards; he couldn't tell the story any other way. In the classical novel, there is a crux to the action: the murder of old Karamzov or the meeting of Édouard and Bernard in Gide's *The Counterfeiters*. One would look in vain for such a crux in *The Sound and the Fury*. Is it the castration of Benjy, Caddy's wretched amorous adventure, Quentin's suicide or Jason's hatred for his niece? Each episode, as soon as you look at it, opens up and reveals other episodes behind it—all the other episodes. Nothing happens; the story doesn't unfold: you discover it beneath every word, like a cumbrous, obscene presence, more or less condensed in each case. It would be wrong to regard these anomalies as gratuitous shows of virtuosity: a novelistic technique always relates to the novelist's metaphysics. The critic's task is to identify the latter before evaluating the former. It is blindingly obvious that Faulkner's metaphysics is a metaphysics of time.

It is man's misfortune that he is a temporal being. 'A man is the sum of his misfortunes. One day you'd think misfortune would get tired, but then time is your misfortune . . .'[1] This is the real subject of the novel. And if the technique Faulkner adopts seems at first a negation of temporality, this is because we are confusing temporality with chronology. It is man who invented dates and clocks: 'Constant speculation regarding the position of mechanical hands on an arbitrary dial which is a symptom of mind-function. Excrement Father said like sweating.'[2] To arrive at real time, we have to abandon this invented measure which in fact measures nothing: '. . . time is dead as long as it is being clicked off by little wheels; only when the clock stops does time come to life.'[3]

Quentin's act of smashing his watch thus has symbolic value: it takes us into clock-less time. And Benjy's time, too, is clock-less, he, the idiot, not knowing how to tell the time.

What is revealed at that point is the present. Not the ideal limit whose place is carefully marked between past and future. Faulkner's present is catastrophic in its essence. It is the event that comes upon us like a thief, enormous and unthinkable. That comes upon us and then disappears. Beyond that present, there is nothing, since the future doesn't exist. The present wells up from we know not where, chasing away another present. It is perpetually beginning anew: 'And . . . and . . . and then . . .' Like Dos Passos, but much more discreetly, Faulkner turns his narrative into an addition. The actions themselves, even when they are seen by those who perform them, break up and scatter as they penetrate into the present:

> I went to the dresser and took up the watch with the face still down. I tapped the crystal on the dresser and caught the fragments of glass in my hand and put them into the ash-tray and twisted the hands off and put them in the tray. The watch ticked on.[4]

The other characteristic of this present is a *sinking-down*. I use this word, for want of a better one, to point up a kind of motionless movement of this formless monster. There is never any progression in Faulkner, never anything that comes from the future. The present was not first a future possibility, as, for example, when my friend eventually appears, after having been *the man I am waiting for*. No, to be present means to appear without reason and to sink down. This sinking-down isn't part of some abstract vision:

it is in things themselves that Faulkner perceives it and attempts to make his readers feel it:

> The train swung around the curve, the engine puffing with short, heavy blasts, and they passed smoothly from sight that way, with that quality of shabby and timeless patience, of static serenity . . .[5]

Or again,

> Beneath the sag of the buggy the hooves neatly rapid like motions of a lady doing embroidery, *diminishing without progress* like a figure on a treadmill being drawn rapidly off-stage.[6]

It seems as though, in the very heart of things, Faulkner grasps a frozen speed: congealed spurting presences brush up against him that grow pale, retreat and reduce without moving.

Yet this elusive, unthinkable immobility can be halted and conceived of. Quentin can say, 'I broke my watch.' Only, when he says it, his act is already past. The past can be named and narrated; it can, to an extent, be grasped in concepts or recognized by the heart. We have already noted, writing of *Sartoris*, that Faulkner always showed events when they were finished. In *The Sound and the Fury*, everything happens in the wings: nothing happens, everything has happened. This is what enables us to understand the strange expression uttered by one of his heroes: 'I was, I am not.'[7] In this sense, too, Faulkner is able to make man a sum total without a future. He is 'the sum of his climatic experiences', 'the sum of his misfortunes', 'the sum of what have you': at every moment a line is drawn under events, since the present is merely a lawless rumbling, a past future. It seems Faulkner's worldview can be compared to that of a man sitting in an open-topped car and looking backwards. At each moment, formless shadows rear up to right and left; flickerings, subdued vibrations, wisps of light, which only become trees, people and cars a little later, as they recede into the distance. The past acquires a sort of surreality in this: its outlines become crisp and hard—changeless. The present, nameless and fleeting, suffers greatly by comparison; it is full of holes and, through these holes, it is invaded by things past, which are fixed, still and silent, like judges or stares. Faulkner's monologues are reminiscent of aeroplane journeys with lots of air pockets. With each new pocket, the hero's consciousness sinks back into the past, rises and then sinks again. The present *is* not; it *becomes*; everything *was*. In *Sartoris*, the past was called 'stories', because these were—constructed—family memories and because Faulkner hadn't found his technique yet. In *The Sound and the Fury*, it is more individual and more undecided. But it is so obsessively there that at times it masks the present. And the present makes its way in the shadows like an underground river, reappearing only when it is, itself, past. When Quentin insults Bland,[8] he doesn't even realize he has done so: he is re-living his dispute with Dalton Ames. And when Bland beats him up, the brawl is overlaid with the one between Quentin and Ames. Later, Shreve *will relate* how Bland struck Quentin: he will relate the scene because it has now become history, but when it was happening in the present, it was merely a veiled, furtive drift of events.

I was told once of a former deputy headmaster who had grown senile and whose memory had stopped like a broken watch: it now stood perpetually at the age of forty. He was sixty years old, but didn't know it and his last memory was of a school playground and the way he used to patrol its covered area each day. As a consequence, he interpreted his present in the light of this final stage of the past and walked round and round his table, convinced he was supervising schoolchildren at play. Faulkner's characters are like this. Worse: their past, though in order, isn't chronologically ordered. It is grouped into affective constellations. Around a number of central themes (Caddy's pregnancy, Benjy's castration and Quentin's suicide), innumerable silent clumps of memories gravitate. Hence the absurdity of chronology, of 'the assertive and contradictory assurance' of watch-faces:[9] the order of the past is the order of the heart. We shouldn't believe that the present, as it passes, becomes our closest memory. Its metamorphosis may sink it to the bottom of our memories, just as it may also leave it on the surface: only its own density and the overall dramatic meaning of our lives determine its level.

* * *

Such is Faulkner's time. And is it not familiar? This ineffable present, shipping water on all sides, these sudden invasions by the past, this affective order that stands opposed to the order of the intellect and the will (which is chronological, but misses reality), these memories, monstrous, intermittent obsessions, these waverings of the heart—is this not the lost—and regained—time of Marcel Proust? I am not unaware of the differences. I know, for example, that salvation, for Proust, lies in time itself, in the reappearance of the past as something whole and entire. For Faulkner, by contrast, the past is never lost—unfortunately. It is always there, an obsession. Only by mystic ecstasies can one escape the temporal world. A mystic is always a man who wants to forget something: his self or, more generally, language or figural representations. For Faulkner, it is time that has to be forgotten:

> Quentin, I give you the mausoleum of all hope and desire; it's rather excruciatingly apt that you will use it to gain the reductio ad absurdum of all human experience which can fit your individual needs no better than it fitted his or his father's. I give it to you not that you may remember time, *but that you might forget it now and then for a moment* and not spend all your breath trying to conquer it. Because no battle is ever won he said. They are not even fought. The field only reveals to man his own folly and despair, and victory is an illusion of philosophers and fools.[10]

It is because he has forgotten time that the hunted negro of *Light in August* suddenly achieves his strange, dreadful happiness:

> It's not when you realize that nothing can help you—religion, pride, anything—it's when you realize that you don't need any aid.[11]

But for Faulkner, as for Proust, time is above all *what separates*. We remember the astonishment of the Proustian heroes who can no longer return to their past loves, of those lovers depicted in *Les Plaisirs et les Jours*, clinging to their passions because they are afraid they may pass and know that they will. We find the same anxiety in Faulkner:

> [P]eople cannot do anything that dreadful they cannot do anything very dreadful at all, they cannot even remember tomorrow what seemed dreadful today . . .[12]

and

> [A] love or sorrow is a bond purchased without design and which matures willy-nilly and is recalled without warning to be replaced by whatever issue the gods happen to be floating at the time.[13]

In truth, Proust's novelistic technique *ought to have* been Faulkner's: it was the logical outcome of his metaphysics. But Faulkner is a lost man and it is because he feels lost that he takes risks, that he carries his thoughts through to their conclusions. Proust is a classicist and a Frenchman. The French lose themselves in a small-time sort of way and always end up finding themselves again. Eloquence, a taste for clear ideas and intellectualism caused Proust to maintain at least the semblance of chronology.

The deep causes of the affinity between the two are to be sought in a very general literary phenomenon: most great contemporary authors—Proust, Joyce, Dos Passos, Faulkner, Gide and Virginia Woolf—have, each in their own way, attempted to mutilate time. Some have shorn it of a past and future and reduced it to the pure intuition of the moment. Others, like Dos Passos, make it a dead, closed memory. Proust and Faulkner simply decapitated it. They took away its future: that is to say, the dimension of acts and freedom. Proust's heroes never undertake anything. Admittedly, they make plans, but their plans remain stuck to them alone; they cannot be thrown beyond the present, as bridges. They are dreams that reality puts to flight. The Albertine who appears isn't the one we were expecting, and the expectation is a mere inconsequential agitation, confined entirely to the present moment. As for Faulkner's heroes, they never see ahead; the car carries them off, facing backwards. The future suicide that throws its dense shadow over Quentin's last day isn't a human possibility: not for a second does Quentin consider that he might *not* kill himself. That suicide is an immobile wall, a *thing* Quentin approaches backwards, which he neither wants nor is able to conceive of: 'You seem to regard it merely as an experience that will whiten your hair overnight so to speak without altering your appearance at all.'[14] It isn't an *undertaking*, but a fateful inevitability. By losing its character as possibility, it ceases to exist in the future. It is already present, and Faulkner's whole art is directed at suggesting to us that Quentin's monologues and his last walk *were already* Quentin's suicide. It is in this way, I think, that the following curious paradox is explained: Quentin thinks his last day in the past tense, like someone remembering. But who is doing the remembering, since the hero's last thoughts coincide more or less with the shattering of his memory and his annihilation? The answer has to be that the novelist's skill lies in the choice of the present from which he narrates the past. And the present Faulkner has chosen here is the infinitesimal moment of death, as Salacrou does in *L'Inconnue d'Arras*.[15] So, when Quentin's memory begins to unfurl his recollections ('Through the wall I heard Shreve's bed-springs and then his slippers on the floor hishing. I got up . . .'[16]), *he is already dead*. All this art and, to tell the truth, all this dishonesty are aimed simply at replacing the intuition of the future which the author lacks. Everything is then explained, beginning with the irrationality of time: since the present is the unexpected, the formless, it can acquire determinacy only by an overload of memories. We can understand, too, why *la durée* is 'man's characteristic misfortune': if the future has a reality, time distances us from the past and *brings us nearer* to the future; but if you abolish the future, time is now merely that which separates the present—which cuts it off—from itself. 'You cannot bear to think that someday it will no longer hurt you like this.' Man spends his time battling against time and it gnaws away at him like an acid, wrenches him away from himself and prevents him from fulfilling his humanity. Everything is absurd: 'Life is a tale told by an idiot, full of sound and fury, signifying nothing.'[17]

But does human time have no future? I can see that, for a nail or a clod of earth, time is a perpetual present. But is man merely a thinking nail? If we begin by plunging him into universal time, the time of nebulae and planets, of tertiary flexures and animal species, as into a bath of sulphuric acid, then that is the case. But a consciousness buffeted about in that way from one moment to another would have to be a consciousness *first* and only *thereafter* something temporal. Do we really believe that time can come to it from outside? Consciousness can 'be in time' only on condition that it becomes time in the very movement that makes it consciousness; it must, as Heidegger says, temporalize itself.[18] Man can no longer be arrested at each present and defined as 'the sum of what he has': the nature of consciousness implies, rather, that, of itself, it projects itself forward, towards the future; we can understand what it is only by what it will be and it is determined in its current being by its own possibilities. This is what Heidegger calls, 'the silent force of the possible'.[19] Faulkner's man, a creature deprived of possibilities, explained solely by what he was, is a being you will not recognize within yourself. Try to seize hold of your consciousness. Probe into it. You will see that it is hollow. You will find in it only futurity. I am not even speaking of your plans and expectations. But the very action you catch in passing has meaning for you only if you can project its completion outside of itself, outside of you, into the 'not yet'. This very cup with its bottom that you do not see—that you could see and that is at the end of a movement you have not yet made—this white sheet of paper, the underside of which is hidden (but you could turn it over) and all the stable, bulky objects surrounding us display their most immediate, most solid qualities in the future. Man is in no sense the sum total of what he has, but the totality of what he doesn't yet have, of what he could have. And if we are immersed, in this way, in futurity, isn't the formless harshness of the present thereby attenuated? The event doesn't spring on us like a thief, since it is, by its very nature, a Having-been-Future. And, in seeking to explain the past, isn't it first the historian's task to research into its future? I rather suspect that the absurdity Faulkner finds in a human life is an absurdity he first put there himself. Not that human life isn't absurd: but there is another form of absurdity.

How does it come about that Faulkner and so many other authors chose that particular absurdity, which is so un-novelistic and so untrue? I believe we have to look for the cause in the social conditions of our present life. Faulkner's despair seems to me to antedate his metaphysics. For him, as for all of us, the future is blocked off. Everything we see and experience suggests to us that 'this cannot last', and yet change is not even conceivable, except in cataclysmic form. We are living in an age of impossible revolutions and Faulkner employs his extraordinary art to describe this world that is dying of old age and our suffocation in it. I love his art; I do not believe in his metaphysics. A blocked-off future is still a future. 'Even when human reality still exists but has nothing more "before it" and has "settled [*abgeschlossen*] its account", its Being is still determined by the "ahead-of-itself". Hopelessness, for example, doesn't tear human reality away from its possibilities, but is only one of its own modes of *Being-towards* these possibilities.'[20]

Notes

1   William Faulkner, *The Sound and the Fury*. Norton Critical Edition, 2nd edn (New York: W. W. Norton & Company, 1994), p. 66.

2   Ibid., p. 49.

3   Ibid., p. 54.

4   Ibid., p. 51.

5   Ibid., p. 56.

6   The italics are Faulkner's.

7   Ibid., p. 110.

8   Ibid., pp. 100–04. See p. 102, the dialogue with Bland inserted into the dialogue with Ames, 'Did you ever have a sister, did you?' etc., and the inextricable confusion of the two battles.

9   Ibid., p. 54.

10 Ibid., p. 48.

11 Ibid., p. 51.

12 Ibid., p. 51.

13 Ibid., pp. 112–13.

14 Ibid., p. 112.

15 Armand Salacrou (1899–1989): a French playwright, who is remembered particularly for *L'Inconnue d'Arras* of 1935. [Trans.]

16 Faulkner, *The Sound and The Fury*, p. 49.

17 William Shakespeare, *Macbeth*, Act V, Scene 5.

18 The reference is presumably to Heidegger's use of the term (*sich*) *zeitigen*. [Trans.]

19 '*Die stille Kraft des Möglichen*'. [Trans.]

20 Martin Heidegger, *Being and Time* (John Macquarrie and Edward Robinson trans.) (Oxford: Basil Blackwell, 1978), p. 279. Translation modified to reflect Sartre's rendering of Dasein as '*la réalité humaine*'. [Trans.]

Monsieur Jean Giraudoux and the Philosophy of Aristotle: *On* Choix des Élues

Everything we are able to know of Monsieur Giraudoux suggests that he is 'normal' in both the most commonplace and the most elevated sense of the term. Furthermore, his critical studies have enabled us to appreciate the supple delicacy of his intelligence. However, as soon as you open one of his novels, you have the impression of entering the universe of one of those waking dreamers, known medically as 'schizophrenics', who are characterized, as we know, by an

122

inability to adapt themselves to reality. The main characteristics of these patients—their stiffness, their efforts to deny change and to mask the present, their geometrism, their taste for symmetry, generalizations, symbols and magical correspondences across time and space—are all taken on by M. Giraudoux and artfully developed: it is in them that the charm of his book resides. I have often been intrigued by the contrast between the man and his work. Might it be that M. Giraudoux finds entertainment in playing the schizophrenic?

Choix des Élues, which was serialized in this very publication,[1] seemed valuable to me because it provided me with an answer. It is probably not M. Giraudoux's best book. But precisely because many of the charms of his style have turned into devices in it, it is easier to grasp the turn of this strange mind. It became clear to me, first of all, that I had been kept from the true interpretation of his work by a prejudice I must share with many of his readers. Up to now, I have always attempted to *translate* his books. In other words, I have acted as though M. Giraudoux had amassed a great many observations and had derived a particular wisdom from them and had then, out of fondness for a certain preciosity, expressed all this experience and wisdom in coded language. My attempts at decipherment had never produced any great results. M. Giraudoux's profundity is genuine, but it is a profundity for his world, not for ours. So on this occasion I did not try to translate, I did not seek out the metaphor, the symbol or the hidden meaning. I took everything at face value with the aim of increasing, not my knowledge of human beings, but my knowledge of M. Giraudoux. To enter fully the universe of *Choix des Élues*, we must first forget the world in which we live. I therefore pretended I knew nothing of our doughy world, rippled by waves whose causes and ends originate elsewhere, nothing of our futureless world made up solely of fresh encounters, in which the present breaks in like a thief, events naturally resist thought and language, and individuals are accidents, lumps of grit, for which the mind retrospectively devises general headings.

I was not wrong to do so. In the America of Edmée, Claudie and Pierre, order and intelligible states of rest exist first; they are the goal of change and its only justification. I was struck from the beginning of the book by these clear little states of rest; the book is made up of rests. A jar of gherkins is not the chance aspect assumed by circling atoms, it is a state of rest, a form closed in upon itself; the mind of a graduate of *Polytechnique*, stuffed with calculations and entitlements, is another state of rest; and rest too is the light head of a painter in the lap of a beautiful, motionless woman—or a landscape, a public park or even the fleeting impression of a morning. These boundaries or limits assigned to the becoming of matter we shall call, as they did in the Middle Ages, 'substantial forms'. M. Giraudoux is so constituted that he first grasps the species in the individual and the thought in matter: 'A truth that was Edmée's face,' he writes. Things are like that in his universe: they are truths first, ideas first, meanings that choose their signs for themselves. 'Jacques, *like an artless little boy*, reticent in his joy and his sorrow alike, had immediately diverted his gaze.' This little Jacques is not first an accident, a rosette of proliferating cells, but the incarnation of a truth. The occasion, the hour and the cast of the times mean that a certain Jacques has a mission to represent, at a certain spot in America, the truth common to artless little boys. But this 'substantial form' is independent of its incarnations and in many other places many other little boys divert their gaze so as not to see their mother's tears. We might say here, to speak like the Schoolmen, that this is a case of matter individualizing. Hence M. Giraudoux's curious penchant for universal judgements: 'All the town's clocks struck ten . . . All cockerels . . . All the villages in France . . .' This is not schizophrenia: these generalizations—wearisome in the world of becoming, where they can be only the inventory of chance encounters—correspond here to exhaustive reviews of all the children charged with personifying the 'artless little boy' and of all the nickel and enamel cylinders whose role it is to embody the 'clock'.

These enumerations often end with the mention of an oddity or exception: 'They ate their lunch on the bench . . . feeding the birds with their crumbs, except for one suspicious individual who was there to watch them, not to eat and who flew off, when they reached the dessert, to deliver his report in some far-off place.' We might term this M. Giraudoux's playfulness. He employs it skilfully, the general survey with a poetic or pleasing or comical exception being one of his most familiar devices. But the disrespect he shows here for the established order has meaning only in relation to that order itself. With M. Giraudoux, as in the wisdom of the old saw, the exception is only there to prove the rule.

We should not believe, however, that M. Giraudoux espouses Platonism. His forms are not to be found in the heaven of ideas, but among us; they are inseparable from the matter whose movements they regulate; impressed, like seals in glass or steel, upon our skins. Nor should they be confused with mere concepts. Concepts contain barely any more than a handful of characteristics common to all the individuals in a group. In truth M. Giraudoux's forms contain no more than that, but all their constitutive features are perfect. Rather than mere general ideas, they are norms and canons. Without a doubt, Jacques spontaneously applies off his own bat all the rules enabling him to achieve, within himself, the perfection of the artless little boy. And the very movement that brought Pierre into being made him the most perfect realization of the Polytechnique-educated husband. 'Edmée's canines, *so distinctly canine . . .*' writes M. Giraudoux. And, further on: 'In order to watch over his mother, Jacques had assumed the tenderest form of Jacques.' And again: 'The annoying thing about Pierre was that he had made such efforts to be representative of humanity that he had genuinely become so. Each of his actions and each of his utterances was now merely the attested sample of human action and language.' It is the same with all of the entities in M. Giraudoux's work: his books are samplings. When questioned by Parmenides, Socrates was reluctant to admit that there was an Idea of dirt, an Idea of the louse. M. Giraudoux wouldn't hesitate. The lice he deals with have the admirable quality of each being the perfection of the louse—all of them equally, though in diverse ways. This is why, rather than the name concept, these substantial forms would deserve that of archetype, and our author does sometimes use this himself: '(Pierre looks at Edmée and) draws back to see only the archetype of Edmée.' But there are also individual perfections. Edmée, who is certainly the most distinctly motherly of mothers—like all mothers—and the most distinctly wifely wife—like all wives—is also most distinctly and perfectly Edmée. And even among the gherkins which, for the most part, limit themselves resignedly to realizing the consummate type of the gherkin, a few rare, privileged ones are nevertheless endowed with a singular archetypal character:

She went to fetch a gherkin. Though one
does not choose gherkins, she obeyed him,
taking the one which, by its architecture,
sculpture and relief could claim the title of
head of household's gherkin.

We can see what the world of *Choix des Élues* is
like: it is a botanical atlas, in which all the species are
carefully classified, in which the periwinkle is blue because it is a periwinkle and the oleanders are pink
because they are pink oleanders. The only causality is
that of archetypes. There is no place in this world for
determinism, the causative action of anterior states.
But you won't find any *events* there either, if by 'event'
one means the irruption of a new phenomenon,
whose very novelty exceeds all expectation and over-
turns the order of concepts. There is hardly any
change here, except for that of matter being acted
upon by form. And the action of this form is of two
kinds. It may act by *innate potentiality*, like fire in the
Middle Ages which burned thanks to phlogiston: in
that case, it implants itself in the matter, shapes it and
moves it at will. Movement is then merely the temporal development of the archetype. In this way, most
of the actions in *Choix des Élues* are the actions of

people possessed. Characters by their acts, and things by their changes, merely realize their substantial forms the more closely:

> No peril hovered around these heads. They were resplendent. They signalled to happiness like beacons, *each with its own lighting system*; Pierre, the husband, with his two smiles, one big, one small, which followed within a second of each other every minute; Jacques, the son, with his face itself, which he raised and lowered, Claudie, the daughter, a more sensitive beacon, with the fluttering of her eyelids.

In this sense, the various alterations of this universe, which we must reluctantly agree to call events, are always the symbols of the forms producing them. But the form may also act by elective affinity. Hence the title *Choix des Élues* (Choice of the Elect). At bottom, every one of M. Giraudoux's creatures is a member of the 'elect'. This is because a form, lurking in the future, lies in wait for its matter. It has chosen it and attracts it to itself. And the second kind of change is of this order: a rapid transition from one form to the other; a becoming that is narrowly defined by its point of origin and its point of arrival. The bud is repose and so too is the flower. Between the two states of rest there is an oriented alteration, the only contingency in this ordered world, a necessary and inexpressible evil. Of this process of becoming, itself, there is nothing to say and M. Giraudoux speaks of it as little as possible. Yet the subject of *Choix des Élues* is a process of becoming. That subject is the becoming of Edmée, the Chosen One. But M. Giraudoux gives us merely its successive stages. Each of his chapters is a 'stasis'; Edmée at her birthday dinner, Edmée in the night, a description of Claudie, Edmée at Frank's, motionless, supporting the weight of a 'light head' on her lap. Edmée at the public park, which is 'outside time', Edmée at the Leeds', etc. The transitions occur off stage, like the murders in Corneille. We are now able to understand that semblance of schizophrenia that had struck us at the outset in Giraudoux's world: it is a world without present indicative. This noisy, shapeless present of surprises and catastrophes has lost its gravity and sparkle; it goes by very quickly and tactfully, excusing itself as it passes. Admittedly, there are, here and there, a few scenes and actions that 'take place', a few adventures that 'occur'. But all that is already more than half generalized away, for the main thing is to describe the symbols of certain archetypes. We repeatedly lose our purchase as we read, sliding imperceptibly from present individuality to timeless forms. At no point do we *feel* the weight of this head lying in Edmée's lap, at no point do we see it in its charming, frivolous individuality, in the light of an American spring. But this is of no importance, since the only concern is to determine whether it is in the nature of a Polytechnic graduate's head to be heavier than the crazy head of an artist. The point is that there are two presents in M. Giraudoux's work: the shameful present of the event, which is concealed as much as possible, like some hereditary defect, and the present of archetypes, which is eternity.

These perpetual limitations of the process of becoming naturally accentuate the discontinuous character of time. Since change is a lesser entity, which exists only for the purpose of rest, time is merely a succession of little jolts, an arrested film. Here is how Claudie thinks of her past:

> There had been a series of a hundred or a
> thousand little girls that had succeeded each
> other day by day to produce the Claudie of

today . . . She gathered together the photographs of this multitude of Claudies, of Claudettes, Claudines and Clo-Clos—there had been a Clo-Clo the country girl for six months—not as photographs of her, but as family portraits.

This is the temporality of *Choix des Élues:* that of the family album. You have to turn the pages, but that is nothing but a little, unremembered disorder between the calm dignity of two portraits.

This is what explains M. Giraudoux's penchant for first beginnings. 'For the first time . . .', 'It was the first time . . .'—perhaps no other phrase recurs so frequently in his work. And perhaps never so frequently as in *Choix des Élues* (see, for example, pages 16, 32, 58, 59, 66, 68, 83, 86, etc.). This is because forces in M. Giraudoux's world are oblivious of progression. In our world, we question the past and seek in vain after origins: 'When did I begin to love her?' To tell the truth, this love never began: it came into being little by little and when I eventually discovered my passion, its freshness was already gone. But in M. Giraudoux, changes are instantaneous, since they obey the famous 'all or nothing' principle. When the conditions are in place, the form appears suddenly and embeds itself in the matter. But if one factor is missing—a single, minuscule factor—nothing happens. Thus our reading carries us, from beginning to beginning, through an awakening world. If we may speak of an atmosphere common to *Simon Le Pathétique, Églantine* and *Jérome Bardini*, it is surely that of morning. From one end of these books to the other, despite ageing and nightfalls, and even massacres, the sun rises. *Électre* closes on a catastrophe and a dawn. Shall I dare say, however, that, reading *Choix des Élues*, I no longer had the impression of those charming daybreaks that Jérôme and Bella chose for their meetings? It seemed to me I was condemned to an eternal morning.

Like the beginnings, the endings are absolute. When the balance is disrupted, the form disappears as it arrived—discreetly, totally: 'In the early morning, Edmée was there without a wrinkle or a smudge on her face, and the long night that had just passed even seemed to have been subtracted from her age.' Marks, wrinkles, blemishes—these are things that properly belong in our world. But M. Giraudoux's world is a world of reconquered virginities. His creatures share a metaphysical chastity. They do, admittedly, make love. But neither love nor motherhood leave a mark on them. The nudity of his women is, admittedly, 'most distinctly nudity'. They are nudes and nothing but nudes; absolutely and perfectly nude, without any of the birthmarks, swellings and subsidings that have no part in the archetype of the nude. Like those film stars Jean Prévost called 'gloveskin women', they have bodies scoured like Dutch kitchens and their flesh gleams with the freshness of scrubbed tiles.

And yet this orderly house stands under the laws of magic. Or, rather, of alchemy, since we find strange transmutations there, in the sense in which the Middle Ages spoke of the transmutation of metals, and of strange remote influences. 'The first week of Claudie's life was the first week Edmée knew a world without spiders, without banana skins, without hairdressers with excessively hot curling tonguess.' Edmée, who is soon going to leave her husband, lies beside him in an off-cream nightdress with Valenciennes lace and a yoke. The objects in the bedroom grew angry and insulted her. She bounded into the bathroom and put on a pair of Pierre's pyjamas.

> The bed fell silent . . . And so the night passed. In these two similar articles of

clothing, they seemed to form a team. Those who can see in the dark would have taken them for twins or a matching pair. Deceived by this sudden mimicry, the objects gradually quietened down . . .

And here we have the description of an exorcism:

Disguised as Claudie, those who wanted to give Edmée white hair, loose teeth and hard skin tried to get into the bed from the space between it and the wall. She had to accept their convention, take them by Claudie's hand, take them back to Claudie's bed and threaten Claudie with no dessert for a week. God knows they didn't care! But, bound by their disguise, they had to obey.

All that is needed, then, to exorcise the demons that have taken on Claudie's shape, is to treat them *as* Claudie. What does all this mean? M. Giraudoux explains it to us himself:

With Claudie, *everything that resembled* Claudie in this lowly world approved of her . . . Her peace with little Claudie was peace with all that is not commonplace, with all that is great, with the mineral and the vegetal, with all that endures.

This is the characteristic feature of all enchant-
ments and spells: resemblance exerts an effect. But we
should be clear here that in Giraudoux resemblance
is not a perception of the mind: it is *realized*. The 'like'
which he employs so generously is never intended to
clarify: it marks a substantial analogy between acts and
between things. We should not, however, be surprised
by this, since M. Giraudoux's universe is a Natural
History. In his eyes, objects are in some sense similar
when, in some aspect or other, they share in the same
form. It is, of course, only with Claudie that Edmée
is seeking peace. But Claudie is, precisely, that which
'is not commonplace'. To make peace with Claudie is
to adapt oneself more closely to the form she currently embodies, to the form of 'all that is great . . .
all that endures'. So, by approaching, out of love for
Claudie, the perishable incarnation of an eternal archetype, Edmée finds herself thereby mysteriously in
tune with all the incarnations of that archetype: with
the desert, the mountains and the virgin forest. But
this is *logical* once we take into account that Edmée
has attuned herself, once and for all, to a universal
form. The magic is merely an appearance, arising from
the fact that this form is refracted through countless

particles of matter. Hence these deep analogies that M. Giraudoux likes to point up between the most diverse objects: the presence of forms divides the universe into an infinity of infinite regions and, in each of these regions, any old object, if we question it in the right way, tells us about all the others. In each of these regions, to love, hate or insult any object is to insult, love and hate all the others. Analogies, correspondences, symbolisms—these are what constitute the marvellous for M. Giraudoux. But, like mediaeval magic, all this is merely a strict application of the logic of the concept.

We have here then a ready-made world, a world that is not in the making. The world of Linnaeus, not of Lamarck. The world of Cuvier, not of Geoffroy Saint-Hilaire. Let us ask now what place M. Giraudoux reserves in it for man. We can sense that it is sizeable. If we remind ourselves that in this world magic is merely an appearance, that it is due simply to a hyperlogicism, we shall first have to record that this world is, to its very core, accessible to reason. M. Giraudoux has banished from it all that might surprise or disconcert us: development, becoming, disorder and novelty. Surrounded by ready-made thoughts, by the reason of trees and stones, the reason of moon and water, man has no other concern than to enumerate and contemplate. And I imagine M. Giraudoux himself has a fondness for the functionaries in the Registry Office: the writer, as he conceives him, is merely a clerk in the Land Registry. And yet a rational world could still be a source of anxiety: think of Pascal's infinite spaces or Vigny's Nature. But there is nothing of that kind here: there is a close affinity between man and world. Remember Claudie and her resemblance to the desert or the virgin forest. Can you not see that the toughness, the strength, the eternity of a forest or desert is also the eternity in the moment, the gentle strength, the frail toughness of a little girl? Humanity finds all the archetypes of nature within itself and, conversely, it finds itself in all of nature. It stands at the crossroads of all 'regions'; it is the centre of the world and a symbol of the world, like the microcosm of the magicians within the great Cosmos. Let us note that the human being, who is so well ensconced in the universe and feels at home everywhere, has not been subjected by M. Giraudoux to the influence of determinism. His character is not the outcome of a thousand imponderables, of his history or his stomach troubles. His character in no way forms as time progresses. On the contrary, it is his history— and even his stomach troubles—that are the products of his character. This is what is called 'having a destiny'. Consider, for example, the terms Edmée uses to warn her young son against love:

> Oh, little Jacques, haven't you seen yourself? Look at yourself in a mirror. It's not that you're bad looking, but you'll see you're a born victim, a ready-made victim . . . You've got just the kind of face for tears, with your head pressed into the pillow, the sort of cheeks for sinking into hands that tremble with despair, the kind of tall body that waits on street corners in the rain . . . the breastbone of those who sob without resorting to tears . . .

For Giraudoux, the character of a human being is not really different from the 'essence' of the gherkin: it is an archetype realized by way of human life through human acts; an archetype for which the human body is the perfect symbol. In this way, through symbols, the most perfect union between mind and body is achieved: the path is open to characterology, to the judgement of character from the face. But if we have swapped the psychologist's determinism for the logical necessity of essences, we don't seem to have gained much in the exchange. Admittedly, there is no longer any psychology, if by that we mean a set of empirically observed laws governing the course of our moods. But we haven't chosen what we are; we are 'possessed' by a form. There is nothing we can do about it. However, we are now protected from universal determinism: there is no danger of our being diluted into the universe. The human being is a finite, *defined* reality and not in any sense an effect produced by the world or a by-product of blind chains of causation. He is a 'man' or a 'Polytechnique-educated husband' or 'a young boy born to suffer for love' in the same way as a circle is a circle. And, for this reason, he is at the origin of first beginnings: his acts emanate from himself alone. Is this freedom? It is, at least, a *certain kind* of freedom. Moreover, it seems M. Giraudoux confers another kind on his creations: man *spontaneously* realizes his essence. For the mineral and vegetal realms, conformity is automatic. Man, by contrast, conforms to his archetype by an act of will; he perpetually *chooses himself* as he *is*. This is, admittedly, a one-way freedom, for if the form is not realized *by* him, it will be realized *through* him and without him. To appreciate the fineness of the line between this freedom and absolute necessity, compare the following two passages. Here is freedom, inspiration:

> Where can we go, Claudie, where we've never been before?'
>
> 'To Washington Park.'
>
> Claudie never hesitated. For every question, even the most embarrassing, she had a ready answer . . . What a happy inspiration to have chosen to come here the very time when parks are useless to humans.

As we can see, there was intuition in this, the poetic creation of an accord between the two women and inanimate objects. But in that very intuition, Claudie couldn't help realizing her essence. She is 'the one who never hesitates'. It was part of her essence to have this intuition. And here, now, is a case where the harmony between our archetype and the world manifests itself through us, without asking our opinion:

> Edmée was amazed at the words that came to her own lips, for they were surprising. But she was *even more amazed at the necessity of what she said* than at its monstrousness.

The difference is not great: in the one case, the form realizes itself through our will; in the other, it spreads through our bodies as though of its own accord. And yet this is what separates man from the gherkin. This fragile, intermittent freedom, which isn't an end in itself but merely a means, is enough to confer a duty upon us. M. Giraudoux has a morality. Man must realize his finite essence freely and thereby attune himself freely to the rest of the world. Every man is responsible for the universal harmony; he must submit himself willingly to the necessity of the archetypes. And at the very moment this harmony appears, when this balance emerges between our deepest inclinations, between nature and spirit, at the moment when man is at the centre of an ordered world, when he is 'most distinctly' man at the centre of a world that is 'most distinctly' world, M. Giraudoux's creation receives his reward. That reward is happiness. And here we see what this author's famous humanism amounts to: a pagan eudaemonism.

A concept-based philosophy, scholastic problems (is it form or matter that individualizes?), a shame-faced conception of becoming, defined as the transition from potential to act, a white magic that is merely

the superficial aspect of a rigorous logicism, a morality of equilibrium, happiness and the golden mean—
this is what we get from a candid examination of
Choix des Élues. We are a long way here from waking
dreamers. But there is an even stranger surprise in
store: for in these few characteristic traits we cannot
fail to recognize the philosophy of Aristotle. Wasn't
it Aristotle who was first a logician—and a logician
of the concept, and a magician through logic? Isn't it
in his work that we find this tidy, finite, hierarchized
world, that is rational to the core. Isn't he the one who
sees knowledge as contemplation and classification?
And—which is even better—isn't it the case that for
him, as for M. Giraudoux, man's freedom resides not
so much in the contingency of his becoming as in the
exact realization of his essence. Both recognize first
beginnings, natural places, the 'all or nothing' principle, and discontinuity. M. Giraudoux has written the
novel of Natural History, Aristotle produced its philosophy. However, Aristotle's was the only philosophy
that could stand atop the science of his time: he
wanted to systematize the wealth of material that had
been amassed by observation and we know that observation, by its nature, culminates in classification;

and classification, by *its* nature, appeals to concepts. We are, by contrast, very much at a loss to understand M. Giraudoux. For four hundred years, philosophers and scholars have been striving to break down rigid conceptual frameworks; to accord preeminence, in all fields, to free creative judgement; to substitute the evolution of species for their fixity. Today, philosophy is foundering, science is shipping water on all sides and morality is drowning. We are everywhere striving to lend the greatest flexibility to our methods and our judgement. No one believes in any sort of pre-established harmony between man and things any longer. No one now dares hope that nature will be accessible to us in its very essence. But suddenly a novelistic universe appears and seduces us with its indefinable charm and air of novelty. We look closer and discover the world of Aristotle, a world that has been buried for four hundred years.

Where has this ghost come from? How has a contemporary writer been able, in all simplicity, to choose to produce fictional illustrations of the views of a Greek philosopher who died three centuries before our era? I have to confess I cannot understand it. It could doubtless be pointed out that we are all

Aristotelian at times. One evening we are walking along the streets of Paris and suddenly things turn still, distinct faces towards us. That evening, of all evenings, is a 'Paris evening' and, out of all the streets that climbs up towards Sacré-Coeur, this little street is a 'Montmartre street'. Time has stopped and we are blessed with a moment of happiness, an eternity of happiness. Which of us has not had such a revelation at least once? I say 'revelation', but I am wrong. Or, rather, it is a revelation that teaches nothing. What I grasp from the pavements, the roadway, the facades of the buildings is merely the concept of street, a concept that has long been in my possession. I have an impression of knowing without there being any knowledge, an intuition of Necessity without any necessity. This human concept, which the street and the evening reflect back like mirrors, dazzles me and prevents me from seeing the inhuman meaning of things, their humble, tenacious thingly smiles. What matter? The street is there and up it climbs—so purely and magnificently a street. There is nothing more to say about it. These unproductive intuitions are comparable not so much to real contemplation as to what our psychologists call illusions of false recognition. Is this the explanation of M. Giraudoux's sensibility? It would be a bold interpretation and I have no idea if it is right. I imagine, too, that a Marxist would call M. Giraudoux's views an urbane rationalism, and that he would explain the rationalism by the triumphant rise of capitalism at the beginning of this century and the urbanity by the very special position M. Giraudoux occupies within the French bourgeoisie: peasant origins, classical culture, a career in the diplomatic corps. I do not know. Perhaps M. Giraudoux knows. Perhaps this writer, so discreet and well hidden behind his fictions, will one day tell us about himself.

March 1940

Note

1 *La Nouvelle Revue Française*, March 1940. [J.-P. S.]
   [The book itself, *Choix des Élues*, was published by
   Grasset (Paris) in 1939. (Trans.)]

The Outsider *Explained*

Hardly was Monsieur Camus's *The Outsider* off the presses than it met with enormous acclaim. It was widely said to be 'the best book since the armistice'. Among the literary productions of its time, the novel was itself an outsider. It came to us from the other side of the line, from across the sea. In that bitter coal-less spring, it spoke to us of the sun, not as an exotic marvel but with the weary familiarity of those who have had too much of it. It wasn't concerned to bury the old regime with its own hands once again, nor to din into us the sense of our unworthiness. Reading it, we remembered that there had, in the past, been works that claimed to stand on their own merits and not prove anything. But, as the price to be paid for this arbitrariness, the novel remained rather ambiguous: what were we to make of this character who, the day after his mother had died, 'was swimming in the sea, entering into an irregular liaison and laughing at a Fernandel film', who killed an Arab 'because of the sun' and who, on the eve of his execution, stating that he had 'been happy, and . . . was still happy', wished for crowds of spectators around the scaffold to 'greet [him] with cries of hatred'.[1] Some said: 'he's a poor fool, an idiot'; others, more insightfully: 'he's an innocent.' And yet the sense of that innocence remained to be understood.

In *The Myth of Sisyphus*, which appeared a few months later, M. Camus provided us with an accurate commentary on his work: his hero was neither good nor evil, moral nor immoral. These are not categories that suit him: he is a member of a very peculiar species, for which the author reserves the name '*absurd*'. But, when M. Camus uses it, this term assumes two very different meanings: the absurd is both a state of fact and the lucid consciousness some people acquire of that state. The 'absurd' man is the one who, from a fundamental absurdity, unfailingly draws the inevitable conclusions. There is the same shift in meaning here as when the young people who dance to 'swing' music are called the 'swing generation'. What, then, is the absurd as a state of fact, as an original datum? It is nothing less than man's relation to the world. Primary absurdity is the expression, first and foremost, of a divorce—between man's aspirations towards unity and the insurmountable dualism of mind and nature, between man's longing for the eternal and the *finite* character of his existence, between the 'concern' that is his very essence and the futility of his efforts. Death, the irreducible pluralism of truths and beings, chance and the unintelligibility of the real—between these poles lies the absurd. To tell the truth, these are not particularly new themes and M. Camus doesn't present them as such. They were enumerated as early as the seventeenth century by a certain sort of hard, terse, contemplative reason that is specifically French: they were commonplaces of classical pessimism. Wasn't it Pascal who stressed 'the natural unhappiness of our feeble, mortal condition, so wretched that nothing can console us when we really think about it'? Wasn't it he who marked out reason's place? Wouldn't he wholly agree with M. Camus when he writes: 'The world is neither (entirely) rational, nor so irrational either'? Didn't he show us that 'custom' and 'distractions' mask man's 'nothingness, his foresakenness, his insufficiency, his dependence, his impotence, his emptiness'? With the frosty style of *The Myth of Sisyphus* and with the subject matter of his essays, M. Camus places himself in the great tradition of those French Moralists whom Charles Andler rightly calls the forerunners of Nietzsche. As for the doubts he raises about the scope of our reason, these are in the most recent tradition of French epistemology. Just think of scientific nominalism, of Poincaré, Duhem and Meyerson,[2] and you will have a better understanding of the criticism our author makes of modern science: '[Y]ou tell me of an invisible planetary system in which electrons gravitate around a nucleus. You explain this world to me with an image. I realize then that you have been reduced to poetry . . .'[3] This is expressed separately, but almost at the same moment, by an author who draws on the same sources, when he writes: '(Physics) employs mechanical, dynamical or even psychological models interchangeably, as though, once freed from ontological pretensions, it were becoming indifferent to the classical antinomies of mechanism or dynamism, which presuppose an innate nature.'[4] M. Camus makes a point of citing passages from Jaspers, Heidegger and Kierkegaard, which, in my view, he doesn't always seem clearly to understand. But his real masters are to be found elsewhere. With the turn of his reasoning, the clarity of his ideas, his essayistic style and a certain kind of sunlit, ordered, formal, desolate grimness, everything about him points to a man of classic temperament, a writer of the Mediterranean. Even his method ('Solely the balance between evidence and lyricism can allow us to achieve simultaneously emotion and lucidity'[5]) is redolent of the old 'impassioned geometries' of Pascal and Rousseau, and brings him considerably closer, for example, to Maurras,[6] that other man of the Mediterranean from whom, however, he differs in so many ways, than to a German phenomenologist or a Danish existentialist.

But M. Camus would doubtless grant us all that. In his eyes, originality means taking his ideas to their limits; it is not his concern to make a collection of pessimistic maxims. Admittedly, the absurd is neither in man nor in the world, if we take the two separately. But, since it is of the essence of man to 'be-in-the-world', the absurd is ultimately of a piece with the human condition. It is not in any sense, therefore, to be grasped as a simple notion; a gloomy insight reveals it to us. 'Get up, tram, four hours in the office or factory, meal, tram, four hours of work, eat, sleep, Monday, Tuesday, Wednesday, Thursday, Friday and Saturday, all to the same rhythm,'[7] and then, suddenly, 'the stage-sets collapse' and we arrive at a lucidity bereft of hope. Then, if we are able to reject the sham succour of religions or existential philosophies, we have acquired a number of essential self-evident truths: the world is chaos, 'a divine equivalence born of anarchy' And there is no tomorrow, since we die.

> [I]n a universe suddenly divested of illusions and lights, man feels an alien, a stranger. His exile is without remedy since he is deprived of the memory of a lost home or the hope of a promised land.[8]

This is because man *is not*, in fact, the world:

> If I were a tree among trees, . . . this life would have a meaning or rather this problem

would not arise, for I should belong to this world. I should *be* this world to which I am now opposed by my whole consciousness . . . This ridiculous reason is what sets me in opposition to all creation.[9]

This already in part explains the title of the novel: the outsider is the man standing over against the world. To describe his work, M. Camus could just as easily have chosen the name of a novel by Gissing, *Born in Exile*.[10] The outsider is also the man among men. '[T]here are days when . . . we see as a stranger [*étrangère*] the one we had loved.'[11] In the end, it is myself in relation to myself: in other words, the man of nature in relation to the mind: 'the stranger who at certain seconds comes to meet us in a mirror'.[12]

But this is not all there is to it: there is a passion of the absurd. *Homo absurdus* will not commit suicide: he wants to live, without abdicating any of his certainties, without tomorrows, without hope, without illusions, but without resignation either. *Homo absurdus* affirms himself in revolt. He confronts death with a passionate attention and that fascination liberates him: he knows the 'divine irresponsibility' of the condemned man. Everything is permitted, since God doesn't exist and we die. All experiences are equivalent; it is just a matter of acquiring as many as possible. 'The present and the succession of presents before a constantly conscious soul is the ideal of the absurd man.'[13] All values crumble before this 'ethics of quantity'; the absurd man, pitched into this world, in revolt and with no one to answer to, has 'nothing to justify'. He is *innocent.* Innocent like those primitives Somerset Maugham writes of, before the arrival of the parson who teaches them Good and Evil, tells them what is permitted and what forbidden.[14] For him, *everything* is permitted. He is innocent as Prince Myshkin,[15] who 'lives in a perpetual present, varied only by smiles and indifference'. An innocent in all senses of the term, and an 'Idiot' too, if you will. And this time we fully understand the title of Camus's novel. The stranger or 'outsider' he wishes to depict is precisely one of those terrible innocents who scandalize a society because they don't accept the rules of its game. He lives among strangers, but for them too he is a stranger. This is why some will love him, like Marie, his mistress, who likes him 'because he is odd', and others will detest him for the same reason, like the crowd in the courtroom whose hatred he can immediately feel rising towards him. And we ourselves who are not yet, when we open the book, entirely familiar with the feeling of the absurd, would seek in vain to judge him by our usual standards: for us, too, he is a stranger.

So when you opened the book and read, 'I realized that I'd managed to get through another Sunday, that Mother was now buried, that I was going to go back to work and that, after all, nothing had changed.,'[16] the shock you felt was intended. It is the outcome of your first encounter with the absurd. But you were probably hoping that as you went on reading, you would find your sense of unease dissipating, that little by little everything would be cleared up, given a rational foundation, explained. Your hopes were dashed: *The Outsider* is not a book that provides explanations. *Homo absurdus* doesn't explain, he describes. Nor is this a book that furnishes proof. M. Camus merely proposes and doesn't trouble to justify that which is, in principle, unjustifiable. *The Myth of Sisyphus* will teach us how to receive our author's novel. We find in that work the theory of the absurdist novel. Although the absurdity of the human condition is its only subject, it isn't a novel that expounds a message; it doesn't emanate from a 'self-satisfied' system of thought intent only on producing evidence for its position. On the contrary, it is the product of a form of thinking that is 'limited, mortal and in revolt'. It proves, in and of itself, the uselessness of abstract reason:

> The preference [the great novelists] have shown for writing in images rather than in reasoned arguments is revelatory of a certain thought that is common to them all, convinced of the uselessness of any principle of explanation and sure of the educative message of perceptible appearance.[17]

Thus the mere fact of delivering his message in the form of a novel reveals a proud humility on M. Camus's part. Not resignation, but the rebellious recognition of the limits of human thought. Admittedly, he felt he had to provide a philosophical translation of his novelistic message and this is precisely what *The Myth of Sisyphus* does. We shall see below what we are to make of this form of duplication. But the existence of this translation in no way detracts from the arbitrary nature of the novel. The absurdist creator has lost even the illusion that his work is necessary. On the contrary, he wants us to be constantly aware of its contingency. He would like to give it the epigraph: 'might never have been', just as Gide wanted to add at the end of *The Counterfeiters* the message: 'could be continued'. It might not have been, like this stone, this stream or this face. It is a present that simply is given, like all the world's presents. It doesn't even have that subjective necessity that artists are wont to claim for their works when they say, 'I simply had to write it; I had to get it out of my system.' This is a theme familiar to us from the Surrealist terrorism, though it is exposed here to the harsh light of classicism: the work of art is merely a leaf torn from a life. It does, indeed, express that life: but it might have not done so. Moreover, everything is equivalent: writing Dostoevsky's *The Demons* or drinking a coffee. M. Camus does not, then, require of his readers that attentive solicitude demanded by the writers who 'have sacrificed their lives to their art'. *The Outsider* is one page of his life. And since the most absurd life must be the most sterile, his novel seeks to be magnificent in its sterility. Art is a useless generosity. But let us not be too horrified by this. Beneath M. Camus's paradoxes, I detect the presence of some very wise remarks by Kant on the 'purposeless purposiveness' of the Beautiful. At any rate, *The Outsider* is there, detached from a life, unjustified, unjustifiable, sterile, instantaneous, already left behind by its author, abandoned in favour of other presents. And this is how we should approach it, as a brief communion between two human beings, the author and the reader, in the absurd and beyond the realm of reason.

This gives us an indication of more or less how we are to view *The Outsider*'s central protagonist. If M. Camus had wanted to write a novel with a message, it would not have been difficult to show a civil servant lording it over his family, then suddenly gripped by a sense of the absurd, battling with it for a while and finally resolving to live out the fundamental absurdity of his condition. The reader would have been convinced at the same time as his character—and by the same arguments. Or, alternatively, he would have recounted the life of one of those saints of absurdity whom he lists in *The Myth of Sisyphus* and of whom he is particularly fond: the Don Juan, the Actor, the Conqueror, the Creator. This is not what he has done and, even for the reader familiar with the theories of absurdity, Meursault, the hero of *The Outsider*, remains ambiguous. We are, admittedly, assured that he is absurd, and pitiless lucidity is his chief characteristic.

Moreover, he is, in more than one respect, constructed in such a way as to provide a concerted illustration of the theories advanced in *The Myth of Sisyphus*. For example, M. Camus writes in this latter work: 'A man is more a man by the things he remains silent about than by the things he says.' And Meursault is an example of this manly silence, of this refusal of idle chatter: '[He was asked] whether he'd noticed that I was at all withdrawn and he simply remarked that I only spoke when I had something to say.'[18] And, indeed, two lines before, the same witness for the defence declared that Meursault 'was a man of the world'. When asked 'what he understood by that . . . he announced that everyone knew what that meant.'[19] Similarly, M. Camus dilates at length on love in *The Myth of Sisyphus*: 'Only by reference to a collective way of seeing for which books and legends are responsible,' he writes, 'do we call what binds us to certain creatures love.'[20] And, in a passage that parallels this one, we read in *The Outsider*: 'A minute later she asked me if I loved her. I told her that it didn't mean anything but that I didn't think so.'[21] From this point of view, the debate that began in the court and in the mind of the reader around the question, 'Did Meursault love his mother?' is doubly absurd. First, as the lawyer says, '. . . after all, is he being accused of burying his mother or of killing a man?'[22] But, above all, the word 'love' is meaningless. Meursault probably put his mother in the Home because he was short of money and 'they had no more to say to each other.' Probably, too, he didn't go to see her often 'because . . . it meant giving up [his] Sunday—let alone making the effort of going to the bus stop, buying tickets and spending two hours travelling.'[23] But what does this mean? Is he not entirely in the present, wrapped up wholly in his present moods? What we call a feeling is simply the abstract unity and the meaning of discontinuous impressions. I am not constantly thinking of those I love, but I claim to love them even when I am not thinking of them—and I would be capable of compromising my peace of mind in the name of an abstract feeling, in the absence of any real, immediate emotion. Meursault thinks and acts differently: he wants nothing to do with these great continuous and indistinguishable feelings. Love doesn't exist for him, nor even love *affairs*. Only the present and the concrete counts. He goes to see his mother when he wants to and that is all there is to it. If the desire is present, it will be powerful enough to make him take the bus, since another concrete desire will have sufficient force to make this lazybones run flat out and jump on to a moving lorry. But he always refers to his mother affectionately and childishly as *maman* and he never misses a chance to understand her and identify with her. 'Of love I know only that mixture of desire, affection and intelligence that binds me to this or that creature.'[24] We can see, then, that the *theoretical* side of Meursault's character shouldn't be overlooked. Similarly, many of his adventures are there mainly to bring out some particular aspect of fundamental absurdity. For example, as we have seen, *The Myth of Sisyphus* extols the 'divine availability of the condemned man before whom the prison doors open in a certain early dawn'[25]—and it was to have us savour this dawn and this 'availability' that M. Camus condemned his hero to capital punishment. 'How had I not seen,' he has him say, 'that nothing was more important than an execution . . . and that, in a sense, it was even the only really interesting thing for a man!'[26] We could quote many more such passages. Yet, this lucid, indifferent, taciturn man is not entirely constructed for the needs of the argument. No doubt, once the character was sketched out, it completed the picture itself; it assumed a substance all its own. And yet Meursault's absurdity appears not to be attained, but given. He is like that, and that is all there is to it. His epiphany will come on the last page, but he had always been living by M. Camus's standards. If there were a grace of the absurd, we should have to say that he has grace. He doesn't seem to ask himself any of the questions that are aired in *The Myth of Sisyphus*; and we don't see him in revolt before he is condemned to death. He was happy, he followed his star, and his happiness doesn't even seem to have known that secret sting to which M. Camus refers several times in his essay and which comes from the blinding presence of death. Even his indifference often seems like indolence, as on that Sunday when he stays at home out of sheer laziness and when he admits that he 'was a little bored'. Thus, even to an absurdist gaze, the character retains an opacity all his own. He is by no means the Don Juan, nor the Don Quixote of absurdity; at many points, we might actually see him as its Sancho Panza. He is there, he exists, and we can neither entirely understand him nor judge him. In a word, he lives, and it is fictional density alone that can justify him in our eyes.

Yet we should not see *The Outsider* as an entirely arbitrary work. As we have said, M. Camus makes a distinction between the *feeling* and the *notion* of the absurd. On this, he writes: 'Like great works, deep feelings always mean more than they are conscious of saying . . . Great feelings carry with them their own universe, splendid or abject.'[27] And, a little further on, he adds: 'The feeling of the absurd is not, for all that, the notion of the absurd. It lays the foundations for it, and that is all. It is not limited to that notion.'[28] We might say that *The Myth of Sisyphus* aims to provide us with this *notion* and that *The Outsider* seeks to inspire in us the *feeling*. The order in which the two works appeared seems to confirm this hypothesis. *The Outsider*, published first, plunges us without further ado into the 'climate' of the absurd; the essay follows, casting its light on the landscape. The absurd is a discrepancy, a gap. *The Outsider* will, as a result, be a novel of gaps and discrepancies, of disorientation. Hence its skilful construction: on the one hand, the amorphous, everyday flow of lived reality; on the other, the edifying recomposition of that reality by human reason and discourse. The point is that the reader, having first been brought into the presence of pure reality, rediscovers it without recognizing it in its rational transposition. This will be the source of the feeling of the absurd or, in other words, of our incapability of *thinking* the events of the world with our concepts and words. Meursault buries his mother, takes a mistress and commits a crime. These various facts are recounted at his trial by the assembled witnesses and explained by the public prosecutor: Meursault will have the impression they are talking about someone else. Everything is so constructed as to lead up suddenly to Marie's outburst. Having given an account framed in terms of human rules in the witness box, she bursts into tears: 'it wasn't like that, there was something else and she was being made to say the opposite of what she thought.'[29] These mirror games have been in common usage since Gide's *Counterfeiters*. This is not where M. Camus's originality lies. But the problem he has to solve will force him to adopt an original literary form. If we are to feel the gap between the prosecutor's conclusions and the actual circumstances of the murder, if, when we close the book, we are to retain the impression of an absurd justice that will never be able to comprehend, nor even ascertain the nature of, the acts it proposes to

punish, we have first to have been brought into contact with reality or with one of these circumstances.
But, in order to establish that contact, M. Camus, like
the public prosecutor, has only words and concepts
at his disposal. Using words and assembling ideas, he
has to describe the world before words. The first part
of *The Outsider* could, like a recent book, be called
Translated from Silence.[30] We touch here on a malady
shared by many contemporary writers, the earliest
signs of which I see in the work of Jules Renard. I
shall call it the obsession with silence. M. Paulhan[31]
would certainly see it as an effect of literary terrorism.
It has assumed a thousand forms, from the 'automatic
writing' of the Surrealists to the famous 'theatre of
silence' of Jean-Jacques Bernard. This is because silence, as Heidegger says, is the authentic mode of
speech. Only he who knows how to speak can be
silent. M. Camus speaks a lot in *The Myth of Sisyphus*.
He even chatters. And yet he tells us of his love of silence. He quotes Kierkegaard's phrase, 'The surest of
stubborn silences is not to hold one's tongue but to
talk.'[32] And he adds, himself, that, 'A man is more a
man by the things he remains silent about than by the
things he says.' So, in *The Outsider*, he set about being

silent. But how can one be silent with words? How, with concepts, can one render the unthinkable, disordered succession of present moments? It is a challenge that requires recourse to a new kind of technique.

What is that technique? 'It's Kafka written by Hemingway,' someone has suggested. I must admit that I don't see Kafka in it. M. Camus's views are wholly down-to-earth. Kafka is the novelist of impossible transcendence. For him, the universe is bristling with signs we do not understand. There is something behind the scenery. For M. Camus by contrast, the human tragedy is the absence of any transcendence.

> I don't know whether this world has a meaning that transcends it. But I know that I do not know that meaning and that it is impossible for me just now to know it. What can a meaning outside my condition mean to me? I can understand only in human terms. What I touch, what resists me—that is what I understand.[33]

There is no question, then, for him of finding arrangements of words that lead us to suspect an indecipherable, inhuman order. The inhuman is merely

167

the disorderly, the mechanical. There is nothing dubious in his work, nothing disquieting, nothing suggested: *The Outsider* presents us with a succession of luminously clear views. If they disorient us, they do so only by their quantity and the absence of any unifying link. Mornings, clear evenings, relentless afternoons—these are his favourite times of day. The perpetual summer of Algiers is his season. There is scarcely any place for night in his universe. If he speaks of it, he does so in the following terms:

> I woke up with stars shining on my face.
> Sounds of the countryside were wafting in.
> The night air was cooling my temples with the
> smell of earth and salt. The wondrous peace
> of this sleeping summer flooded into me.[34]

The person who wrote these lines is as far as can be from the *Angst* of a Kafka. He is thoroughly calm amid the chaos. The stubborn blindness of nature irritates him certainly, but it also reassures him. Its irrationality is merely a negative factor: *homo absurdus* is a humanist, he knows only the blessings of this world.

The comparison with Hemingway seems more fruitful. There is an obvious affinity of style. In both texts, we find the same short sentences: each refuses to profit from the impetus of the preceding one; each is a new beginning. Every sentence is like a snapshot of an action or an object. Each new action and each new object has its corresponding new sentence. And yet I am not satisfied: the existence of an 'American' narrative technique has, without doubt, assisted M. Camus. But I doubt that it has, strictly speaking, influenced him. Even in *Death in the Afternoon*, which is not a novel, Hemingway retains this jolting mode of narration, which conjures each sentence out of nothingness in a kind of respiratory spasm: the style is the man. We already know that M. Camus has a different style, a ceremonial style. But even in *The Outsider*, he occasionally raises the tone: the sentence then has a broader, continuous flow:

> The cries of the newspaper sellers in the languid evening air, the last few birds in the square, the shouts of the sandwich sellers, the moaning of the trams high in the winding streets of the town and the murmuring of the sky before darkness spills over onto the port, all these sounds marked out an invisible route which I knew so well before going into prison.[35]

Showing through Meursault's breathless narrative, I glimpse a broader underlying poetic prose, which must be M. Camus's personal mode of expression. If *The Outsider* bears such visible marks of the American technique, that is because there is a deliberate borrowing. Among the instruments available to him, M. Camus has chosen the one that seemed best to fit his purpose. I doubt if he will use it again in his future works.

Let us look more closely at the framework of his narrative. We shall get a clearer idea of his methods.

Men too secrete the inhuman. At certain moments of lucidity, the mechanical aspect of their gestures, their meaningless pantomime make silly everything that surrounds them.[36]

Here, then, is what must first be conveyed: *The Outsider* must put us, from the outset, into 'a state of unease at man's inhumanity'. But what are the particular occasions that can provoke in us this unease? *The Myth of Sisyphus* gives us an example:

A man is talking on the telephone behind a glass partition; you cannot hear him but you see his incomprehensible dumb-show; you wonder why he is alive.[37]

This tells us what we need to know. It almost tells us too much, for the example reveals a certain bias on the part of the author. The movements of the man on the phone, whom you cannot hear, are only *relatively* absurd: the fact is that he is part of an incomplete circuit. Open the door, put your ear to the receiver and the circuit is re-established: human activity is senseless no longer. Sincerely, then, we would have to say that there are only relative absurdities— and then only by comparison with 'absolute rationalities'. Yet it is not a question of sincerity, but of art. M. Camus has a ready-made method: he will insert a glass screen between the characters he is talking about and the reader. What could be more inept than men behind a window? The glass seems to let everything through, but it actually cuts out just one thing: the meaning of their actions. All that remains is to choose the window. In this case, it will be the Outsider's consciousness. It is, in fact, a transparent medium: we see everything that it sees. Only it has been so constructed as to be transparent to things and opaque to meanings:

> From that point on everything happened very quickly. The men moved towards the coffin with a pall. The priest, his followers,

the warden and myself all went outside. By
the door there was a woman I hadn't seen
before. 'This is Mr Meursault,' the warden
said. I didn't hear the woman's name, I just
understood that she was the duty nurse. She
bowed her head, without a trace of a smile
on her long, bony face. We stood aside to
make way for the body.[38]

People are dancing behind a glass screen.
Between them and the reader a consciousness has
been inserted—almost nothing, a pure translucency,
a purely passive thing recording all the facts. But this
has done the trick: precisely because it is passive, the
consciousness records only the facts. The reader has
not noticed the interposing of the screen. But what,
then, is the assumption implied by this kind of narrative? In short, a melodic organization has been turned
into an assemblage of invariant elements; it is being
claimed that the succession of *movements* is strictly
identical with the *act* conceived as a totality. Are we
not confronted here with the analytic presupposition
that all reality is reducible to a sum total of elements?
But if analysis is the instrument of science, it is also
the instrument of humour. If I want to describe a

rugby match and write: 'I saw adults in short trousers fighting and throwing themselves on the ground in an effort to get a leather ball through two wooden posts,' I have summed up what I *saw*, but I have deliberately omitted its meaning: I have created something humorous. M. Camus's narrative is analytical and humorous. He lies—like every artist—because he is claiming to render raw experience and yet he is slyly filtering out all the meaningful connections, which are also part of the experience. This is what David Hume did when he announced that all he could find in experience was isolated impressions. This is what today's American new realists do when they deny that there is anything between phenomena but external relations. Contrary to that view, contemporary philosophy has established that meanings are also immediate data. But that would carry us too far from our subject here. Let us simply note that the universe of *homo absurdus* is the analytical world of the new realists. In the literary world, this is an approach with a strong track record. It is Voltaire's approach in *L'Ingénu* and *Micromégas*, and Swift's in *Gulliver's Travels*. For the eighteenth century had its outsiders too—'noble savages' as a rule, who, when carried off to unfamiliar civilizations, perceived the facts before they could grasp their meaning. Wasn't the effect of this discrepancy precisely to prompt in the reader a sense of absurdity? M. Camus seems to remember this on several occasions, particularly when he shows us his hero pondering the reasons for his imprisonment.[39]

It is this analytic method that explains the use of the American technique in *The Outsider*. The presence of death at the end of our road has sent our futures up in smoke; there is 'no tomorrow' to our lives; they are a succession of present moments. What does this express, other than that *homo absurdus* applies his analytical spirit to time? Where Bergson saw a form of organization that cannot be broken down into smaller units, *his* eye sees only a series of instants. It is the plurality of the incommunicable instants that will, in the end, account for the plurality of beings. What our author borrows from Hemingway, then, is the discontinuity of his chopped-up sentences, which precisely apes the discontinuity of time. We are now better able to understand the cast of his narrative: each sentence is a present moment. But it is not a vague present that smudges and runs into the following one. The sentence is distinct, crisp, self-contained; an entire void separates it from the next one, just as Descartes's moment is separated from the moment that follows. Between each sentence and the next, the world is annihilated and reborn: as it emerges, the word is a creation *ex nihilo*; a sentence in *The Outsider* is an island. And we tumble from sentence to sentence, from void to void. It is to accentuate the solitude of each sentence unit that M. Camus chose to narrate his story in the present perfect tense.[40] The French past definite is the tense of continuity: '*Il se promena longtemps.*' These words refer us to a *plu*perfect, and to a future. The reality of the sentence is the verb, the act, with its transitive character, its transcendence. '*Il s'est promené longtemps*' conceals the verbalness of the verb. The verb here is shattered, broken in two: on the one hand, we find a past participle that has lost all transcendence and is as inert as a thing; on the other, there is the verb 'to be' which functions merely as a copula, joining participle to noun as it might join complement to subject. The transitive character of the verb has vanished and the sentence has become frozen; its reality now is the noun. Instead of projecting itself between past and future, like a bridge, it is merely a little, isolated, self-sufficient substance. If, moreover, one takes care to reduce it as much as possible to the main clause, then its internal structure becomes perfect in its simplicity; and it gains all the more in cohesiveness. It is truly indivisible, an atom of time. Of course, the sentences are not articulated together: they are merely juxtaposed. In particular, all causal relations are avoided, as they would introduce a glimmer of explanation into the narrative and bring an order to its moments that differed in some way from pure succession. Take the following passage:

> A minute later she asked me if I loved her. *I told her that it didn't mean anything but that I didn't think so. She looked sad.* But as we were getting lunch ready, and for no apparent reason, she laughed again, so I kissed her. It was at that point that we heard a row break out in Raymond's room.[41]

I have underlined two sentences which, as carefully as possible, conceal a causal link beneath the mere appearance of succession. When it is absolutely necessary to allude to the previous sentence, the words 'and', 'but', 'then' and 'it was at that moment that' are used, all of which suggest only disjunction, opposition or pure addition. The relations between these temporal units are external ones, just like the relations new realism establishes between things. The real appears without being brought on to the scene and disappears without being destroyed. The world collapses and is reborn with each pulse of time. But do not go thinking it generates itself: it is inert. Every activity on its part would tend to substitute fearful powers for the reassuring disorder of chance. A nineteenth-century naturalist would have written, 'A bridge bestrode the river.' M. Camus rejects such anthropomorphism. He will say, 'Over the river there was a bridge.' In this way the thing immediately imparts its passivity to us. It simply *is there*, undifferentiated:

> There were four men in black in the room . . .
> By the door there was a woman I hadn't seen
> before . . . Outside the gate stood the hearse
> . . . Next to it stood the funeral director.[42]

It was said of Jules Renard that he would end up writing, 'The hen lays.' M. Camus and many contemporary authors would write, 'There's the hen and she lays.' The fact is that they like things for what they are in themselves; they do not wish to dilute them into the flow of time. 'There is water': this is a little piece of eternity—passive, impenetrable, incommunicable, sparkling. What sensual delight if one can touch it!

For *homo absurdus* this is the one and only blessing of this world. This is why the novelist prefers this shimmering of short-lived moments of brilliance, each of which is a delight, to an organized narrative. This is why, in writing *The Outsider*, M. Camus is able to believe he is being silent: his sentences don't belong to the universe of discourse; they have neither ramifications, continuations, nor internal structure. A sentence from the novel might be defined, like Valéry's 'Sylph' as

> Unseen, never happened:
> The instant of a naked breast
> Between two chemises.

The span of time it takes for a silent intuition to emerge covers it very precisely.

Given this state of affairs, can we speak of a totality we might describe as M. Camus's novel? All the sentences in his book are equivalent, as are all the experiences of *homo absurdus*. Each one takes its place in its own right and sweeps the others into the void. As a consequence, however, except in the rare moments when the author betrays his own principles and *makes* poetry, none stands out from the others. Even the dialogues are integrated into the narrative. Dialogue provides a moment of explanation, of meaning: to give it prominence would be to admit that meanings exist. M. Camus shaves it down, summarizes it, expressing it often in indirect style. He denies it any typographical distinction, so that the phrases uttered seem to be events just like any other; they shimmer for a moment and disappear, like a sudden pulse of heat or a sound or a smell. When you begin reading the book, you don't seem to be in the presence of a novel, but rather of a monotonous chanting, of the nasal singing of an Arab. You have the impression that the book will be like one of those tunes Courteline[43] speaks of, which 'drift away and never return' and which stop suddenly without you knowing quite why. Gradually, however, before the reader's very eyes, the work, by its own dynamic, assumes organized form; it reveals the solid substructure that underpins it. There isn't a single useless detail. Not one that isn't taken up again later and put to use. And when we have closed the book, we realize it could not have begun differently, that it could have had no other ending. In the world that is being presented to us as absurd, from which causality has been carefully extirpated, the tiniest incident has weight. Every single one contributes to leading the hero towards the crime and execution.

The Outsider is a classical work, a work of order, written about the absurd and against the absurd. Is this entirely what the author intended? I do not know; it is the reader's opinion I am conveying.

And how are we to classify this crisp, clear work—a work that is so carefully put together beneath its apparent disorder, so 'human' and so unsecretive once one has the key to it? We cannot call it a story [*récit*]: the story explains and coordinates as it reproduces events; it substitutes causal order for chronological sequence. M. Camus calls it a 'novel'. Yet the novel requires a continuous flow of time, a development, the manifest presence of the irreversibility of time. Not without some reluctance would I grant that name to this succession of inert present moments, beneath which we can just make out the mechanical economy of a deliberate contrivance. Or we might see it as a *moraliste's* novella, like *Candide* or *Zadig*, with a discreet strain of satire and a series of ironic portraits[44] which, despite what it takes from the German existentialists and the American novelists, is ultimately very much akin to one of Voltaire's tales.

February 1943

Notes

1 Albert Camus, *The Outsider* (Joseph Laredo trans.) (London: Penguin Classics, 2000), pp. 91, 99, 117.

2 Henri Poincaré (1854–1912) and Pierre Duhem (1861–1916): prominent French mathematicians and philosophers of science; Émile Meyerson (1859–1933): a Polish-born, German-educated, French chemist and philosopher of science. [Trans.]

3 Albert Camus, *The Myth of Sisyphus* (Justin O'Brien trans.) (London: Penguin, 2005), p. 18.

4 Maurice Merleau-Ponty, *La Structure du Comportement* (Paris: La Renaissance du Livre, 1942), p. 1.

5 Camus, *The Myth of Sisyphus*, p. 3.

6 Charles Maurras (1868–1952): essayist and leader of the extreme Right Action française movement. [Trans.]

7 Ibid., p. 11 (translation modified).

8 Ibid., pp. 4–5.

9 Ibid., pp. 49–50

10 George Gissing (1857–1903): a prolific Yorkshire-born novelist, his *Born in Exile* (1892) was translated into French by Marie Canavaggia and published in 1932. [Trans.]

11 Camus, *The Myth of Sisyphus*, p. 13.

12 Ibid., p. 13.

13 Ibid., pp. 61–2.

14 William Somerset Maugham (1874–1965): one of the most popular English novelists of his day. Sartre is probably thinking of novels such as *The Moon and Sixpence*, based on the life of Paul Gauguin among the 'primitives' of Tahiti. [Trans.]

15 The central character of Dostoevsky's novel *The Idiot*. [Trans.]

16 Camus, *The Outsider*, p. 28.

17 Camus, *The Myth of Sisyphus*, pp. 97–8.

18 Camus, *The Outsider*, p. 89.

19 Ibid.

20 Camus, *The Myth of Sisyphus*, p. 71 (translation modified).

21 Camus, *The Outsider*, p. 38.

22 Ibid., p. 93.

23 Ibid., p. 11.

24 Camus, *The Myth of Sisyphus*, p. 71.

25 Ibid., p. 57.

26 Camus, *The Outsider*, p. 109.

27 Camus, *The Myth of Sisyphus*, p. 9 (translation modified).

28 Ibid., p. 27.

29 Camus, *The Outsider*, p. 91.

30 The reference is to Joë Bousquet, *Traduit du Silence* (Paris: Gallimard, 1941). [Trans.]

31 Jean Paulhan (1884–1968): a French writer, literary critic and publisher, and director of the literary magazine *Nouvelle Revue Française*. [Trans.]

32 Camus, *The Myth of Sisyphus*, p. 24. Compare also Brice Parain's theory of language and his conception of silence.

33 Ibid., p. 49.

34 Camus, *The Outsider*, p. 116.

35 Ibid., p. 93.

36 Camus, *The Myth of Sisyphus*, p. 13.

37 Ibid.

38 Camus, *The Outsider*, p. 19.

39 Ibid., pp. 76–7.

40 The use of the present perfect in French is quite different from its use in English. In particular, it is used for completed actions in the past, whereas the English present perfect requires almost always either that an action is continuing into—or is of some continuing relevance to—the present. [Trans.]

41 Ibid., p. 38.

42 Ibid., p. 19.

43 Georges Courteline (1858–1929): one of the leading French dramatists in the early decades of the twentieth century. [Trans.]

44 Of the pimp, the investigating magistrate, the public prosecutor, etc.

Aminadab:
Or the Fantastic Considered as a Language

> Thought taken ironically for an object
> by something other than thought.
>
> Maurice Blanchot, *Thomas l'Obscur*[1]

Thomas is moving through a small town. Who is Thomas? Where is he from? Where is he going? We shall have no answers to these questions. A woman beckons to him from a house. He goes in and suddenly finds himself in a strange community of tenants, in which everyone seems both to lay down the law and to be subject to it. He is made to undergo some incoherent initiation rites; he is chained to an almost speechless companion and wanders, still yoked to that companion, from room to room and floor to floor, often forgetting what he is looking for, but remembering always just in time when they try to detain him. After many adventures, he changes, loses his companion and falls ill. It is at this point that he receives his last warnings. An old employee tells him, 'The person you should be interrogating is yourself,'[2] and a nurse adds, 'you have been the victim of an illusion; you thought someone was calling you, but no one was there, and the call came from you.'[3] He persists nonetheless, gets to the upper floors and finds the woman who had waved to him. But he does so only to be told, 'No order called you here, and someone else was expected.'[4] Thomas has gradually weakened. At nightfall, the companion to whom he was earlier chained comes back to see him and explains that Thomas has taken a wrong turning.

> You didn't recognize your own way . . . I was like another you. I knew all the pathways of the house, and I knew which one you ought to have followed. All you had to do was ask me.[5]

Thomas asks a last question, but it remains unanswered and the room is flooded with the darkness from outside, 'beautiful and soothing . . . a vast dream which is not within the reach of the person it envelops'.[6] Summarized like this, M. Blanchot's intentions seem very clear. What is even clearer is the extraordinary resemblance of his book to the novels of Kafka. The same meticulous, urbane style, the same nightmarish civility, the same weird, starchy ceremoniousness, the same pointless quests—pointless since they lead to nothing; the same exhaustive, stagnant reasoning; and the same sterile initiations—sterile because they are not initiations into anything. M. Blanchot states that he had read nothing of Kafka's when he wrote *Aminadab*. This leaves us even greater scope to marvel at the strange encounter that led this young and as yet uncertain writer to rediscover, in his quest to express some banal ideas on human life, the instrument that once produced such unprecedented sounds in other hands.

I don't know how this conjunction came about. It interests me only because it enables me to draw up the 'latest balance sheet' of the literature of the fantastic. For fantasy, like the other literary genres, has an essence and a history, the latter being merely the development of the former. What, then, must the nature of the contemporary fantastic genre be if a French writer—and, moreover, one convinced of the need to 'think French'[7]—is able to find himself at one with a writer from Central Europe as soon as he adopts this mode of expression?

To achieve the fantastic, it is neither necessary nor sufficient to depict the extraordinary. If it occurs singly in a law-governed world, then the oddest event will become part of the order of the universe. If you make a horse talk, then I shall believe it is momentarily bewitched. But if it goes on talking amid trees that don't move and on ground that remains where it is, I shall grant him the natural power of speech. I shall no longer see the horse, but the man in the horse costume. If, on the other hand, you manage to persuade me that this horse is fantastical, then the trees, earth and rivers are so too, even if you haven't mentioned the fact. One doesn't make occasional allowances for the fantastical; either it doesn't exist or it extends to the whole of the universe; it is a complete world in which things manifest a captive, tormented form of thinking, both whimsical and connected, that gnaws away from below at the linkages of the mechanism, without their ever managing to express themselves. In that world, matter is never wholly matter, since it offers only the perpetually thwarted rudiments of determinism, and mind is never wholly mind, since it has sunk into slavery and been impregnated and coarsened by matter. All is woe: things suffer and tend towards inertia, without ever quite achieving it; the humiliated, enslaved mind strives unsuccessfully after consciousness and freedom. The fantastic offers an inverse image of the union of soul and body: the soul takes the place of the body and the body that of the soul. And we cannot form clear, distinct ideas with which to think this image; we have to resort to confused thoughts that are themselves fantastical; in short, though we are wide-awake, fully mature and entirely civilized, we have to give in to the 'magical' mentality of the dreamer, the child and the primitive. There is no need, then, to resort to fairies; in themselves, fairies are simply pretty women; what is fantastical is nature when it bends to the fairies' will; this is nature outside of man or within man, when man is conceived as a creature turned upside down.

So long as we thought it possible to escape the human condition by asceticism, mysticism, the metaphysical disciplines or the practice of poetry, the genre of fantasy had a clearly defined role to fulfil. It manifested our human power to transcend the human. We strove to create a world that was not this world, either because, like Poe, we preferred artifice in principle, because we believed, with Cazotte,[8] Rimbaud and all those who strove to see 'a drawing-room at the bottom of a lake'[9] that the writer had a magical mission, or, alternatively, because, like Lewis Carroll, we wanted to apply systematically to literature that unconditional power the mathematician has of engendering a universe from a small number of conventions or, lastly, because, like Nodier,[10] we had recognized that the writer is, first, a liar and we wanted to achieve the absolute lie. The object thus created was entirely self-referential; its aim was not to depict, but only to exist; it compelled acceptance through its own density alone. If certain authors happened to take over the language of the fantasy genre to express some philosophical or moral ideas under cover of agreeable fictions, they willingly acknowledged that they had diverted this mode of expression from its usual ends and had merely created, so to speak, a *trompe-l'oeil* form of the fantastic.

M. Blanchot is beginning to write in a period of disillusionment. After the great metaphysical carnival of the post-war years, which ended in disaster, the writers and artists of the new generation have, out of pride, humility and seriousness, made a widely-trumpeted return to the human. This trend has had an impact on the fantastic itself. For Kafka, who figures as a forerunner here, there was no doubt a transcendent reality, but it is out of reach and serves only to make us feel man's abandonment within the realm of the human the more cruelly. M. Blanchot, who doesn't believe in transcendence, would no doubt subscribe to the following opinion expressed by Eddington: 'We have found a strange footprint on the shores of the unknown. We have devised profound theories, one after another, to account for its origins. At last, we have succeeded in reconstructing the creature that made the footprint. And lo! It is our own.'[11] Hence the tentative moves towards a 'return to the human' on the part of the literature of fantasy. Admittedly, it will not be used to prove anything or to enlighten. M. Blanchot, in particular, denies that he has written one of those allegories whose 'meaning', as he puts it, 'corresponds unequivocally to the story, but can also be explained entirely apart from it'. It is simply the case that, to take its place within contemporary humanism, the fantastic is domesticating itself like the other genres, giving up on the exploration of transcendent realities, and resigning itself to transcribing the human condition. And at around this same moment, as a result of internal factors, this literary genre has been pursuing its own line of development and getting rid of fairies, genies and hobgoblins as useless, time-worn conventions. Dali and de Chirico showed us a nature that was haunted, but freed, nonetheless, from the supernatural: the one depicted the life and sufferings of stones, while the other illustrated an accursed biology, showing us the horrible sprouting of human bodies or of metals contaminated with life. By a curious twist, the new humanism further hastens this development: M. Blanchot, following Kafka, is no longer concerned to recount the bewitchings of matter; Dali's monsters of meat probably seemed like clichés to him, as haunted castles had to Dali. For him, only one fantastical object remains: man. Not the man of religion and spiritualism, who is only half-committed to the things of this world, but given man, natural man, social man—the man who acknowledges a hearse as it passes, who shaves by a window, who kneels in churches, who marches behind a flag. That being is a microcosm. He is the world, the whole of nature: in him alone can the whole of spellbound nature be revealed. In him. Not in his body—M. Blanchot renounces physiological fantasies; his characters are physically undistinguished; he describes them with a single word, in passing—but in his total reality as *homo faber, homo sapiens.* And so the fantastic, in humanizing itself, comes closer to the ideal purity of its essence and becomes what it was. It has rid itself, it seems, of all its trickery. There is nothing up its sleeve now and we recognize that the footprint on the shore is our own. No succubi, no ghosts, no weeping fountains—there are only human beings and the fantasy creator announces that he identifies with the fantasy object. For contemporary man, the fantastic is now just one way among a hundred others of reflecting back his own image.

It is on the basis of these remarks that we can try to gain a better understanding of the extraordinary resemblance between *Aminadab* and Kafka's *Castle.* We have seen that the essence of the fantastic is to offer an inverted image of the union between soul and body. Now, we have seen that in both Kafka and Blanchot, the fantastic confines itself to expressing the human world. Is it not going to find itself subject, in the work of both authors, to new conditions? And what can the inversion of human relations mean here?

When I come into a café, the first things I see are implements. Not things, not raw materials, but utensils, tables, benches, mirrors, glasses and saucers. Each of them represents a piece of subjugated matter. Taken together, they are part of a manifest order. And the meaning of their ordering is a purpose, an end— an end that is myself or, rather, the man in me, the consumer that I am. This is what the human world is like, when it is *the right way up*. We would look in vain for a 'raw' material: the means functions here as the matter, and the form—the spiritual order—is represented by the end or purpose. Let us now depict this café *turned upside down*. We shall have to show ends that are crushed by their very own means, which are attempting unsuccessfully to burst through enormous thicknesses of matter; or, alternatively, objects which of themselves show their instrumentality, but do so with a force of indiscipline and disorder, a kind of woolly independence that causes their purpose to elude us just when we think we have grasped it. Here is a door, for example: it is there with its hinges, handle and lock. It is carefully bolted, as though protecting some treasure or other. After trying various different approaches, I manage to procure the key: I unlock it and find that it opens on to a wall. I sit down and order a coffee. The waiter has me repeat the order three times and repeats it himself to eliminate all possibility of error. He dashes off, passes my order on to a second waiter, who writes it in a notebook and hands it to a third. In the end, a fourth waiter comes back; 'Here you are,' he says, and places an inkwell on my table. 'But I ordered a coffee,' I say. 'That's right,' he says, as he walks off. If, when reading tales of this sort, the reader is able to think this is a practical joke being played by the waiters or some collective psychosis, then we have failed in our efforts. But if we have managed to convey the impression that we are speaking to him of a world in which these bizarre happenings represent normal behaviour, then he will be plunged at once into the heart of the fantastic. This *human* form of the fantastic is the revolt of means against ends: either the object in question noisily asserts itself as a means and, by the violence of that assertion, conceals its own end or purpose, or it refers on to another and another in an infinite succession without our ever being able to discover any supreme end or, by some confusion of means that really belong to unrelated series, we are left with a glimpse of a scrambled, composite image of contradictory ends.

Let us imagine, on the other hand, that I have managed to perceive an end. In that case, I find all my bridges are burned. I cannot discover or devise any means to achieve it. I have an appointment with someone on the first floor of this café; I have to get up there urgently. I can see this first floor from down below. Its balcony is visible from a large circular opening. I can even see tables and customers at those tables. But though I walk a hundred times round the room I cannot find a stairway. In this case, the means is precisely specified; everything points to and calls for it; it is latent in the manifest presence of the end. But things have reached such an extreme that it simply doesn't exist. Is this to be described as an 'absurd' world, such as M. Camus speaks of in his *Outsider*? But the absurd is a total absence of ends. The absurd can be conceived clearly and distinctly; it belongs to the world *the right way up*, as limited *de facto* by human powers. In the obsessive, hallucinatory world we are trying to describe, the absurd would be an oasis, a respite; hence there is no place for it. I cannot pause there for a moment. Every means sends me relentlessly to the ghost of an end that haunts it, and every end to the ghost of a means by which I could achieve it. I cannot form any kind of thought, except in slippery, shimmering notions that fall to pieces as I examine them.

Given all this, it is not surprising that, in authors as different as Kafka and Blanchot, we find strictly identical themes. Is it not this same preposterous world they are attempting to depict? It will be the first concern of both to exclude 'impassive nature' from their novels: hence the stifling atmosphere that is common to both. The struggle of the hero of Kafka's *Trial* takes place in a city; he crosses streets and enters buildings. Thomas in *Aminadab* wanders around the interminable corridors of a block of flats. Neither of them ever sees forests, meadows or hills. And yet how restful it would be if they could find themselves in the presence of a mound of earth, of a fragment of matter that had *no purpose*! But, were they to do so, the fantastic would vanish in an instant. The law of the genre condemns them never to encounter anything but tools. These tools, as we have seen, are not intended to serve them, but to provide relentless evidence of a strange, elusive purpose: hence this labyrinth of corridors, doors and staircases that lead nowhere; hence these signposts indicating nothing, the countless signs that stud the roads and have no meaning. We should cite as a particular case of the theme of signs the message motif that is so important to both Kafka and Blanchot. In the right-way-up world, the existence of a message implies a sender, a messenger and a recipient. It is itself merely a means; its content is the end. In the upside-down world, the means becomes autonomous and self-contained: we are plagued by messages without content, messengers or senders. Or, alternatively, the end exists, but the means gradually gnaws away at it. In one of Kafka's tales, the emperor sends a message to one of the townspeople, but the messenger has such a long way to go that the message will never reach its destination. For his part, M. Blanchot tells us of a message whose contents change progressively in the course of its journey. He writes:

> All these hypotheses . . . make the following conclusion seem most likely; namely that, despite his good will, the messenger, upon arriving upstairs, will have forgotten his message and will be unable to transmit it; or else, assuming he has scrupulously retained the terms in which it was formulated, it will be impossible for him to understand its meaning, for what has a certain meaning here must have a completely different one there, or perhaps none at all; . . . What he himself will have become, I refuse to imagine, for I assume that he will be as different from what I am as the transmitted message will be different from the one that is received.[12]

It may also happen that a message reaches us and is partially decipherable. But we learn later that it wasn't intended for us. In *Aminadab*, M. Blanchot discovers another possibility: a message comes through to me, which is, of course, incomprehensible. I enquire into it and find out, in the end, that I was the sender. Needless to say, these eventualities do not represent strokes of ill luck among other possible outcomes. They are part of the *nature* of the message. The sender knows this and the recipient isn't unaware of it; yet they go on relentlessly sending and receiving messages, as though the great thing were the message itself, not its content. But the means has absorbed the end as surely as a blotter absorbs ink.

For the same reason as they banish nature from their narratives, our two authors also banish natural man, that is to say, the isolated person, the individual, the one Céline calls a 'fellow of no collective importance', who can be no other than an absolute end. The fantastic imperative stands the Kantian imperative on its head. 'Act always in such a way,' it tells us, 'that you treat the human in yourself and in others as a means and never as an end.' In order to plunge their heroes into feverish, exhausting, unintelligible activity, Messrs. Blanchot and Kafka have to surround them with instrument-men. Sent from instrument to man as he might be from means to end, the reader discovers that man, in his turn, is merely a means. Hence the functionaries, soldiers and judges who people Kafka's works, and the domestics, also known as 'employees', in *Aminadab*. As a result, the fantastic universe assumes the appearance of a bureaucracy: it is, in fact, the great departments of state that most resemble a society turned upside down; Thomas in *Aminadab* goes from office to office, from clerk to clerk, without ever finding the employer or the man in charge, like those visitors petitioning a ministry who are sent endlessly from one department to another. Moreover, the acts of these functionaries remain wholly unintelligible. In the normally constituted world, I can distinguish reasonably well a magistrate's sneeze, which is an accident, or his whistling, which is a matter of whim, from his juridical activity, which is the application of the law. In the upside-down world, the meticulous, pernickety employees of the fantastical world will seem at first to be diligently carrying out their functions. But I shall soon learn that their zeal is bereft of meaning—or even reprehensible: it is mere whim. By contrast, some sudden action that outrages me by its inappropriateness turns out, on closer examination, to be entirely in keeping with the social dignity of the character concerned; it was carried out according to the law. In this way, the law collapses into whim and whim affords a sudden insight into the law. I would look in vain here for rulebooks, regulations and decrees: ancient commands lie around on desks and the employees conform to them without it being clear whether these orders have been issued by someone in authority, whether they are the product of centuries-old, anonymous routines or whether indeed they have not been invented by the functionaries themselves. Even the scope of these orders is ambiguous and I shall never be able to decide whether they apply to all members of the community or only to me. Yet this ambiguous law, which wavers between rule and whim, between the universal and the singular, is present everywhere. It holds you in its grip, overwhelms you. You transgress it when you think you are obeying and, when you think you are rebelling, you find your are obeying it unwittingly. Ignorance is no excuse and yet no one knows what the law actually is. Its aim is not to maintain order or regulate human relations. It is simply the Law, without purpose, meaning or content, and no one can escape it.

But the circle must be closed: no one can enter the world of dreams other than by sleeping; similarly, no one can enter the world of the fantastic other than by becoming fantastical themselves. Now, we know that when the reader begins reading he identifies with the hero of the novel. It is, then, the hero who, by lending us his point of view, provides the only path of access to the fantastic. The old technique presented him as a normally constituted individual transported miraculously into a world turned upside down. Kafka employed this process at least once. In *The Trial*, K. is a normal man. We can see the advantage of this technique; by creating a contrast, it throws the strange character of the new world into relief and the fantastic novel becomes an *Erziehungsroman*. The reader shares in the protagonist's amazement and follows him from discovery to discovery. Only, at the same time, he sees the fantastic *from the outside*, as a spectacle, as though a waking rational consciousness were peacefully contemplating the images of our dreams. In *The Castle*, Kafka perfected his technique. Here, the protagonist is himself a fantastic creature. We know nothing about this surveyor, whose adventures and views we are to share, other than his unintelligible determination to remain in a forbidden village. To achieve this goal, he sacrifices everything; he treats himself as a means. But we shall never know the value this goal had for him, nor whether it was worth so much effort.

M. Blanchot has adopted the same method; his Thomas is no less mysterious than the domestic servants in the building. We don't know where he comes from, nor why he is so eager to get to the woman who beckoned to him. Like Kafka, like Samsa, like the Surveyor, Thomas *is never surprised*: he is, however, outraged, as though the series of events he witnesses seemed perfectly natural to him, but reprehensible, as though he had within him a strange norm of Good and Evil about which M. Blanchot has carefully omitted to inform us. So we are forced, by the very laws of the novel, to espouse a viewpoint that is not our own, to condemn without comprehending and to contemplate with no surprise things that astound us. Furthermore, M. Blanchot opens and closes his hero's soul like a box. We can at times get inside it, at others we are left outside. And when we are inside, we find lines of reasoning that have already begun, that link together in mechanical sequence and presuppose principles and purposes of which we know nothing. We fall into line, because we *are* the hero and reason with him; but these lines of thinking never come to anything, as though the reasoning alone were all that counted. Once again, the means has consumed the end. And our reason, which was about to set aright a world turned upside down, is swept up in the nightmare and becomes, itself, fantastical. M. Blanchot has gone even further than this. In an excellent passage in *Aminadab*, his hero suddenly discovers that he is, without knowing it, employed in the building and that he has the role of executioner there. We had patiently questioned the functionaries, since it seemed to us that they knew the law and the secrets of the universe, and suddenly we learn that we were ourselves functionaries and didn't know it. So now the others turn imploring gazes on us and question us in turn. Perhaps we know the law after all. 'To know,' says Alain, 'is to know that we know.' But this is a maxim from the normally constituted world. In the world turned upside down, we don't know that we know what we know; and when we know that we know, we don't know. In this way, our last resort, that self-consciousness in which stoicism sought refuge, eludes us and disintegrates. Its transparency is the transparency of the void; our very being is outside and in the hands of others.

These, in outline, are the central themes of *The Castle* and *Aminadab*. I hope I have shown that they are inevitable once the decision has been made to depict a world turned upside down. But, you will object, why does it have to be depicted that way? What a stupid plan, to show human beings with their legs in the air! This world is not, in fact, fantastical, for the very good reason that everything in it is the right way up. A horror novel might present itself as a mere transposition of reality, because one does meet with some horrible situations in the normal course of events. But, as we have seen, there cannot be any *fantastical* events, because the fantastic can exist only as a universe. Let us examine this more closely. If I am the wrong way up in a topsy-turvy world, then to me everything seems the right way up. If I were fantastical and inhabited a fantastical world, I could in no way regard it as such. This will help us to understand our authors' intentions.

I cannot, then, judge this world, because my judgements are part of it. If I conceive it as a work of art or as a complicated mechanism, I do so employing human notions. And if, on the other hand, I declare it absurd, I do so again by means of human concepts.

As for the ends pursued by our species, how am I to describe them, except in relation to other ends? I may hope, at a pinch, to know the detail of the mechanism surrounding me one day, but how could man judge the world in its totality—that is to say, the world with man in it? It is, however, my ambition to know what really goes on; I would like to contemplate humanity as it is. The artist stubbornly persists when the philosopher has given up. He invents convenient fictions to satisfy our curiosity: Micromégas,[13] the noble savage, the dog Riquet[14] or that 'Outsider' M. Camus recently told us about—pure gazes that stand outside the human condition and are, therefore, able to inspect it. In the eyes of these angels, the human world is a *given* reality; they can say that it is this or that and that it could be different. Human ends are contingent; they are mere facts that the angels consider, as we consider the ends of bees and ants. Human progress is a mere running on the spot, since man can no more jump out of this finite, limited world than the ant can escape from his ant's universe. Only, by forcing the reader to identify with an inhuman hero, we send him soaring above the human condition. He escapes; he loses sight of that prime necessity of the universe he is contemplating—namely, that man is inside it. How can we have him see *from outside* this obligation to be inside? Ultimately, this is the problem Blanchot and Kafka set themselves. It is an exclusively literary and technical problem, which would have no meaning at the philosophical level. And here is the solution they have found: they have eliminated the angelic perspective and have plunged the reader into the world, with K. and with Thomas. But they have left to hover within this immanence something like a ghost of transcendence. The instruments, actions and purposes are all familiar to us, and we are on such intimate terms with them that they are barely noticeable. But at the very point when we feel enveloped, with them, by a warm atmosphere of organic sympathy, they are presented to us in a cold, strange light. This brush is here in my hand. I merely have to pick it up to brush my clothes. But on the point of touching it, I stop. It is a brush seen from outside. It is there in all its contingency; it refers to contingent ends, as seems to be the case to human eyes with the white pebble the ant stupidly pulls towards its hole. 'They brush their clothes every morning,' the Angel would say. And that is all it would take for the activity to seem obsessive and unintelligible. In M. Blanchot's case, there is no angel, but the effort is made, nonetheless, to make us conceive *our* ends—those ends that arise with us and give meaning to our lives—as *ends for others*. We are shown merely the external aspect of these alienated, paralysed ends, the side that they show to the outside, the side that makes them *facts*. These are petrified ends, ends seen from their underside, invaded by materiality and registered before our will has willed them. As a consequence, the means are cast adrift again. If it is no longer clear you have to brush yourself every morning, then the brush comes to seem like an indecipherable implement, the relic of some vanished civilization. It still signifies something, like those pipe-shaped tools they found at Pompeii. But no one now knows what it signifies. What, pray, is the world of the fantastic but the combination of these immobilized ends and these monstrous, futile means? The method is clear here: since human activity, when seen from outside, seems upside down, Kafka and Blanchot, seeking to have us see our condition from the outside but without resorting to angels, have depicted a world turned upside down. A contradictory world, in which mind becomes matter, since values appear as facts, and in which matter is grawed away by mind, since everything is simultaneously both a means and an end—a world in which, while continuing to be inside it, I see myself from the outside. We can conceive this world only with evanescent, self-destroying concepts. Or, more accurately, we cannot conceive it at all. This is why M. Blanchot writes, '[The meaning] can be grasped only through a fiction and dissipates as soon as we try to understand it in itself . . . The story . . . seems mysterious, because it expresses everything that will not, in fact, bear expression.' There is a kind of marginal existence of the fantastic: look it directly in the eye, try to express its meaning in words and it vanishes, because you have to be either inside it or outside. But if you read the story without attempting to translate it, it attacks you from the sides. The few truths you fish out of *Aminadab* will become colourless and lifeless the moment they are out of the water. Yes, of course, man is alone, he decides his destiny alone, he invents the law to which he is subject; each of us, though a stranger to himself, is a victim and a tormentor for everyone else; in vain do we try to transcend the human condition; it would be better to acquire a Nietzschean sense of earthliness. Yes, of course, M. Blanchot's wisdom seems to belong among those 'transcendences' Jean Wahl referred to when speaking of Heidegger. But in the end, none of this has a particularly new ring to it. And yet when these truths were slipping upstream, through the currents of the narrative, they had a strange gleam about them. This is because we were seeing them wrong side up: they were fantastical truths.

Our authors, who had travelled such a long way together, part company at this point. Of Kafka I have nothing to say, except that he is one of the rarest, greatest writers of our time. And then he came first. In him the chosen technique met a need. If he shows us human life perpetually disturbed by an impossible transcendence, he does so because he believes in the existence of that transcendence. It is simply beyond our grasp. His universe is both fantastical and rigorously true. M. Blanchot has, admittedly, considerable talent. But he comes second and the artifices he employs are already too familiar to us. Commenting on Jean Paulhan's *Les Fleurs de Tarbes*, he has written:

> Those who, by prodigious efforts of asceticism, had the illusion of distancing themselves from all literature through the attempt

to rid themselves of conventions and forms, in order to gain direct access to the secret world and profound metaphysics they wished to reveal . . . contented themselves in the end with using that world, that secret and that metaphysics as conventions and forms which they displayed with self-satisfaction and which constituted the visible armature and core of their works . . . For that kind of writer, metaphysics, religion and feelings take the place of technique and language. They are a system of expression, a literary genre— in a word, literature.[15]

I am rather afraid that this criticism, if it is a criticism, may be directed at M. Blanchot himself. The system of signs he has chosen doesn't entirely correspond to the thought he expresses. To depict for us the 'nature of the mind, its deep division, this battle of the Same with the Same, which is the means of its power, its torment and its apotheosis', there was no point resorting to artifices that introduce an external gaze into the heart of consciousness. I would happily say of M. Blanchot what Lagneau said of Barrès: 'He stole the tool.'[16] And this slight discrepancy between sign and signified relegates what in Kafka were living themes to the rank of literary conventions. Thanks to M. Blanchot, there is now a stereotype of the 'Kafkaesque' fantastic, in the same way as there is a stereotype of haunted castles and blood-spattered monsters. And I know that art lives by conventions, but they have, at least, to be properly chosen. Seen against a transcendence tinged with Maurrassianism, the fantastic looks like something that has been tacked on.

The reader's unease increases further because M. Blanchot doesn't remain faithful to his original intention. He has told us that he wants the meaning of *Aminadab* to 'dissipate as soon as we seek to understand it for itself'. Well and good, but why then does he offer us a perpetual translation of its symbols and a copious commentary on them? In many places, the explanations become so insistent that the story comes to look like an allegory. Select at random any page of the long narrative in which the myth of the domestics is developed. Take the following, for example:

> I have told you that the staff is invisible most of the time. What a foolish thing to say; I gave in to a prideful temptation and am now ashamed of it. The staff invisible? Invisible most of the time? We never see them, ever,

not even from a distance; we do not even know what the word *see* could mean when it comes to them, nor if there is a word to express their absence, nor even if the thought of this absence is not a supreme and pitiful resource to make us hope for their coming. The state of negligence in which they keep us is, from a certain point of view, unimaginable. We could therefore complain about how indifferent they are to our interests, since many of us have seen our health ruined or have paid with our lives for mistakes made by the service. Yet we would be prepared to forgive everything if from time to time they gave us some satisfaction . . .[17]

Take the above passage and replace the word 'staff' with the word 'God', the word 'service' with 'providence' and you will have an entirely intelligible account of a certain aspect of the religious feeling. Often, too, the objects of this falsely fantastical world yield their meaning 'the right way up', without need of any commentary, such as the companion in chains that so clearly stands for the body—the body humiliated and mistreated in a society that has divorced the physical from the spiritual. At this point we seem to be translating a translation, to be translating back words that had originated in our own language.

I don't, in fact, claim to have grasped all the author's intentions and perhaps I am wrong about many of them. It was a sufficient source of unease that these intentions were obvious, even when they were obscure. It was always in my mind that, with more application or more intelligence, I would have got to the bottom of them. In Kafka, the various accidents of the narrative are connected by the needs of the plot: in *The Trial*, for example, we never for a moment lose sight of the fact that K. is fighting for his dignity and his life. But what is Thomas fighting for? He has no clear-cut character, he has no aim, he is barely of any interest. And events accumulate capriciously. As in life, one might say. But life isn't a novel, and these successions of events, with no rhyme or reason to them, that we can discern in the work itself, send us back, in spite of ourselves, to the author's secret intentions. Why does Thomas lose his partner in chains, and does he fall ill? Nothing in the world turned upside down prepares or explains this illness. Its *raison d'être* must lie outside that world, in the author's providential intentions. Most of the time, then, M. Blanchot is wasting his effort; he doesn't succeed in ensnaring his reader in the nightmarish world he is depicting. The reader escapes; he is outside, outside with the author himself. He is contemplating these dreams as he would a well-oiled machine; only at very rare moments does he lose his foothold.

As it happens, these moments are enough to show up M. Blanchot as a writer of quality. He is ingenious and subtle, sometimes profound, and he loves words. All that is missing is for him to find his style. His incursion into the realm of the fantastic is not without consequence: it makes something clear. Kafka was inimitable. He remained on the horizon as a perpetual temptation. By having imitated him unwittingly, M. Blanchot frees us from his thrall; he brings his methods out into the open. Once catalogued, classified, ossified and useless, they lose their frightening or dizzying effects. Kafka was merely a stage; through him, as through Hoffmann, Poe, Lewis Carroll and the Surrealists, the literature of the fantastic continues the steady progress that will inevitably unite it, ultimately, with what it has always been.

Notes

1 Maurice Blanchot, *Thomas the Obscure* (Robert Lamberton trans.) (New York: Hill Press, 1988), p. 14.

2 Maurice Blanchot, *Aminadab* (Jeff Fort trans.) (Lincoln and London: University of Nebraska Press, 2002), p. 123.

3 Ibid., p. 154.

4 Ibid., p. 192.

5 Ibid., p. 184.

6 Ibid., p. 196.

7 M. Blanchot was, I believe, a disciple of Charles Maurras. [J.-P. S.] On Maurras, see NOTE 6, p. 181. [Trans.]

8 Jacques Cazotte (1719–92): a French author of fantastical tales and romances. [Trans.]

9 Arthur Rimbaud, *A Season in Hell* (Oliver Bernard trans.) (London: Penguin, 1995), p. 37.

10 Charles Nodier (1780–1844): a French novelist and author of fantastical tales. [Trans.]

11 The quotation is from Sir Arthus Eddington's *Space, Time and Gravitation* (Cambridge: Cambridge University Press, 1920). [Trans.]

12 Blanchot, *Aminadab*, p. 147.

13 Micromégas is the hero of Voltaire's satirical *conte* of the same name, which was originally published in London in 1752. He is a 120,000-foot-tall inhabitant of Sirius who visits Earth in 1737. [Trans.]

14 Riquet is the dog of Monsieur Bergeret, a recurring character in the novels of Anatole France. [Trans.]

15 Maurice Blanchot, *Comment la littérature est-elle possible?* (Paris: José Corti, 1942), p. 23.

16 Maurice Barrès (1862–1923): a novelist, journalist and political activist; close to the Symbolist movement in his youth, he came to be associated with extreme nationalism and a current of pre-fascist romanticism in early-twentieth-century French literature. [Trans.]

17 Blanchot, *Aminadab*, p. 75.

A New Mystic

I

There is a crisis of the essay. Elegance and clarity
seem to demand that, in this kind of work, we employ
a language deader than Latin: the language of Voltaire.
I have remarked on this before in relation to *The Myth
of Sisyphus.*[1] But if we really try to express today's
thoughts using yesterday's language, what a lot of
metaphors, circumlocutions and imprecise images
ensue: you would think we were back in the age of

Delille.[2] Some, like Alain[3] and Paulhan,[4] try to be economical with words and time, to rein in, by means of
numerous ellipses, the florid prolixity that characterizes that language. But how obscure this becomes!
Everything is covered with an irritating veneer, whose
shimmering surface conceals the ideas. With the
American writers, with Kafka and with Camus in
France, the contemporary novel has found its style.
The style of the essay remains to be discovered. And
the style of criticism, too, in my opinion, for I am not
unaware, as I write these lines, that I am using an outdated instrument which academic tradition has preserved into our own day.

This is why we must point out a work like that of
M. Bataille as deserving of special attention. It is an
essay that I would happily describe as agonized (and
I have its author's authority to do so, since there are
so many mentions of torture and torment in the
book). M. Bataille forsakes both the stony speech of
the great minds of 1780 and with it, inevitably, the
objectivity of the classics. He strips himself bare; he
lays himself before us; he isn't pleasant company. If
human wretchedness is his theme, then look, he says,
at my sores and ulcers. And he opens his clothing to

show them to us. Yet lyricism isn't his aim. If he shows himself, he does so in pursuit of proof. Barely has he let us glimpse his wretched nudity and he is covered up again and off we go with him in reasoned discussions of Hegel's system or Descartes's *cogito*. But then the reasoning comes to an abrupt halt and the man reappears. 'I could say,' he writes, for example, in the middle of an argument about God, that 'this hatred is time, but that bothers me. Why should I say time? I feel this hatred when I cry; I analyze nothing.'[5]

Actually, this form which still seems so new, is already part of a tradition. The death of Pascal saved his *Pensées* from being written up into a strong and colourless Apologia. By delivering them to us all jumbled up, by striking down their author before he had the time to muzzle himself, that death made them the model for the genre that concerns us here. And there is, in my view, more than a little of Pascal in M. Bataille, particularly the feverish contempt and the desire to get his words out quickly, to which I shall return. But it is to Nietzsche that he himself refers explicitly. And, indeed certain pages of *Inner Experience*, with their breathless disorder, their passionate symbolism and their tone of prophetic preaching, seem to come straight out of *Ecce Homo* or *The Will to Power*. Lastly, M. Bataille was once very close to the Surrealists and no one cultivated the agonized essay so much as the Surrealists. Breton's voluminous personality found itself at ease in that genre: coldly, in the style of Charles Maurras, he demonstrated the incomparable excellence of his theories, and then suddenly went off on to the most puerile details of his life, showing photographs of the restaurants in which he had had lunch and the shop where he bought his coal. There was, in that exhibitionism, a need to destroy all literature and, to that end, suddenly to reveal, behind the 'monsters imitated by art', the true monster. There was probably also a taste for scandal, but mainly a preference for direct contact. The book had to establish a kind of fleshly closeness between author and reader. Lastly, in the case of these authors impatient for commitment, who felt contempt for the quiet occupation of writing, every work had to involve risk. As Michel Leiris did in his admirable *Manhood*,[6] they revealed of themselves everything that could shock, annoy or prompt laughter, in order to lend their undertakings the perilous seriousness of a genuine act. Pascal's *Pensées*, Rousseau's *Confessions*, Nietzsche's *Ecce*

Homo, *Les Pas Perdus* and *L'Amour Fou* by Breton, *Le Traité du Style* by Aragon and *Manhood*—it is within this series of 'passionate geometries' that Bataille's *Inner Experience* has its place.

Right from the preface, the author informs us that he wants to achieve a synthesis of '*rapture*' and '*rigorous intellectual method*'; that he is trying to make 'rigorous, shared emotional knowledge (laughter)' and 'rational knowledge' coincide.[7] No more is needed for us to see that we are going to find ourselves in the presence of a demonstrative apparatus with a powerful affective potential. But M. Bataille goes further. For him, feeling is both at the origin and at the end: 'Conviction,' he writes, 'does not arise from reasoning, but only from the feelings which it defines.'[8] We know these famous ice-cold, yet fiercely blazing lines of reasoning, troubling in their harsh abstraction, that are deployed by the passionate and the paranoid: their rigour is, from the outset, a challenge and a threat; their suspicious immobility harbours forebodings of stormy lava-flows. M. Bataille's syllogisms are like that. They are the proofs supplied by an orator, jealous lover, barrister or madman. Not by a mathematician. We can sense that this plastic, molten substance, with its sudden solidifications that liquify again as soon as we touch them, needs to be rendered in a special form and can never be at home with an all-purpose language. At times, the style is close to choking or drowning in its efforts to render the gasping suffocations of ecstasy or anguish (Pascal's 'Joy, joy, tears of joy' will find a counterpart in such sentences as the following: 'One must. Is this to moan? I no longer know. Where am I going to?' etc. . . .);[9] at others, it is broken up with little bursts of laughter; at yet others, it sprawls out into the balanced periods of reasoning. The sentence of intuitive rapture, condensed into a single instant, is found side by side, in *Inner Experience*, with the leisurely discursive mode.

It is, in fact, only reluctantly that M. Bataille employs this discursive mode. He hates it and, through it, he hates all language. M. Bataille shares this hatred—which we also noted recently in Camus—with a great many contemporary writers. But the reasons he gives for it are all his own: it is the mystic's hatred to which he lays claim, not the terrorist's. First, he tells us, language is a project: the speaker has an appointment with himself at the end of the sentence. Speech is a construction, an undertaking; the octogenarian who speaks is as mad as the octogenarian who plants. To speak is to rend oneself apart; to put existence off until later, until the end of the discourse; to be torn between a subject, a verb and a complement. M. Bataille wants to exist fully and immediately—this very instant. Moreover, words are 'the instruments of useful acts': hence, to name the real is to cover it over or veil it with familiarity, to bring it into the ranks of what Hegel termed 'das Bekannte': the *too well known*, which goes unnoticed. To tear away the veils and swap the opaque quietude of knowledge for the astonishment of non-knowledge, a 'holocaust of words' is needed, that holocaust that has already been carried out by poetry:

> Should words such as *horse* or *butter* come into a poem, they do so detached from interested concerns . . . When the farm girl says *butter* or the stable boy says *horse*, they know butter and horses . . . But, *on the contrary, poetry leads from the known to the unknown*. It can do what neither the boy nor the girl can do: introduce a butter horse. In this way, it sets one before the unknowable.[10]

But poetry doesn't propose to communicate a precise experience. M. Bataille, for his part, has to identify, describe, persuade. Poetry confines itself to sacrificing words; M. Bataille aims to explain to us the reasons for this sacrifice. And it is with words that he must exhort us to sacrifice words. Our author is very conscious of this circle. It is partly for this reason that he situates his work 'beyond poetry'. As a result of this, he becomes subject to a constraint similar to those the tragedians imposed on themselves. Just as Racine could wonder, 'how to express jealousy and fear in rhyming twelve-foot lines' and just as he drew his force of expression from that very constraint, so M. Bataille asks himself how he can express silence with words. Perhaps this is a problem that has no philosophical solution; perhaps, from this angle, it is merely a case of wordplay. But from our standpoint, it looks like an aesthetic rule as valid as any other, a supplementary difficulty the author freely imposes on himself, like a billiards player marking out limits for himself on the green baize. It is this difficulty freely consented to that lends the style of *Inner Experience* its particular savour. First, we find in M. Bataille a mimesis of the moment. Silence and the moment being one and the same thing, it is the configuration of the moment he has to impart to his thought. 'The expression of inner experience,' he writes, 'must in some way respond to its movement.'[11] He therefore eschews the carefully composed work and an ordered development of argument. He expresses himself in short aphorisms, spasms, which the reader can grasp at a single glance and which stand as instantaneous explosions, bounded by two blanks, two abysses of repose. He himself provides the following explanation:

> A continual challenging of everything deprives one of the power of proceeding by separate operations, obliges one to express oneself through rapid flashes, to free as much as is possible the expression of one's thought from a project, to include everything in a few sentences: anguish, decision and the right to the poetic perversion of words without which it would seem that one was subject to a domination.[12]

As a result, the work assumes the appearance of a string of remarks. It is odd to record that the anti-intellectualist Bataille meets up here with the rationalist Alain in his choice of mode of exposition. This is because this 'continual questioning of everything' may just as well proceed from a mystic negation as from a

Cartesian philosophy of free judgement. But the resemblance goes no further than this: Alain trusts in
words. Bataille, by contrast, will attempt to consign
them, in the very weft of his text, to the most minor
role. They have to be shorn of their ballast, emptied
out and imbued with silence, in order to lighten them
to the extreme. He will try, then, to use 'slippery sentences', like soapy planks that have us suddenly falling
into the ineffable; slippery words too, like this very
word 'silence'. He will write of 'the abolition of the
sound which the word is; among all words . . . the
most perverse and the most poetic.'[13] Alongside those
words which signify—words indispensable, after all,
to understanding—he will slip into his argument
words that are merely suggestive, such as 'laughter',
'torment', 'agony', 'rending', 'poetry', etc., which he
diverts from their original meaning to confer on them
gradually a magical evocative power. These various
techniques lead to a situation in which M. Bataille's
deep thought—or feeling—seems entirely encapsu-
lated in each of his 'Reflections'. It doesn't build up,
isn't progressively enriched, but rises, undivided and
almost ineffable, to the surface of each aphorism, so
that each presents the same formidable, complex

meaning with a different lighting. By contrast with the analytical methods of the philosophers, we might say that M. Bataille's book presents itself as the product of a totalitarian thinking.

But this thinking itself, syncretic as it may be, could still aim for—and attain to—the universal. M. Camus, for example, no less struck by the absurdity of our condition, has still attempted an objective portrait of 'homo absurdus', irrespective of historical circumstances, and the great exemplary Absurd individuals to whom he refers—such as Don Juan—have a universality that is every bit the equal of that of Kant's moral agent. Bataille's originality lies in his having, despite his angry, peevish reasoning, deliberately chosen history over metaphysics. Here again, we have to look back to Pascal, whom I would happily call the first *historical* thinker, because he was the first to grasp that, in man, existence precedes essence. There is, in his view, too much grandeur in the human creature for us to understand him on the basis of his wretchedness, too much wretchedness for us to deduce his nature from his grandeur. In a word, something *happened to* man, something undemonstrable and irreducible, and hence something *historical*: fall and redemption.

As a historical religion, Christianity stands opposed to all metaphysics. M. Bataille, who was a devout Christian, has retained Christianity's deep sense of historicity. He speaks to us of the human condition, not of human nature: man is not a nature, but a drama; his characteristics are *acts*: project, torment, agony, laughter—so many words referring to temporal processes of realization, not qualities given passively and passively received. This is because M. Bataille's work is, like most mystical writings, the product of a *re-descent*. M. Bataille is returning from an unknown region; he is coming back down among us. He wants to carry us with him: he describes our wretchedness which once was his; he tells us the story of his journey, his long-held delusions, his arrival. If, like the Platonic philosopher brought out from the cave, he had found himself suddenly in the presence of an eternal truth, the historical aspect of his account would probably have been eliminated, giving way to the universal rigour of Ideas. But his encounter was with non-knowledge, and non-knowledge is essentially historical, since it can be described only as a particular experience had by a particular person on a particular date. For this reason, we have to see *Inner Experience* both as a

Gospel (though he doesn't impart any 'good news' to us) and an Invitation to the Voyage.[14] Edifying Narrative—that is what he could have called his book. With this—through this mix of proof and drama—the work takes on an entirely original flavour. Alain first wrote his objective *Propos* (Remarks) and only later, as a conclusion to his life's work, his *Histoire de mes Pensées* (History of My Thoughts).[15] But the two are in one here, entangled in the same book. Barely have the proofs been laid before us than they suddenly appear historical: a man thought them, at a certain point in his life, and became a martyr to them. We are reading not just Gide's *The Counterfeiters*, but at the same time 'Édouard's Journal'[16] and *The Journal of the Counterfeiters*.[17] In conclusion, the subjectivity closes over both the reasoning and the rapture. It is a man that stands before us, a man naked and alone, who disarms all his deductions by dating them, a man both unlikable and 'captivating'—like Pascal.

Have I conveyed the originality of this language? One last feature will help me to do so: the tone is constantly scornful. It recalls the disdainful aggressiveness of the Surrealists; M. Bataille wants to rub his readers up the wrong way. Yet, he writes to 'communicate'.

But it seems that he speaks to us reluctantly. And is he actually addressing us? Indeed he is not—and he is at pains to let us know. He 'loathes his own voice'. Though he regards communication as necessary—for ecstasy without communication is mere emptiness—he says: 'I become irritated when I think of the time of 'activity' which I spent—during the last years of peacetime—in forcing myself to reach my fellow beings.'[18] And we must take this term 'fellow beings' in its strictest sense. It is for the mystic's apprentice that M. Bataille writes, for the person who, in solitude, is making his way, through laughter and world-weariness, towards his final torment. But there is nothing comforting for our author in the hope that he will be read by this very particular sort of Nathanaël.[19] 'Even in preaching to the converted, there is, in its predication, a distressful element.'[20] Even if we were this potential disciple, we have the right to listen to M. Bataille, but not—he loftily warns us—to judge him: 'There are no readers, nevertheless, who have in them anything to cause . . . [my] disarray. Were the most perspicacious of them to accuse me, I would laugh: it is of myself that I am afraid.'[21] This puts the critic at his ease. M. Bataille opens up here, strips himself bare before our very eyes, but at the same time he curtly rejects our judgement: it is for him alone to judge and the communication he wishes to establish is without reciprocity. He is on high, we are down below. He delivers us a message and it is for us to receive it if we can. But what adds to our difficulty is that the summit from which he speaks to us is at the same time the 'abyssal' depth of abjection.

The proud and dramatic preaching of a man more than halfway committed to silence, who, to go as quickly as he can, reluctantly speaks a feverish, bitter and often incorrect language and who exhorts us, without looking at us directly, to join him proudly in his shame and darkness—this is what *Inner Experience* seems at first to be. Apart from a little empty bombast and some clumsiness in the handling of abstractions, everything in this mode of expression is praiseworthy: it presents the essayist with an example and a tradition; it takes us back to the sources, to Pascal and Montaigne, and at the same time it offers us a language and a syntax better adapted to the problems of our age. But form isn't everything. Let us look at the content.

II

There are people you might call survivors. Early on, they lost a beloved person—father, friend or mistress—and their lives are merely the gloomy aftermath of that death. Monsieur Bataille is a survivor of the death of God. And, when one thinks about it, it would seem that our entire age is surviving that death, which he experienced, suffered and survived. God is dead. We should not understand by that that He does not exist, nor even that He now no longer exists. He is dead: he used to speak to us and he has fallen silent, we now touch only his corpse. Perhaps he has slipped out of the world to some other place, like a dead man's soul. Perhaps all this was merely a dream. Hegel tried to replace Him with his system and the system has collapsed. Comte tried with the religion of humanity, and positivism has collapsed. In France and elsewhere, around the year 1880, a number of honourable Gentlemen, some of them sufficiently logical to demand they be cremated after their deaths, had the notion of developing a secular morality. We lived by that morality for a time, but then along came M. Bataille—and so many others like him—to attest to its bankruptcy. God is dead, but man has not, for all that, become atheistic. Today, as yesterday, this silence of the transcendent, combined with modern man's enduring religious need, is the great question of the age. It is the problem that torments Nietzsche, Heidegger and Jaspers. It is our author's central personal drama. Coming out of a 'long Christian piety', his life 'dissolved into laughter'. Laughter was a revelation:

> Fifteen years ago . . . I was returning from I don't know where, late at night . . . Crossing the rue du Four, I suddenly became unknown to myself in this "nothingness" . . . I denied the grey walls that enclosed me, I plunged into a kind of rapture. I was laughing divinely: the umbrella that had come down over my head covered me (I deliberately covered myself with this black shroud). I was laughing as no one perhaps had laughed before; the bottom of every thing lay open, was laid bare, as though I were dead.[22]

For some time, he attempted to sidestep the consequences of these revelations. Eroticism, the all-too-human 'sacred' of sociology, offered him some precarious havens. And then everything collapsed and here he is before us, lugubrious and comical, like an inconsolable widower indulging, all dressed in black, in 'the solitary vice' in memory of his dead wife. For M. Bataille refuses to reconcile these two immovable and contradictory demands: God is silent, I cannot budge an inch on that; everything in me calls out for God, I cannot forget Him. At more than one point in *Inner Experience*, you would think you had Stravogin or Ivan Karamazov before you—an Ivan who had known André Breton. From this there arises, in Bataille's case, a particular experience of the absurd. In fact, that experience is found in one form or another in most contemporary authors. One thinks of the 'fissure' in Jaspers, death in Malraux, Heidegger's 'abandonment', Kafka's temporarily reprieved creatures, the pointless, obsessive labour of Sisyphus in Camus, or Blanchot's Aminadab.

But it must be said that modern thought has encountered two kinds of absurd. For some, the fundamental absurdity is 'facticity' or, in other words, the irreducible contingency of our 'being-there', of our existence that has neither purpose nor reason. For others, faithless disciples of Hegel, it resides in the fact that man is an insoluble contradiction. It is this absurdity M. Bataille feels most sharply. Like Hegel, whom he has read, he takes the view that reality is conflict. But, for him, as for Kierkegaard, Nietzsche and Jaspers, there are conflicts that have no resolution. He eliminates the moment of synthesis from the Hegelian trinity, and, for the dialectical view of the world, he substitutes a tragic—or, as he would put it, dramatic—vision. The reader will perhaps be put in mind of Camus here, whose fine novel we commented on recently. But for Camus, who has barely dipped into the phenomenologists and whose thinking falls within the tradition of the French moralists, the original contradiction is a matter of fact. There are forces in presence—which are what they are—and the absurdity arises out of the relation between them. The contradiction comes retrospectively. For M. Bataille, who is more intimately familiar with existentialism and has even borrowed his terminology from it, the absurd is not given, but *produces itself*. Man creates himself as conflict. We are not made of a certain stuff in which fissures might appear through wear and tear or the action of some external agent. The 'fissure'[23] fissures only itself; it is its own substance and man is the unity of that substance: a strange unity that inspires nothing at all, but, rather, destroys itself to maintain the opposition. Kierkegaard called this ambiguity: in it contradictions co-exist without merging; each one leads on indefinitely to another. It is this perpetual evanescent unity that M. Bataille experiences immediately within himself; it is this which provides him with his original vision of the absurd and the image he constantly employs to express that vision: the image of a self-opening wound whose swollen lips gape open towards the heavens. Should we then, you will ask, place M. Bataille among the existentialist thinkers? That would be too hasty. M. Bataille doesn't like philosophy. His aim is to relate a certain experience to us or, rather, we should say, a certain *lived experience*, in the sense of the German word *Erlebnis*.[24] It is a question of life and death, pain and delight, not tranquil contemplation. (M. Bataille's mistake is to believe that modern philosophy has remained contemplative. He has clearly not understood Heidegger, of whom he speaks often and ineptly). As a result, if he does use philosophical techniques, he does so as a more convenient way of expressing an adventure that lies beyond philosophy, on the borders of knowledge and non-knowledge. But philosophy takes its revenge:

this technical material, employed without discernment, bowled along by polemical or dramatic passion and dragooned into rendering the pantings and spasms of our author, turns round against him. When inserted in M. Bataille's texts, words that had precise meanings in the works of Hegel or Heidegger lend it a semblance of rigorous thought. But as soon as you attempt to grasp that thought, it melts like snow. The emotion alone remains, that is to say, a powerful inner disturbance in respect of vague objects. 'Of poetry, I will now say that it is . . . the sacrifice in which words are victims,' writes M. Bataille.[25] In this sense, his work is a burnt offering of philosophical words. As soon as he uses one, its meaning immediately curdles or goes off like warm milk. Moreover, in his haste to *bear witness*, M. Bataille regales us with thoughts from very different dates in no particular order, but he doesn't tell us whether we are to regard them as the paths that have led him to his current state of feeling or as ways of seeing that he still holds to today. From time to time, he seems in the grip of a feverish desire to unify them; at other times, he relaxes, abandons them and they go back to their isolation. If we attempt to organize this vague assemblage, we must first remind ourselves that each word is a trap and that he is trying to trick us by presenting as thoughts the violent stirrings of a soul in mourning. Furthermore, M. Bataille, who is neither a scholar nor a philosopher, has, unfortunately, a smattering of science and philosophy. We run up straight away against two distinct attitudes of mind that co-exist within him, without his realizing it, and that are mutually detrimental: the existentialist attitude and what I shall dub, for want of a better word, the scientistic. As we know, it was scientism that scrambled Nietzsche's message, deflecting him into childish views on evolution and masking his understanding of the human condition. It is scientism too that will distort the whole of M. Bataille's thought.

The starting point is that man is born from—'is begotten of'—the earth: We may take this to mean that he is the product of one of the countless possible combinations of natural elements. A highly improbable combination, we guess, as improbable as cubes with letters on them rolling on the ground arranging themselves in such a way as to spell out the word 'anticonstitutional'. 'A single chance decided the possibility of this *self* which I am: in the end the mad improbability of the sole being without whom, *for me*, nothing would be, becomes evident.'[26] There you have a scientistic, objective viewpoint if ever there was one. And, indeed, in order to adopt it, we have to assert the anteriority of the object (Nature) over the subject; we must, from the outset, place ourselves outside of inner experience—the only experience available to us. We have to accept the value of science as a basic assumption. And yet science doesn't tell us that we came from the earth: it simply tells us about earth. M. Bataille is scientistic in the sense that he makes science say much more than it really does. We are, then, it seems, poles apart from an *Erlebnis* on the part of the subject, from a concrete encounter of existence with itself: at the moment of the *cogito*, Descartes never saw himself as a product of Nature; he registered his own contingency and facticity, the irrationality of his 'being-there', not his improbability. But here everything changes suddenly: this 'improbability'—which can be deduced only from the calculation of the *chances* of the play of natural forces producing just *this*, this *Self*—is presented to us as the original content of the *cogito*. 'The feeling of my fundamental improbability situates me in the world,' writes M. Bataille.[27] And, a little further on, he rejects the reassuring constructs of reason in the name of the 'experience of the self, of its improbability, of its insane demands'.[28] How can he not see that improbability is not an immediate given, but precisely a construct of the reason? It is the *Other* who is improbable, because I apprehend him from outside. But, in an initial conceptual slide, our author equates facticity, the concrete object of an authentic experience, with improbability, a pure scientific concept. Looking further, we find that, according to Bataille, this feeling brings us into contact with our deepest being. What a mistake! Improbability can only be a hypothesis that is closely dependent on earlier presuppositions. I am improbable if a certain universe is assumed to be true. If God created me, if I was subject to a particular decree of Providence or if I am a mode of Spinozist substance, my improbability disappears. Our author's starting point is, then, *something deduced*; it is in no way encountered by feeling. But we shall see another piece of trickery: M. Bataille goes on to equate improbability with irreplaceability: 'I,' he writes, 'that is to say, the infinite, painful improbability of an irreplaceable being, which I am.'[29] And this identification is even clearer a few lines later:

The empirical knowledge of my similarity
with others is irrelevant, for the essence of
my self arises from this—that nothing will
be able to replace it: the feeling of my fundamental improbability situates me in the
world where I remain as though foreign to
it, absolutely foreign.[30]

In this same way, Gide didn't need to advise
Nathanaël to *become* the most irreplaceable of human
beings: irreplaceability, which makes every person a
Unique Entity, is given from the outset. It is a quality
we are endowed with, since what is *unique* in me is, in
the end, the '*single* chance' that 'decided the possibility
of this self'.[31] Thus, in conclusion, this self is not me:
it eludes me; it no more belongs to me than the movement belongs to the billiard ball. It was imparted to
me from the outside. M. Bataille calls this external
idiosyncracy 'ipseity' and the very name he gives to it
reveals his perpetual confusion with regard to scientism and existentialism. The word 'ipseity' is a neolo-
gism he takes from Corbin, Heidegger's translator. M.
Corbin uses it to render the German term *Selbstheit*,
which means existential return towards oneself on the
basis of the project. It is from this return to oneself

243

that the *self* emerges. Hence, ipseity is a reflexive relationship that one creates by living it out. Once in possession of the word, M. Bataille applies it to knives, machines and even attempts to apply it to the atom (then thinks better of it). This is because he understands it merely to mean *natural individuality*. The rest follows automatically: noticing its 'ipseity', the product of the 'most madly improbable chance', the self sets itself up defiantly above the void of Nature. We come back here to the inner attitude of existentialism: 'Human bodies are erect on the ground like a challenge to the Earth . . .'[32] Improbability has been internalized; it has become a fundamental, lived, accepted, claimed experience. This brings us back to the 'challenge' that lies, for Jaspers, at the beginning of all history. The self demands its ipseity; it wishes to 'climb to the pinnacle'. And M. Bataille tops Jaspers off with Heidegger: the authentic experience of my improbable ipseity is not given to me ordinarily, he tells us:

> As long as I live, I am content with a coming and going, with a compromise. No matter what I say, I know myself to be a member of a species and I remain in harmony, roughly speaking, with a common reality; I

take part in what, by all necessity, exists—
in what nothing can withdraw. The Self-
that-dies abandons this harmony: it truly
perceives what surrounds it to be a void and
itself to be a challenge to this void.[33]

This is the meaning of human reality in the light
of its 'being-for-death'. Just as Heidegger speaks of a
freedom that launches itself against death (*Freiheit zum
Tod*), so M. Bataille writes: 'the *self* grows until it
reaches the pure imperative: this imperative . . . is formulated "die like a dog".[34] Isn't this irreplaceability
of 'human reality', experienced in the blinding light
of being-for-death, precisely the Heideggerian experience? Yes, but M. Bataille doesn't stop at that: the
fact is that this experience, which ought to be pure,
suffered apperception of the self by itself, bears within
it a seed of destruction; in Heidegger we discover only
the *inside* and we are nothing except insofar as we discover ourselves; being coincides with the movement
of discovery. For his part, M. Bataille has poisoned
his experience, since he actually makes it bear upon
improbability, a hypothetical concept borrowed from
external reality. In this way, the outside has slipped
inside myself; death illumines only a fragment of

Nature; at the point where the urgency of death reveals me to myself, M. Bataille has silently arranged that I should see myself through the eyes of another. The consequence of this piece of legerdemain is that 'Death is in a sense an imposture.' Since the Self is an external object, it has the 'exteriority' of natural things.[35] This means, first of all, that it is *composite* and that the grounds of its compositeness lie outside itself: 'A being is always a set of particles whose relative autonomies are maintained'[36] and 'This being *ipse*, itself constituted from parts and, as such—being result, unpredictable chance—enters the universe as the will for autonomy.'[37] These remarks are made, once again, from the scientific standpoint: it is science which, by its desire for analysis, dissolves individualities and relegates them to the realm of appearances. And it is the scientist again who, looking at human life *from the outside*, can write:

> What you are stems from the activity which links the innumerable elements which constitute you to the intense communication of these elements among themselves. These are contagions of energy, of movement, of warmth, or transfers of elements, which con-

stitute inevitably the life of your organized being. Life is never situated at a particular point; it passes rapidly from one point to another (or from multiple points to other points), like a current or like a sort of streaming of electricity. Thus, where you would like to grasp your timeless substance, you encounter only a slipping, only the poorly coordinated play of your perishable elements.[38]

Moreover, ipseity is subject to the solvent action of time. M. Bataille takes over Proust's remarks on time as separator. He doesn't see the balancing element: namely, that *durée* also—and primarily—fulfils a binding role. Time, he says, 'signifies only the flight of the objects that seemed true'[39] and, he adds, 'as is the case with time, the self-that-dies is pure change, and neither one nor the other have real existence.'[40]

What, then, but scientific time is this time that gnaws away and separates—this time each instant of which corresponds to a position of a moving object on a trajectory? Is M. Bataille sure that a genuine *inner* experience of time would have yielded the same results? The fact remains that, for him, this 'reprieved' self that is never finished, made up of components external to one another is—though it reveals itself to the dying subject—merely a sham. We see the emergence of the tragic here: we are an appearance striving to be a reality, but whose very efforts to leave its phantom existence behind are mere semblance. We can, however, also see the *explanation* for this sense of the tragic: the fact is that M. Bataille adopts two contradictory viewpoints simultaneously. On the one hand, he seeks—and finds—himself by a procedure analogous to the *cogito*, which reveals to him his irreplaceable individuality; on the other hand, he suddenly steps outside himself to examine that individuality with the eyes and instruments of the scientist, as though it were a thing in the world. And this latter point of view assumes that he has taken on board a certain number of postulates on the value of science and analysis and on the nature of objectivity, postulates he would have to sweep away if he wanted immediate access to himself. As a result, the object of his enquiry seems a strange, contradictory entity, very similar to Kierkegaard's 'ambiguous creatures': it is a reality that is, nonetheless, illusory, a unity that crumbles into multiplicity, a cohesion that time tears apart. But these contradictions are not to be wondered at: if M. Bataille found them in himself, that is because he put them there, forcibly introducing the transcendent into the immanent. If he had kept to the viewpoint of inner discovery, he would have understood: 1) that the data of science have no part in the certainty of the *cogito* and that they have to be regarded as merely probable; if one confines oneself to one's inner experience, one cannot come out again to observe oneself from the outside; 2) that in the field of inner experience, there no longer are any appearances; or, rather, that, in that experience, appearance is absolute reality. If I dream of a perfume, it is not a real perfume. But if I dream that I take pleasure in smelling it, then that is *true* pleasure; you cannot dream your pleasure, you cannot dream the simplicity or unity of your *Self.* If you discover them, then they exist, because you give them existence by discovering them; 3) that there is nothing troubling about the famous temporal rending of the Self. For time also binds and the Self in its very being is temporal. This means that, far from being nullified by Time, it has need of Time to realize itself. And I shall have nothing of the objection that the Self fades away by fragments, by moments, for the Time of inner experience is not made up of moments.

But M. Bataille is at the second stage of the analysis now, the stage that will reveal to us the permanent contradiction that we *are*. The *ipse*, the unstable unity of particles, is itself a particle in larger entities. This is what M. Bataille calls *communication*. He notes quite rightly that the relations established between human beings cannot be limited to mere relations of juxtaposition. Human beings do not first exist and then communicate afterwards; communication constitutes them in their being from the outset. Here again, we might at first believe we are in the presence of the latest philosophical advances of Phenomenology. Isn't this 'communication' reminiscent of Heidegger's *Mitsein*? But, as before, this existential resonance appears illusory as soon as we look more closely. 'A man,' writes M. Bataille, 'is a particle inserted in unstable and tangled groups,'[41] and elsewhere,

> Knowledge which the male neighbour has of his female neighbour is no less removed from an encounter of strangers than is life from death. *Knowledge* appears in this way like

an unstable biological bond—no less real, however, than that of cells of a tissue. The exchange between two persons possesses in effect the power to survive momentary separation.[42]

He adds that 'Only the instability of the relations . . . permits the illusion of a being which is isolated . . .' In this way, the *ipse* is doubly illusory: illusory because it is composite and illusory because it is a component. M. Bataille brings out the two complementary and opposing aspects of any organized ensemble: 'constitution transcending the constituent parts, relative autonomy of the constituent parts'.[43] This is a good description: it is akin to Meyerson's insights into what he termed 'the fibrous structure of the universe'. But he was, precisely, describing the universe or, in other words, Nature outside the subject. To apply these principles to the community of subjects is to reinsert them into Nature. How, in fact, can M. Bataille apprehend this 'constitution transcending the constituent parts'? It can only be by observing his own existence, since he is merely an element within an ensemble. The floating unity of the elements can be evident only to an observer who has deliberately placed himself outside this totality. But only God is outside. And even then, we would have to be speaking of a God that is different from Spinoza's. Moreover, the discovery of a reality that is not *our* reality can be made only through a hypothesis and its status is never anything more than probable. How are we to align the inner certainty of our existence with this probability that it may belong to these unstable ensembles? And, logically, shouldn't the subordination of the terms be reversed: isn't it our autonomy that becomes certainty and our dependency that is consigned to the realm of illusion? For if I am the consciousness *of* my dependency, then dependency is an object and consciousness is independent. Moreover, the law M. Bataille establishes isn't limited to the field of human interrelations. In the texts we have cited, he extends it expressly to the entire organized universe. If it applies, then, to living cells as much as to subjects, this can only be insofar as subjects are regarded as cells or, in other words, as things. And the law is no longer the simple description of an inner experience, but an abstract principle, akin to those that govern mechanics and, at the same time, several regions of the universe. If it were sentient, the falling stone wouldn't discover the law of gravity in its own fall. It would experience its fall as a unique event. The law of gravity would, for that stone, be a law applying to *other stones*.

Similarly, when he legislates on 'communication', M. Bataille is necessarily speaking of the communication of the Others amongst themselves. We recognize this attitude: the subject establishes a law by induction from the empirical observation of other human beings, then employs analogical reasoning to place himself under the sway of the law he has just established. This is the attitude of the sociologist. Not for nothing was M. Bataille a member of that strange and famous Collège de Sociologie that would have so surprised the honest Durkheim, whom it claimed, among others, as its inspiration and each member of which was using an emergent science to pursue extra-scientific designs. In the Collège M. Bataille learned to treat human beings as things. These volatile, incomplete totalities that suddenly form and become entangled, only to decompose immediately and re-form elsewhere, are more akin to the 'unanimist lives' of Romains[44] and, above all, to the 'collective consciousnesses' of the French sociologists than to Heideggerian *Mitsein*.

Was it by chance that these sociologists—Durkheim,[45] Lévy-Bruhl[46] and Bouglé[47]—were the ones, towards the end of the last century, who vainly attempted to lay the foundations of a secular morality? Is it any accident that M. Bataille, the bitterest witness to their failure, has taken over their vision of the social, transcended it and stolen the notion of the 'sacred' from them, in order to adapt it for his personal ends? But the point is that the sociologist cannot integrate himself into sociology: he remains the one creating it. He cannot be part of it, any more than Hegel can be part of Hegelianism or Spinoza of Spinozism. In vain does M. Bataille attempt to enter into the machinery he has set up: he remains outside, with Durkheim and Hegel and God the Father. We shall see, shortly, that he surreptitiously sought out that privileged position.

However this may be, we have now pinned down the contradiction: the self is autonomous and dependent. When it considers its autonomy, it wants to be *ipse*: 'I want to carry my person to the pinnacle,' writes our author.[48] When it experiences its dependence, it wants *to be everything*, that is to say, it wants to expand to the point where it embraces within itself the totality of the constituent parts:

The uncertain opposition of autonomy to transcendence puts being into a position which slips: each being *ipse*—at the same time that it encloses itself in autonomy, and for this very reason—wants to become the whole of transcendence: in the first place, the whole of the constitution of which it is a part, then one day, without limits, the whole of the universe.[49]

The contradiction becomes glaringly obvious: it lies both in the situation of the subject that is split in this way between two opposing exigencies and in the very end it wishes to attain:

The universal God . . . is alone at the summit, even allows himself to be taken for the totality of things and can only arbitrarily maintain "ipseity" within himself. In their history, men are thus engaged in the strange battle of *ipse*, which must become everything and can only become it by dying.[50]

I shall not, with M. Bataille, go over the ins and outs of this vain struggle—this battle that is lost before it begins. At times man wishes to be everything (the desire for power, for absolute knowledge), at times 'the individual, lost in the multitude, delegates to those who occupy its centre the concern for taking on the totality of "being". He is content to "take part" in total existence, which maintains, even in simple cases, a diffuse character.'[51]

Our existence is, in any event, 'an exasperated attempt to complete being'.[52] The horror of our condition is such that most of the time we give up and attempt to escape from ourselves into the *project* or, in other words, into those thousand little activities that have a merely limited meaning and that mask the contradiction by the purposes they project forward. But in vain:

> Man cannot, by any means, escape insufficiency, nor renounce ambition. His will to flee is the fear which he has of being man: its only effect is hypocrisy—the fact that man is what he is without daring to be so . . . There is no concurrence imaginable, and man, inevitably, must wish to be everything, remain *ipse*.[53]

'Project' here is another existentialist's word. It is the received translation of a Heideggerian term. And, as a result, M. Bataille, who undoubtedly borrowed the word from Corbin, seems at times to conceive the project as a fundamental structure of human reality—as when he writes, for example, that 'the world . . . of project is the world in which we find ourselves. War disturbs it, it is true: the world of project remains, but in doubt and anguish,' and we 'emerge through project from the realm of project'. [54] But even though there still seems to be some vacillation in our author's thinking here, a rapid examination is enough to set us right: the project is only a particular form of flight: if it is essential, it is so only to the modern Westerner. The equivalent is not so much to be sought in Heidegger's philosophy as in Kierkegaard's 'ethical man'. And the opposition between project and 'torment' strangely resembles the opposition Kierkegaard establishes between the moral and the religious life. In fact the project pertains to the concern to compose one's life. The man who makes projects thinks of the morrow and the day after that. He sketches out the plan of his entire life and sacrifices each detail—that is to say, each moment—to the order of the whole. This is what Kierkegaard symbolized in the example of the married man, the head of the family. This perpetual sacrificing of immediate life to the laid-out, fissured life of discourse, M. Bataille likens to the *esprit de sérieux*: project is 'the serious side of existence'.[55] A wretched seriousness that *takes* time, that throws itself into time: 'It is a paradoxical way of being in time: *it is the putting off of existence to a later point*.'[56] But he is more scornful of the serious man than Kierkegaard was of the ethical: this is because seriousness is a *fuite en avant*. M. Bataille is reminiscent of Pascal when he writes: 'One has egotistical satisfaction only in projects . . . one falls in this way into flight, like an animal into an endless trap; on one day or another, one dies an idiot.'[57] The fact is that the project is, in the end, identical with Pascal's *divertissement*; our author would happily condemn the man of projects for 'being unable to sit still in a room'. Behind our agitation, he uncovers—and wishes to get back to—an atrocious stillness. We shall speak of this in a moment. What we must note at this point is that, in his horror of the temporal fissure, M. Bataille has affinities with an entire family of thinkers who, whether mystical or sensual, rationalistic or otherwise, envisaged time as a separating, negating power and believed that man won himself from time by cleaving to himself in the moment. For these thinkers—Descartes must be ranked among them, as must Epicurus, Rousseau and Gide—discourse, planning, utilitarian memory, *la raison raisonnante* and enterprise wrest us from ourselves. Against this they oppose the moment—the intuitive moment of Cartesian reason, the ecstatic moment of mysticism, the anguished, eternal instant of Kierkegaardian freedom, the moment of Gidean enjoyment, the instant of Proustian remembrance. What unites thinkers who are otherwise so different is the desire to exist right now and to the full. In the *cogito* Descartes believes he grasps himself in his totality as 'res cogitans'; similarly, 'Gidean purity' is the entire possession of oneself and the world in the enjoyment and plundering of the instant. This is the ambition of our author too: he too wishes to 'exist without delay'. His project is to exit from the world of projects.

It is laughter that will enable him to do this. Not that the man-in-project, so long as he continues to battle, is comical: 'everything remains suspended within him.' But a new vista can open up: with a failure or setback, suddenly laughter peals out, just as, for Heidegger, the world suddenly begins to glow with the prospect of machines getting out of kilter, tools being broken. We recognize this laughter of Bataille's: it isn't the plain, inoffensive laughter of Bergson. It is a forced laughter. It has its forerunners: it was through humour that Kierkegaard escaped the ethical life; it was irony that was to liberate Jaspers. But there is, above all, the laughter of Nietzsche: it is that laughter, first and foremost, that M. Bataille wants to make his own. And he quotes this note penned by the author of *Zarathustra*: 'To see tragic natures sink and to be able to laugh at them, despite the profound understanding, the emotion and the sympathy which one feels—that is divine.'[58] However, Nietzsche's laughter is lighter: he terms it 'exuberance' and Zarathustra likens it explicitly to dance. M. Bataille's laughter is bitter and studied; it may be that M. Bataille laughs a lot when he is alone, but nothing of it passes into his work. He tells us that he laughs, but he doesn't make us laugh. He would like to be able to write of his work what Nietzsche writes of *The Gaya Scienza*: 'in practically every sentence of this book profundity and exuberance go hand in hand.'[59] Yet the reader cries out here: profundity maybe, but exuberance!

Laughter is 'a *communal* and *disciplined* emotional knowledge'.[60] The laughing subject is 'the unanimous crowd'. By that, M. Bataille seems to accept that what is described is a collective phenomenon. Yet there he is, laughing alone. No matter: this belongs, no doubt, among those countless contradictions we shall not even attempt to point up. But *of what* is there knowledge here? This, our author tells us, is 'the puzzle . . . which, solved, would itself solve everything.'[61] That certainly pricks our curiosity. But what disappointment a little later on when we get the solution: man is characterized by his desire for sufficiency and laughter is caused by the sense of an insufficiency. More precisely, it *is* the sense of insufficiency.

> If I pull the rug out from under . . . the sufficiency of a solemn figure is followed suddenly by the revelation of an ultimate insufficiency.[62] I am made happy, no matter what, by failure experienced. And I myself lose my seriousness as I laugh. As if it were a relief to escape the concern for my sufficiency.[63]

Is this everything? So *all forms* of laughter are revelations of insufficiency? *All encounters with insufficiency* express themselves through laughter? I can hardly believe this: I could cite a thousand individual cases . . .

But I am not criticizing at this point, just laying out the argument. It is merely to be regretted that M. Bataille's 'ideas' should be so formless and flabby when his feeling is so firm. To summarize, laughter now grows up: at first it has children and fools as its butt, whom it throws off towards the periphery, but in a reversal it turns back on the father, the leader and all those charged with ensuring the permanence of social combinations and symbolizing the sufficiency of all that the *ipse* wishes to be:

> If I now compare the constitution of society to a pyramid, it appears as domination by the summit . . . The summit incessantly consigns the foundation to insignificance and, in this sense, waves of laughter traverse the pyramid, contesting step by step the pretence of self-importance of the beings placed at a lower level. But the first pattern of these waves issued from the summit ebbs and the second pattern traverses the pyramid from bottom to top: in this instance the backwash contests the self-importance of the beings placed at a higher level . . . it cannot fail . . . to strike at [the summit] . . . And if it strikes

at it, what ensues are the death throes of God in darkest night.[64]

A strong image, but loose thinking.[65] We are familiar with this wave that rises to the rafters and leaves only scattered stones in the shadows. But there is no other reason to call it laughter than M. Bataille's arbitrary decision to do so. It is also the critical spirit, analysis, dark revolt. It may even be noted that revolutionaries, who are the most convinced of the insufficiency of the commanding heights, are the most serious people in the world. Satire and pamphleteering come from on high. Conservatives excel at it; by contrast, it took years of labour to build up a semblance of revolutionary humour. And even then it looked less a direct insight into the ridiculous and more a painful translation of serious considerations.

However this may be, M. Bataille's laughter is not an inner experience. For himself, the *ipse* seeking 'to become everything' is 'tragic'. But, by revealing the insufficiency of the total edifice in which we believed we occupied a reassuring, comfortable place, laughter, at its height, plunges us suddenly into horror: not the slightest veil subsists between ourselves and the dark night of our insufficiency. We are not everything; no one is everything; being is nowhere. Thus, just as Plato accompanies his dialectical movement with the *askesis* of love, we might speak in M. Bataille's thinking of a kind of *askesis* through laughter. But laughter here is *the negative* in the Hegelian sense. 'At first I had laughed, upon emerging from a long Christian piety, my life having dissolved, with a spring-like bad faith, in laughter.'[66] This negative dissolution that wanders off into all the Surrealist forms of disrespect and sacrilege, must, by dint of the fact that it is experienced, have its positive balancing element. Thus Dada, which was pure solvent laughter, transformed itself through reflection upon itself into the clumsy dogmatism of Surrealism. Twenty-five centuries of philosophy have left us familiar with those unforeseen turnabouts in which everything is saved when all seemed lost. Yet M. Bataille doesn't wish to save himself. Here, we might say, it is almost a question of taste: 'What characterizes man . . . ,' he writes, 'is not only the will to sufficiency, but the cunning, timid attraction toward insufficiency.'[67] This may perhaps be true of mankind; it is certainly true of M. Bataille. How are we to explain this taste for abjection which makes him write, 'I take pleasure today in being the object of disgust for the sole being to whom destiny links my life,' a sentiment in which his sensitive pride is thoroughly steeped? Is it perhaps the remnant of a long period of Christian humility? At all events, this duly elaborated inclination has become a method: how could we believe that, after ten years of Surrealist sorcery, our author could quite simply plan to achieve salvation?

> Salvation is the summit of any possible project and the pinnacle where projects are concerned . . . At the extreme limit, the desire for salvation turns into the hatred of any project (of putting off existence until later), and of salvation itself, suspected of having a mundane motive . . . salvation *was* the sole means of dissociating eroticism . . . from the nostalgia for existing without delay.[68]

With M. Bataille, we remain entirely in the realm of black magic. If he quotes the famous maxim, 'whosoever would save his life shall lose it, but whosoever would lose his life . . . shall save it,' he does so only to reject it with all his might. The point is, indeed, to lose oneself. But 'to lose oneself in this case would be to lose oneself and *in no way to save oneself.*[69] This taste for perdition is utterly *outmoded*: we need only think back to the host of experiences the young people of 1925 engaged in: drugs, eroticism and all the lives lived on the toss of a coin out of a hatred for 'making plans'. But Nietzschean intoxication now comes and puts its stamp on this gloomy determination. M. Bataille sees this useless, painful sacrifice of self as the extreme of generosity: it is freely given. And precisely because of its gratuitousness, it cannot be done coolly; it makes its appearance at the end of Bacchic revels. Sociology can, once again, provide his imagery: what one glimpses beneath the icy exhortations of this solitary is nostalgia for one of those primitive festivals in which an entire tribe becomes inebriated, laughs, dances and copulates randomly; for one of those festivals that are both consumption and consumation, in which everyone, in wild, joyous frenzy, engages in self-mutilation, gaily destroys a whole year's worth of patiently amassed wealth and ends in self-destruction, going to their death singing, with neither God nor hope, carried by wine and shouting and rutting to the extremes of generosity, killing themselves *for nothing*. Hence a rejection of *askesis.* Asceticism would, in fact, put a mutilated man on the pyre. But for the sacrifice to be entire, it would have to consume man in his totality, with his laughter, passions and sexual excesses: 'If ascesis is a sacrifice, it is the sacrifice of only a part of oneself which one loses with the intention of saving the other part. But should one desire to lose oneself completely, one can do so from a movement of drunken revelry, but in no way without emotion.'[70]

Here, then, is the invitation to lose ourselves without calculation, without *quid pro quo*, without salvation. Is it sincere? We spoke not so long ago of a turnabout. It seems to me that M. Bataille has masked his own turnabout, but he has not, for all that, eliminated it. For, in the end, this loss of self is, above all, *experience*. It is 'the questioning (testing), in fever and anguish, of what man knows of the fact of being'.[71] As a result, it realizes that existence without delay that we were seeking in vain. The *ipse* is drowned in it, no doubt, but another 'oneself' arises in its stead: 'Oneself is not the subject isolating itself from the world, but a place of communication, of fusion of the subject and the object.'[72] And from this conversion M. Bataille promises us marvels:

I am and you are, in the vast flow of things, only a stopping-point favourable to resurgence. Do not delay in acquiring an exact awareness of this anguishing position. If it happened that you attached yourself to goals confined to limits in which no one was at stake but you, your life would be that of the great majority; it would be shorn of 'the marvellous'. A brief moment's halt and the complex, gentle, violent movement of worlds will make a splashing foam of your death. The glories, the marvels of your life are due to this resurgence of the wave that formed within you, to the immense cataract-like sound of the sky.[73]

And then anguish becomes frenzy, excruciating joy. Isn't this worth risking the journey for? Especially as one returns from it. For, in the end, M. Bataille writes; he has a job at the Bibliothèque Nationale; he reads, makes love and eats. As he says, in a phrase that he surely couldn't blame me for laughing at, 'I crucify myself when the fancy takes me.'[74] Why not? And we are so *won over* to this little exercise that M. Bataille calls it, 'the distance man has covered in search of himself, of his glory'. He calls those who haven't been to the extremes of the possible, servants or enemies of man, not men. And suddenly this unnameable destitution takes on shape: we thought we were irredeemably lost and we were, quite simply, thereby realizing our essence: we were becoming what we are. And, at the very end of our author's explanations, we glimpse a quite different way of losing ourselves irredeemably—namely, to remain willingly within the world of the project. In that world, man flees himself and loses himself on a daily basis. He hopes for nothing and he will receive nothing. But the auto-da-fé M. Bataille offers us has all the characteristics of an apotheosis.

However, let us look at this more closely. It is, we are told, a *death agony*. We have arrived at this agony through laughter, but we could have got to it by other methods. In particular, by systematic diligence in feeling our abjection. The key thing is that we should, from the outset, *experience* this fundamental truth: being is nowhere; we are not everything, there is no everything. As a result, we can no longer 'desire to be everything'.[75] And yet 'man cannot, by any means, escape insufficiency, nor renounce ambition . . . There is no concurrence imaginable, and man, inevitably, must wish to be everything.'[76] There is no contradiction. Or, rather, this new contradiction is in the subject: we are dying from wishing for what we cannot give up wishing for. But this death agony is a passion: we have the duty to agonize, to raise up the whole of Nature with us to the point of agony. For it is through us that the world exists, through us, who are merely a delusion and whose ipseity is illusory. If we disappear, the world will fall back into darkness. And here we are, a flickering flame, always on the point of extinction; and the world flickers with us, it vacillates with our light. We take it in our hands and raise it to the heavens as an offering for the heavens to mark it with their seal. But the heavens are empty. Then man understands the sense of his mission. He is the One called on by all things to ask heaven for an answer that heaven refuses. 'Completed "being", from rupture to rupture, after a growing nausea had delivered it to the emptiness of the heavens, has become no longer "being", but wound, and even "agony" of all that is.'[77] And this gaping wound, which opens in the earth, beneath the endless desert of the sky, is simultaneously supplication and challenge. It is a supplication and an imploring questioning, for it seeks in vain for the All that would give it its meaning, but which hides itself. It is challenge since it knows that the All conceals itself, that it alone is responsible for the inert world, that it alone can invent its own sense and the meaning of the universe. This aspect of M. Bataille's thinking is very deeply Nietzschean. He himself uses a 'fragment' written by Nietzsche in 1880 to designate his 'Experience' more precisely: 'But where do those waves of everything which is great and sublime in man finally flow out? Isn't there an ocean for these torrents?—Be this ocean: there will be one,' wrote Nietzsche. And M. Bataille adds: 'the being lost of this ocean and this bare requirement: "be that ocean", designate experience and the extreme limit to which it leads'.[78] Man, an absurd creature, protesting against creation, a martyr to absurdity but re-creating himself by giving himself a meaning of his own beyond the absurd, man defiant, laughing man, Dionysian man— here, it seems to me, are the foundations of a humanism common to Nietzsche and our author.

But, thinking about it, we are not so sure of ourselves any more. M. Bataille's thought is changeable. Is he going to be content with this human, all-too-human heroism? First, let us note that he cannot properly hold to this dionysian passion he proposes; as the reader may already have noticed, by the terms of the long argument that precedes it, that passion is a swindle, a more subtle way of identifying oneself with the all, the 'everything'. Didn't M. Bataille write, in a passage we quoted above, 'Man (at the end of his quest) is . . . agony of *all that is*,' and does he not prescribe for us, in the chapter devoted to Nietzsche, 'a sacrifice in which everything is victim'?[79] At the bottom of all this, we find the old initial postulate of dolorism, formulated by Schopenhauer and taken over by Nietzsche, that the man who suffers takes up and founds within himself the pain and evil of the entire universe. This is what Dionysianism or the gratuituous affirmation of the metaphysical value of suffering amounts to. There are many excuses for such an affirmation: a little distraction is permitted when one is in pain, and the idea of taking on universal suffering may serve as a balm if one manages to convince oneself of this at the appropriate point. But M. Bataille wants to be sure. He has, then, to acknowledge his bad faith: If I suffer for *everything*, I am everything, at least where suffering is concerned. If my death throes (*agonie*) are the death throes of the world, I am the world in its death throes. In this way, I shall, by losing myself, have gained *everything*.

Moreover, M. Bataille doesn't linger in this safe haven. Yet, if he leaves it, it is not for the reasons we have just stated. He does so because he wants more. The savour of Nietzschean thought derives from the fact that it is profoundly and solely earthly. Nietzsche is an atheist who harshly and logically draws all the consequences from his atheism. But M. Bataille is a shamefaced Christian. He has thrown himself into what he calls a cul-de-sac. His back is to the wall. He sums up the situation himself: 'The sky is empty . . . The ground will give way beneath my feet. I will die in hideous conditions . . . I solicit everything negative that a laughing man can experience.'[80] And yet this hard-pressed, cornered man will not make the admission we await from him: he will not acknowledge that *there is no* transcendence. He will prefer to play on the words, 'there is no' and 'transcendence'. We have him here and his only thought is of escape. In spite of everything, he remains what Nietzsche called, one of the 'Afterworldsmen' [*Hinterweltler*].[81] With this, the work he sets before us assumes its true meaning: the Nietzschean humanism was merely a stopping-point on his way. The true reversal comes a little later. We believed it was a question of finding man amid his wretchedness. But no, it was in fact God we had to find. Once we are aware of this, all the sophisms we have identified can be seen in a new light: they didn't arise inadvertently in some way or from precipitate judgements; they had their role to play; it was for them to persuade M. Bataille that a new kind of mysticism is possible. They were to lead us by the hand to mystical experience. It is this experience we are now going to contemplate.

III

Mysticism is *ek-stasis* or, in other words, a wresting from oneself towards, and intuitive enjoyment, of the transcendent. How can a thinker who has just asserted the absence of any transcendence achieve, in and by that very move, a mystical experience? This is the question our author has to face. Let us see how he answers it.

Jaspers showed him the way. Has M. Bataille read the three volumes of *Philosophy*?[82] I am assured that he has not. But he is probably aware of the commentary Jean Wahl has made of it in the *Études kierkegaardiennes*. The similarities of thought and vocabulary are disquieting. For Jaspers, as for M. Bataille, the key thing is the absolute, irremediable failure of any human enterprise, which shows existence to be a 'thinking unintelligibility'. On that basis, one must 'make the leap where thought ceases'. It is the 'choice of non-knowledge' into which knowledge throws itself and in which it loses itself. For him, too, the abandonment of non-knowledge is passionate sacrifice to the world of darkness. '*Non-savoir*', '*déchirure*', '*monde de la nuit*' and '*extrême de la possibilité*'—all these expressions are common to Wahl translating Jaspers and to M. Bataille.

Our author does, however, diverge from Jaspers on one essential point. I said just now that he was in search of God. But he wouldn't agree on this. 'Mockery! that one should call me pantheist, atheist, theist! But I cry out to the sky, "I know nothing".'[83] God is still a word, a notion that helps you to leave knowledge behind, but that remains knowledge: 'God, final word meaning that all words will fail further on.'[84] M. Bataille starts out from a meditation on failure, as does Jaspers: 'Lost and pleading, blind, half-dead. Like Job on the dung-heap, in the darkness of night, but imagining nothing—defenceless, knowing that all is lost.'[85] Like Jaspers, he comes to know himself as thinking unintelligibility. But as soon as he has shrouded himself in non-knowledge, he refuses any concept enabling him to designate and classify what he then attains to: 'If I said decisively: "I have seen God", that which I see would change. Instead of the inconceivable unknown—wildly free before me, leaving me wild and free before it—there would be a dead object and matter for the theologian.'[86]

Yet not everything is so clear. He now writes: 'I have of the divine an experience so mad that one will laugh at me if I speak of it' and, further on, 'God speaks to me, the idiot, face to face . . .'[87] Lastly, at the beginning of a curious chapter that contains a whole theology,[88] he again explains his refusal to name God, but in a rather different way: 'What, at bottom, deprives man of all possibility of speaking of God, is that, in human thought, God necessarily conforms to man insofar as man is weary, famished for sleep and for peace.'[89] These are no longer the scruples of an agnostic who, faced with atheism and faith, intends to keep matters in suspense. This is genuinely a mystic speaking, a mystic who has seen God and rejects the all-too-human language of those who have not. The distance separating these two passages contains the whole of M. Bataille's bad faith. What has happened?

We had left our author in a cul-de-sac, with his back to the wall. In a state of atrocious, unavoidable disgust. And yet, 'man's "possible" cannot be confined to this constant disgust at himself, this dying man's rejected denial.'[90] It *cannot* be—and yet there is nothing else. The heavens are empty and man knows nothing. This is the situation M. Bataille rightly terms 'torment' and that is, if not the torment of human beings in general, at least his individual torment, his initial situation. There is no need, then, to go looking very far. This is the primary fact: M. Bataille disgusts himself. A fact considerably more terrifying in its simplicity than two hundred pages of loaded considerations on human wretchedness. Through it, I glimpse the man and his solitude. At present I know I can do nothing for him and he won't be able to do anything for me. He looks like a madman to me and I know, too, that he regards me as a madman. It is what he *is* that draws me on to the path of horror, not what he says.

But he has necessarily to fight back. Against himself. Has he not said as much? The torment he cannot escape is a torment he cannot bear either. Yet there is *nothing* but that torment. So it is this very torment that is going be doctored. The author admits this himself: 'I teach the art of turning anguish to delight.'[91] And here is where the slippage comes: I know nothing. Alright. That means my knowledge goes so far and no further. Beyond that nothing exists, since nothing is for me only what I know. But what if I substantify my ignorance? What if I transform it into the 'night of non-knowledge'? Then it becomes something positive: I can touch it, meld myself with it. 'With non-knowledge attained, then absolute knowledge is simply one knowledge among others.'[92] Better, I can settle into it. There was a light that lit up the darkness weakly. Now, I have withdrawn into the darkness and I look on the light *from the standpoint of darkness*:

> Non-knowledge lays bare. This proposition is the summit, but must be understood in this way: lays bare, therefore I see what knowledge was hiding up to that point, but if I see, I *know*. Indeed, I know, but non-knowledge again lays bare what I have

known. If nonsense is sense, the sense which
is nonsense is lost, becomes nonsense again
(without possible end).[93]

Our author is not to be caught so easily. If he sub-
stantifies non-knowledge, he nonetheless does so with
caution, as a movement, not as a thing. Nonetheless,
he has pulled off the trick: non-knowledge, which previously was *nothing*, becomes the 'beyond' of knowledge. By throwing himself into it, M. Bataille suddenly
finds himself *in the realm of the transcendent*. He has broken clear: the disgust, shame and nausea are left behind
with knowledge. After that, little matter that he tells
us 'Nothing, neither in the fall nor in the void, is
revealed,'[94] for the essential thing is revealed: that my
abjection is a nonsense and there is a nonsense of this
nonsense (which is not, in any way, a return to the original sense). A passage from M. Blanchot cited by M.
Bataille[95] shows us the trick: 'The night soon appeared
to him to be darker, more terrible than any other night
whatsoever, as it had really emerged from a wound of
thought which could no longer think itself, *of thought
captured ironically as object by something other than thought*.'[96]

But M. Bataille precisely will not see that non-
knowledge is immanent to thought. A thinking that

thinks it doesn't know is still thinking. It discovers its limits *from the inside*. Yet this doesn't mean it has an overview of itself. You might as well say that *nothing* has become something on the grounds that one has given it a name.

Indeed our author does go that far. It isn't hard to do so. You and I just write, quite straightforwardly, 'I know nothing.' But let us suppose I put inverted commas around this *nothing*. Suppose that I write, like M. Bataille, 'And, above all, "nothing", I know "nothing".' This is a *nothing* that takes on a strange form; it detaches itself, isolates itself—it is not far from existing on its own. We have only now to call it the *unknown* and our goal is achieved. The nothing is what doesn't exist at all; the unknown is what in no way exists for me. By calling the nothing the unknown, I make it the entity whose essence it is to elude the grasp of my knowledge; and if I add that I know nothing, this means that I communicate with that entity by some means other than knowledge. Here again, M. Blanchot's text, to which our author refers, brings enlightenment:

> Through this void, therefore, it was his gaze
> and the object of his gaze which became

mingled. Not only did this eye *that saw nothing*
apprehend something, but it apprehended
the cause of his vision. *It saw as an object that
which caused him not to see.*[97]

Here, then, is this unknown, wild and free, to
which M. Bataille at times gives—and at times refuses—the name of God. It is a pure hypostatized
nothingness. One last effort and we shall ourselves
dissolve into the night that previously only protected
us: it is knowledge that creates the *object* over against
the subject. Non-knowledge is 'suppression of the
object and of the subject: the only means of not resulting in the possession of the object by the subject'.[98] There remains 'communication' or, in other
words, the absorbtion of everything by the night. M.
Bataille forgets that he has, by his own hand, constructed a universal object: Night. And this is the moment to apply to our author what Hegel said of
Schelling's absolute: 'It is the night in which all cows
are black.' It would seem that this abandonment to
the night is a source of delight: that comes as no surprise. It is, in fact, one particular way of dissolving
oneself into the *nothing*. But that nothing is skilfully
contrived in such a way that it becomes *everything*. M.

Bataille, as in the case of his Nietzschean humanism above, is here satisfying in a roundabout way his desire to 'be everything'. With the words 'nothing', 'night/darkness', 'non-knowledge that lays bare', he has quite simply prepared a nice little pantheistic ecstasy for us. We remember what Poincaré said of Riemannian geometry: replace the definition of the Riemannian plane by the definition of the Euclidian sphere and you have Euclid's geometry. Similarly, just replace M. Bataille's absolute nothing by the absolute being of substance and you have Spinoza's pantheism. We must concede, of course, that Riemann's geometry isn't Euclid's. In the same way, Spinoza's system is a white and M. Bataille's a black pantheism.

We can, as a result, understand the function of scientism in our author's thinking. True inner experience is, in fact, poles apart from pantheism. When once one has found oneself through the *cogito*, there is no longer any question of losing oneself: farewell to the abyss and the night, man takes himself with him everywhere. Wherever he is, he casts light and sees only what he casts light on; it is he who decides the meaning of things. And if somewhere he apprehends an absurd being, even if that absurd being is himself, that absurdity is still a human signification and it is he who decides on it. Man is immanent to the human; man's universe is finite, but not limited. If God speaks, he is made in the image of man. But if he remains silent, he is still human. And if there is a 'torment' for man, it is not being able to stand outside the human to judge himself, not being able to read the underside of the cards. Not because they are hidden from him, but because even if he could see them, he would be able to judge them only by his own lights. From this point of view, mystical experience must be considered as one human experience among others; it enjoys no privilege. Those who find this torment of immanence unbearable devise ruses by which to see themselves with inhuman eyes. We have seen M. Blanchot resorting to the fantastic to present us with an inhuman image of humanity. With similar motivations, M. Bataille wants to get at the human without human beings, in much the same way as Loti described 'India without the English'.[99] If he manages to do this, then the game he is playing is already more than half won: he is already outside himself, has already situated himself in the realm of the transcendent. But—differing in this respect from the author of *Aminadab*—he doesn't resort to literary methods, but to the scientific attitude.

We remember Durkheim's famous precept that we should 'treat social facts as things.' This is what tempts M. Bataille in Sociology. If only he could treat social facts and human beings and himself as things, if his inexpiable individuality could only appear to him as a certain given quality, then he would be rid of himself. Unfortunately for our author, Durkheim's Sociology is dead: social facts are not things; they have meanings and, as such, they refer back to the being through whom meanings come into the world, to man, who cannot be both scientist and object of science at the same time. You might just as well try to lift the chair you are sitting on by grabbing it by its crossbars. Yet M. Bataille revels in this vain effort. It is not by chance that the word 'impossibility' flows frequently from his pen. He belongs, without a doubt, to that spiritual family whose members are susceptible, above all, to the acid, exhausting charm of impossible endeavours. It would be more appropriate to symbolize his mysticism, rather than M. Camus's humanism, by the myth of Sisyphus.

What remains of such an undertaking? First, an undeniable experience. I don't doubt that our author is familiar with certain ineffable states of anguish and torturous joy. I merely note that he fails in his attempt to impart to us the method that would enable us to obtain them in our turn. Moreover, although his avowed ambition was to write a mystical *Discourse on Method*, he confesses several times that these states come and go as and when it suits them. For my part, I see them, rather, as defensive reactions specific to M. Bataille, appropriate to his case alone. In the way that hunted animals sometimes react with what is known as 'the fake death reflex', the supreme escapism, our author, pinned to the rear wall of his cul-de-sac, escapes his disgust by a sort of ecstatic fainting fit. But even if he were able to make available to us a rigorous method for obtaining these delights at will, we would be within our rights to ask: what of it? Inner experience, we are told, is the opposite of the 'project'. But we *are* projects, despite what our author says. And we are not so out of cowardice or to flee from anxiety: we are projects from the first. If such a state is to be pursued, then, it is to be sought as a basis for new projects. Christian mysticism is a project: it is eternal life that is at issue. But, if the joys to which M. Bataille invites us are to be purely self-referential, if they are not to be part of the fabric of new undertakings and contribute to shaping a new humanity that will surpass itself towards new goals, then they are of no greater value than the pleasure of drinking a glass of brandy or of sunning oneself on a beach.

Rather than with this unusable experience, then, we shall concern ourselves more with the man who reveals himself in these pages, with his 'sumptuous, bitter' soul, his pathological pride, his self-disgust, his eroticism, his often magnificent eloquence, his rigorous logic that masks the incoherence of his thought, his passion-induced bad faith and his fruitless quest for impossible escape. But literary criticism runs up against its limits here. The rest is a matter for psychoanalysis. Yet before anyone protests, I do not have in mind the crude, questionable methods of Freud, Adler or Jung; there are other schools of psychoanalysis.

December 1943

Notes

1 See *Cahiers du Sud* (February 1943).

2 Jacques Delille (1738–1813): a poet renowned for his elaborate circumlocution. [Trans.]

3 See 'Monsieur François Mauriac and *Freedom*', pp. 81–2, NOTE 8. [Trans.]

4 See '*The Outsider* Explained', p. 183, NOTE 30. [Trans.]

5 Georges Bataille, *Inner Experience* (Albany: State University of New York Press, 1988), p. 102.

6 Michel Leiris, *Manhood* (London: Jonathan Cape, 1968).

7 Bataille, *Inner Experience*, p. xxxiii.

8 Ibid., p. 18.

9 Ibid., p. 55. It even seems at times that M. Bataille amuses himself by pastiching Pascal's style: 'Should one look at last at the history of men, man by man', etc. (ibid., p. 38).

10 Ibid., pp. 135–6 (translation modified).

11 Ibid., p. 6.

12 Ibid., pp. 28–9.

13 Ibid., p. 16.

14 'Invitation au Voyage' is the title of a famous and

much-translated poem in Baudelaire's *Les Fleurs du Mal* [Trans.]

15 Alain wrote a series of 'Propos', including *Propos sur le bonheur* (Paris: Gallimard, 1925), *Propos de politique* (Paris: Éditions Rieder, 1934) and *Propos de littérature* (Paris: Paul Hartmann, 1934); his *Histoire de mes pensées* was published by Gallimard in 1936. [Trans.]

16 This journal maintains the purported narrator's running commentary within the novel on André Gide's *Les Faux-Monnayeurs* (1925). [Trans.]

17 The latter journal, published separately in 1927, was (or at least claims to be) Gide's journal at the time of writing *Les Faux-Monnayeurs.* [Trans.]

18 Bataille, *Inner Experience*, p. 92.

19 Nathanaël is the disciple to whom André Gide's *Les nourritures terrestres* (1928) is addressed. [Trans.]

20 Bataille, *Inner Experience*, p. 92. The original French here is: '*Même à prêcher des convaincus, il est dans la prédication un élément de détresse.*' It seems odd to read '*prédication*' here in the grammatical sense of 'predication', rather than to take it to refer to its everyday meaning of 'preaching'. [Trans.]

21 Ibid., p. 66.

22 Ibid., p. 34 (translation modified).

23 This '*déchirure*' or 'fissure' is found in Jaspers and in M. Bataille. Is this evidence of influence? M. Bataille doesn't quote Jaspers, but he seems to have read him.

24 It is, in fact, only in the German language, as *Das innere Erlebnis*, that the book's title will have its full meaning. The French word 'expérience' misrepresents our author's intentions.

25 Ibid., p. 135.

26 Ibid., p. 69.

27 Ibid.

28 Ibid., p. 70.

29 Ibid., p. 69.

30 Ibid.

31 'Linked to the birth then to the union of a man and a woman, and even, at the moment of their union . . .' (ibid.).

32 Ibid., p. 78 (translation modified).

33 Ibid., p. 71.

34 Ibid., p. 72.

35 In the sense in which Hegel tells us, 'Nature is externality.'

36 Ibid., p. 85 (translation modified).

37 Ibid., p. 74 (translation modified).

38 Ibid., p. 94 (translation modified).

39 Ibid., p. 74 (translation modified).

40 Ibid.

41 Ibid., p. 84.

42 Ibid.

43 Ibid., p. 85.

44 Jules Romains (1885–1972): a French novelist and the founder of the Unanimist literary movement. [Trans.]

45 Émile Durkheim (1858–1917): one of the founding fathers of modern sociology. [Trans.]

46 Lucien Lévy-Bruhl (1857–1939): a sociologist and ethnologist with a strong interest in what was known in his day as 'the primitive mind'. [Trans.]

47 Célestin Bouglé (1870–1940): a philosopher who turned to the social sciences and became, alongside Durkheim, one of the first editors of *L'Année Sociologique*. [Trans.]

48 Ibid., p. 66.

49 Ibid., p. 85 (translation modified).

50 Ibid., pp. 87–8.

51 Ibid., p. 87.

52 Ibid., p. 89.

53 Ibid., p. 91.

54 Ibid., p. 46.

55 Ibid., p. 48.

56 Ibid., p. 46 (translation amended).

57 Ibid., p. 49.

58 Ibid., p. xxxi.

59 Friedrich Nietzsche, *Ecce homo. How One Becomes What One Is* (R. J. Hollingdale trans.) (London: Penguin, 1979), p. 98.

60 Bataille, *Inner Experience*, p. xxxiii.

61 Ibid., p. 66.

62 Here again, a German word would render M. Bataille's thought better, the word being *Unselbstständigkeit.*

63 Ibid., p. 89 (translation modified).

64 Ibid., p. 90 (translation modified).

65 A conception akin to the Surrealists' notion of 'black humour', which is also radical destruction.

66 Ibid., p. 66.

67 Ibid., p. 88 (translation modified).

68 Ibid., p. 47 (translation modified).

69 Ibid., p. 22.

70 Ibid., p. 23 (translation modified).

71 Ibid., p. 4 (translation modified).

72 Ibid., p. 9.

73 Ibid., p. 95 (translation amended).

74 Ibid., p. 55 (translation amended).

75 Ibid., p. x.

76 Ibid., p. 91.

77 Ibid., p. 80 (translation modified).

78 Ibid., p. 27.

79 Ibid., p. 130.

80 Ibid., p. 79.

81 See Friedrich Nietzsche, *Thus Spoke Zarathustra* (R. J. Hollingdale trans.) (London: Penguin, 1961), p. 58.

82 Karl Jaspers, *Philosophy* (Chicago: University of Chicago Press, 1969–71).

83 Bataille, *Inner Experience*, p. 37.

84 Ibid., p. 36.

85 Ibid., p. 35.

86 Ibid., p. 4 (translation modified).

87 Ibid., pp. 33, 36.

88 Bataille, *Inner Experience*, Part Four, pp. 99–157. [Trans.]

89 Ibid., pp. 102–03 (translation modified).

90 Ibid., p. 34 (translation amended).

91 Ibid., p. 35.

92 Ibid., p. 55 (translation modified).

93 Ibid., p. 52.

94 Ibid.

95 Albert Camus pointed out to me that *Inner Experience* is the exact translation of, and commentary on, Maurice Blanchot's *Thomas l'Obscur* (*Thomas the Obscure*, 1941).

96 From Blanchot, *Thomas the Obscure*. Cited in Bataille, *Inner Experience*, p. 101 (translation modified; Sartre's italics [Trans.]).

97 Ibid., p. 101 (translation extensively modified).

98 Ibid., p. 53.

99 Pierre Loti (1850–1923): a naval officer from Rochefort (Charente-Maritime) who became one of France's leading novelists. He first published *L'Inde* (*sans les Anglais*) in 1903. It has recently (2008) been republished by Phébus of Paris in the 'Libretto' Collection. [Trans.]

There and Back[1]

Parain is a man on the move. He hasn't arrived yet,
nor does he even know precisely where he wants to
get to, but we can get a general sense of his direction
of travel. I would describe it as a return. He himself
entitled one of his works *Retour à la France* and, in that
book, he wrote:

> I have learned, after a long period of uncon-
> straint, that the mediating powers have the
> role of forbidding man to step outside his

domain. At his extreme limits, they set up barriers, beyond which destruction threatens him.

These few words might be enough to date his undertaking: he journeyed to the extremes, tried to step outside of himself, and now he is coming back. Isn't this the entire literary history of the post-war period? People had great, inhuman ambitions. The aim was to grasp nature—both within man and outside him—as it was when human beings were absent from it; one tiptoed into the garden to catch it unawares and see it at last as it was when there was no one there to see it. And then, somewhere around the nineteen-thirties, encouraged and urged on by publishers, journalists and picture dealers—and channelled through them— came the beginnings of a return to the human. A return to order. The aim now was to define a modest, practical wisdom in which contemplation would be subordinated to limited, effective action and the ambitious values of truth would yield to those of honesty; it was a wisdom that wasn't a pragmatism, nor an opportunism, but a new mix of values, illuminating action with knowledge and subordinating knowledge to action, subjecting the individual to the social order and yet refusing to sacrifice him to it; in short, an economical wisdom whose main concern was to strike a balance.

I fear that the youngest among us have gone far beyond it today: events seem to require both less and more. But it was, after all, an adventure of the mind, as valid as all the others, such as Surrealism or Gidean individualism, and one to be judged, in times to come, by its consequences. In any event, it was through this adventure—and in it—that Parain chose who he was to be. There is, however, something we must be clear about: there have been some fake 'returns'. Some, like Schlumberger,[2] who believed they had never left, merely wanted to force others to return. 'We must turn around and go back,' they said, but it was evident that the 'we' was just a polite formula. A sad, severe younger generation, conscious of the shortness of their lives, hastily took their places in the marching troop—a group who, as the popular quip has it, 'have lost all their illusions, without ever having had any in the first place'. We even saw a curious species of sad *arriviste*, a thin-blooded Julien Sorel,[3] like Petitjean, who exploited this deflation to make his bid for success.[4] For his part, Parain made a genuine return. He knew and experienced the temptation of the inhuman and now he is returning slowly and clumsily to human beings, with memories the young do not possess. Think of the 'return' of Aragon and his new arthritic Surrealist style,[5] shot through with sudden bolts of lightning that recall the extravagances of yesteryear; think of the 'return' of La Fresnaye,[6] coming back from Cubism and eliciting a timid, hesitant meaning from the stony faces he paints. Parain is their brother. But his bouts of excess and repentance, his fits of anger and despair were always worked out between himself and language. We should, then, see the *Recherches sur la nature et les fonctions du langage* as a stage in a return to order or, more accurately, in a *re-descent.* He writes:

> You climb up to the plateau to see as far as is possible; you climb up to the plateau, where the wind blows . . . where life is solitary . . . You go back down to the valley, back to sea level, to gardens and houses, to where the farrier and wheelwright are, below the cemetery and the church; you go back down for evening, as the darkness begins to fall . . . Everything climbs up out of the valley and returns to the valley.[7]

It is this itinerary we are going to attempt to retrace, step by step. First the ascent, then the re-descent. Parain is a lyrical writer: by a very peculiar stroke of good fortune, despite having more concern for others than for himself, this honest, good man, with his precise, impartial intelligence, nonetheless speaks about himself. And this is the case whatever he may say, and even if he does not realize it. But, you will say, that is true of everyone. And so it is. But at least his testimony is perfectly dechipherable: we shall draw on it to reconstitute the history of this great re-descent, sadder than a bout of despair, which, after what Daniel-Rops termed the 'turning years' of the late twenties and early thirties,[8] characterized the second half of the post-war period.

I. INTUITION

In Parain's journey, the departure is marked by an intuition, while an experience initiates the return. When, at the age of twenty-five, one writes of 'the signs establishing imperfect communication between men, governing social relations in the manner of a shaky lever',[9] and, twelve years later, that

There is just one problem . . . the problem
posed by the non-necessity of language.
Through it human energy seems not to
transmit itself fully as it goes through its
transformations . . . There's too much play
in the gears,[10]

then one offers a fine example of consistency of
thinking and persistence in one's metaphors. The fact
is that these comparisons express a fundamental
intuition which Parain, in his *Essai sur la Misère humaine*,
calls: 'the dizzying sense of language's inexactness'.
This tells us what we need to know: Parain doesn't
begin his research with the inhuman impartiality of
the linguist. He is suffering from word-sickness and
wants to be cured. He feels out of phase with
language.

That is enough to tell us that this is not the place
to be looking for an an objective study of linguistic
sounds. The linguist usually acts like a man who is
confident in his ideas, concerned only to know
whether language, an ancient traditional institution,
renders them with precision. So, for example, the 'par-
allelism' between logic and grammar will be studied,
as though logic were given, on the one hand, in the

heaven of ideas, and grammar were given on earth. A French equivalent for the German word *Stimmung* will be sought, for example, which assumes that the corresponding notion exists for a French speaker as it does for a German, and all that arises is the question of its expression. But language regarded in this way is anonymous: the words are thrown on the table like dead fish, already killed and cooked. In short, the linguist studies language when no one is speaking it. Dead words, dead concepts. He studies the word 'Freedom' as you might fish it out of texts, not the living, intoxicating, irritating, lethal word as it resonates today in an angry or an eager mouth. Parain, by contrast, is concerned with language 'as it is spoken'. In other words, he sees it as a link in the chain of concrete action. What he grapples with is the language of this particular soldier or worker or revolutionary. In this sense, how can words be distinguished from ideas? The orator speaks and says 'Justice' or 'Democracy' and the whole auditorium applauds. Which part of this is the 'thought' and which the 'verbal material'? What strikes the listener is the whole thing together: what Claudel so felicitously calls 'the intelligible mouthful'. And it is this intelligible mouthful that Parain will examine. 'Words are ideas,' he writes in *Recherches*, for he has already adopted a practical, political perspective, as has Heidegger, who refuses to distinguish between body and soul, a problem of contemplative philosophy, and who would happily write that, from the point of view of action, which is the only real standpoint, the soul is the body and the body is the soul. As a peasant, an 'assiduous warrior' of World War I and a citizen, Parain deliberately rejects the joys of contemplation. His first—unpublished—essay was concerned with the pursuit of an 'art of living'. 'War,' he wrote, 'has made us see the value of life, and has shown us not to waste a single moment of it.' Since then, morality and politics, indissolubly linked, are his great concern. 'A theory of knowledge,' he writes in 1934, 'can only ever be a theory of the reform of the understanding and, in the end, a treatise on morality.' And by this he meant to underline that he granted primacy to the *practical* sphere over all others. Man is a being who acts. Science, metaphysics and language have their scope and meaning within the narrow limits of that action. One might be tempted to compare Parain with Auguste Comte: they share a lapidary, forceful sense of

seriousness, a determination not to distinguish morality from politics, and a deep sense of human solidarity.
But Comte is an engineer. Behind his theory of action, we sense the machine-tool or the locomotive.
Parain is of peasant stock; he was, like all the men of
the 1920s, fired with a great anger against machinism.
Behind his morality and his critique of language, we
glimpse the pick and the shovel, the workbench. In
any event, the two thinkers have the same concern to
think their age through and to do so with ideas that
are 'of the times'; they distrust the universal and the
eternal. It is the language of 1940 that Parain studies,
not universal language. It is language with its sick
words, in which 'Peace' means aggression, 'Freedom'
oppression and 'Socialism' a regime of social inequal-
ity. And if he examines those words, he does so not
as a biologist but as a doctor. By this I mean that it is
not his aim to isolate organs and examine them in a
laboratory; it is the whole organism that he studies
and intends to cure.

'It wasn't I,' writes Parain, 'who invented the distrust of language . . . We have been fed it by the whole
of our civilization.'[11] It is his intention, thereby, to date
his investigations in the same way as Hegel dated

Hegelianism. But this dating is too crude an approximation. For you are not the author of the *Recherches*—and neither am I. You may perhaps be too old and I am a little too young. Look at the thinkers who came out of this last war: they praise Parain; they approve of what he is doing. But they no longer entirely understand him, and they inflect his findings towards their own ends—Blanchot, for example, using them for purposes of political protest. If we want to understand his message fully, we must bear in mind that it comes from a man of the inter-war years. It is, then, arriving slightly belatedly; it wasn't transmitted at the appointed time—just like the work of Proust, written before the 1914 war and read after it—and it is this delay, this slight dissonance that no doubt makes it so fruitful. Parain is a man of forty-six. He is a peasant who was sent to the front in the last years of the first war: it is this that will explain his original intuition to us.

The peasant works alone amid the forces of nature, which act without any need of being named. He says nothing. Parain has written of his 'stupour' when he gets back to the village after ploughing his field and hears human voices. He has written, too, of the social destruction of the individual which . . . tends to continue today in the transformation of the peasant into an agricultural worker . . . For a peasant, the earth is the intermediary that binds his thought solidly to his action and enables him to judge and act . . . For a worker or for any member of industrial civilization, this bond or intercessor is the plan, the scientific hypothesis of construction that provides him with the idea of his place in the whole and assigns him his collective usefulness, his social and inner value. It is language that is the vehicle of intelligence. In moving . . . from the field that is to be tilled to the part that is to be manufactured, we move from a thinking that is more concrete and closer to its object to a thought that is more abstract and further iremoved from its object.[12]

Like so many others, Parain came into the city. But what he encountered there first wasn't the technical language of the factories and building sites, but rhetoric. At the École Normale Supérieure, I knew many of these peasants' sons, who had been wrested from the soil by their exceptional intelligence. For long periods, they were as silent as the soil, but would suddenly break that silence to expatiate on the most abstract subjects. Like the Socrates of *The Clouds*, they would argue both sides of the case with equal virtuosity and a pedantry that was its own source of amusement. And then they would sink back into silence. Visibly, this intellectual gymnastics remained something alien; it was merely a game to them, a murmur of noise on the surface of their silence. Parain was one such student. In November 1922 (he had just sat the *agrégation* in philosophy), he himself wrote: 'I have at last completed my studies in a University where the art of persuasion has replaced the art of living and thinking.' He was taught at that time the brilliant, weightless language of polemic. A young worker has to decide for or against Marx. Parain didn't have to decide between Voltaire and Rousseau, but he knew how properly to compare them, reconcile them or condemn them both equally. He has remained a formidable dialectician. He has the art of responding quickly and sharply, of going off at a tangent, breaking off a line of thought, or halting a discussion with a single word when he is in difficulty. But he *hears himself* speak, with a kind of scandalized amusement. He hears himself speak from the depths of his silence. And this affords an initial distance with regard to language. He will always see words through a layer of dumbness, the way fish probably see bathers on the surface of the water. 'When we understand each other well,' he says, 'we remain silent.' At home, he remains silent. What is there to say? One person is repairing a wobbly table, another is sewing; the house is there around them. This alternative between quickfire speech and silence is a characteristic feature of his person. In 1922 he calls this mutism *instinct* and contrasts it with speech, which is 'eloquence' or 'polemic'. 'When we understand each other well, we remain silent.' The lamp is on the table; everyone is working and senses the mute presence of the others: there is an order of silence. Later, for Parain, there will be an order of instinct. As for these little verbal cracklings on his surface, they are not his. They have been given—or, rather, lent—to him. They come from the town. In the fields and the house, they are redundant.

This peasant fought in the war, which is another factor setting him apart. The unified language he had just learned in the town, that language of academics and industrialists, seemed to him, in a way, like an impersonal Reason in which every individual could participate. The war taught Parain there were several Reasons—the reason of the Germans, that of the Russians and ours—and that each corresponds to an objective system of signs and that they are all engaged in a trial of strength. He learned this lesson amid a new silence, full of explosions and violent wrenches, amid a mute solidarity. Words still run along the surface of this silence. Articles by Barrès,[13] communiqués, patriotic speeches really become 'words' for these men standing silent in their trenches. They are 'words, words!' They have lost their affective roots and no longer culminate in action. But this ineffectuality unmasks them. When a word is a link in a chain— 'pass me the . . . there . . .'—it fades from view; you obey it without hearing it or seeing it. But when it is no longer the vehicle of anything, it displays and reveals itself *as word*, in the same way as, for Bergson, it is indetermination in reaction that carves out an image of the world. It is this language, still fully armed, fully alive, coming warm out of human mouths, this language cut off from any practical application and all the more haunting for that, which will, from this point on, be the subject of Parain's studies. I was saying just

307

now that he didn't wish to carry out the linguist's dessicating experiments on words, that he refused to form them arbitrarily into an isolated system. But events effected for him what in methodology is called a 'passive experiment'. The word isolated itself of itself, spontaneously, while retaining nonetheless a human flavour. For the peasant that was Parain, language was, until not so long ago, the town. Now, for the soldier, it is 'the home front'.

And then back he comes. As though his whole life were to have this there-and-back rhythm to it. The return of the young intellectual to the fields for his vacations; the return of the demobilized soldier to Paris for Peace. And it was a return to put language to the test once more. All the words were there around him as willing servants; he had only to take them. And yet as soon as he wanted to use them, they betrayed him. When it comes to describing to women or old men what the war was like, he has only to reach out his hand: the words 'horror', 'terror', 'boredom', etc., will be there for the taking. But, like the message in *Aminadab* that changes meaning as it is passed along, the words are not understood in the sense in which they were meant. What does 'terror' mean to a woman? And what is boredom? How is one to insert into language an experience that was had without it? He will at least, we might suppose, be able to depict himself, to find names to name himself, to describe himself. But the instruments that he uses in all good faith have unexpected repercussions. He offers to give lessons to a banker's children to earn a little money? Immediately, the banker asks around: *who* is Parain? In 1920, that means: was he in the war? And as what? What will Parain's answer be? That he served as a private? This is the truth. But what truth? It is, without a doubt, a social truth that has its place in a system of files, notes and signs. But Parain is also an ex-student of the *grandes écoles* and has the *agrégation*: as such, he *should have been* an officer. 'In saying "private soldier", I am saying for the worker a pal, for the banker a suspect . . . perhaps a rebel—at any rate a problem and not inspiring immediate trust.'[14] And Parain adds:

> If I said "private", I would be thinking, a casual attitude at the beginning, an honest lack of desire to command, despite the advantages, because I didn't believe myself capable of it, youthful scruples and also friendships already formed, habits of life, and a sense of

> trust keeping me where I am . . . Will [the
> banker] not think: lack of dignity, love of
> the common herd, lack of patriotism? . . . In
> telling the truth, I deceive him more than if
> I lie.

Parain will choose, then, to say he was a lieutenant. Not
in order to lie, but precisely so as to be understood: 'In
saying officer, I am saying: one of your kind whom you
can recognize'. By officer, then, he means non-revolu-
tionary—a truth he cannot express at the same time as
that other truth—that he was a private. This is the experience of the demobilized soldier, which Parain will
later record in *Essai sur la Misère humaine*:

> The image of an object . . . evoked by a word
> is more or less identical for two people,
> though only on condition that they speak the
> same language, belong to the same class of
> society and the same generation; that is to
> say, ultimately, that it is more or less identical
> within a norm in which the differences be-
> tween the two persons can be regarded as
> practically negligible.[15]

From this he will derive this moral precept: 'If you do
not react towards other people's remarks in terms of

norms set socially by your milieu and your period, you do not know how to understand them and interpret them,' and this first generalization: 'Taken in isolation, the sign has no other relation to the object signified than one of designation . . . it is, so to speak, floating . . . it acquires reality only within an ordered system.'[16]

In which system does the word 'private' have a meaning—the banker's or Parain the soldier's? But the point is precisely that Parain the soldier would look in vain for a language that is valid for him. He is alone. For the moment there is only one language, the one that the bankers, the industrialists and the old men behind the lines share with the other inhabitants of the towns and cities. You have to choose either to get by with the existing system or to remain silent. But the person who remains silent in the town becomes 'frantic, half-mad'.

> Reduce yourself to silence, even an inner silence, and you will see how some bodily desires intensify to the point of obsession, and how you lose the notion of the social. You will see how you no longer know how to behave, how you cease to understand and have only your feelings, how you become an idiot

in Dostoyevsky's sense. You have separated yourself from collective experience.[17]

Should one lie, then? And what exactly is it to lie? It is to give up on expressing an impossible truth and use words not in order to make oneself understood, but so as to be accepted, to 'be loved'. Parain, the most honest of thinkers, the one who indulges least in fine words, is also the one with the greatest indulgence for lying. Or, rather, it seems to him that there are no lies: it would be too much to hope that everyone could lie. That would mean that words have rigorous meanings, that you can put them together to express a precise truth or prefer deliberately to turn your back on that truth. To lie would be to know the truth and reject it, in the same way as doing Evil is rejecting Good. But one can no more lie in Parain's world than one can do evil in Claudel's. For precisely the opposite reasons: for Claudel, the Good is Being. For Parain, Being is imprecise; it floats. I cannot reject the True, because the True is indeterminate: 'Communication is imperfect, not only because thought doesn't wholly contain the individual that it expresses, but also because no word, sentence or work has a necessary meaning without there being a need to interpret

312

it.'[18] Given that state of affairs, in which I perhaps tell an untruth when I want to be truthful, can I be sure of telling an untruth when I mean to lie? We know of those mental patients suffering from the 'psychosis of influence', who complain that their 'thought is being stolen' or, in other words, that their thought is being deflected from its original meaning before it reaches its conclusion. They are not so mad and this is something that befalls every one of us: words drink our thought before we have the time to recognize it; we had a vague intention, we put it clearly into words and now here we are saying something quite different from what we meant. There are no liars. There are only oppressed individuals getting by as best they can with language. Parain never forgot the story of the banker or other similar stories. He still remembers it when he speaks, twenty years later, of his daughter's lies:

> When my daughter tells me she has done her homework even though she has not, she doesn't do so . . . *with the intention* of misleading me, but to indicate to me that she could have done it, that she wanted to do it, that she should have done it, but that none of

313

that is of any great importance. She does so,
then, more to get rid of someone who is annoying her than to say something untrue.[19]

These are, no doubt, the thoughts that were running through the mind of the poor demobbed soldier,
half-liar, half-mute, part Myshkin,[20] part Julien Sorel,
when he came away from seeing his banker. As he did
so, language, a product of towns and cities, of the
'home front', came to be seen by him as a privilege of
the rich. Parain borrowed it, but it belonged to others—to the bankers, generals and prelates and, indeed,
to all those who handled it with insouciance and consummate, indolent artistry, sure of their ability to be
understood by their peers and to impose their words
on their underlings. He had the right to use it, but only
in the sense—and within the limits—prescribed by
the powers that be. With words, the bankers and industrialists wormed their way into him and stole his
most secret thoughts, diverting them to their advantage. Language became the most insinuating of instruments of oppression. Worse still, it became the
characteristic medium and essential tool of the unproductive, parasitic class of intermediaries. He didn't
make this discovery by chance: at the front, as in the

fields, Parain had encountered the world of work, for war is hard industrial and agricultural work. He had returned to the peacetime world the way the peasant returns to the village or the miner, after his day's work, comes back to the surface of the earth. He was back in the world of ceremony and good manners, the world of intermediaries in which man is no longer dealing with the soil or the seam or the explosive shell, but with man. Language became an intermediary between man and his desire, between man and his work, in the same way as there are intermediaries between the producer and the consumer. Between man and himself: if I name what I am, I allow myself to be defined within a particular social order and become complicit with it. Yet I cannot be silent. What, then, am I to become?

At about the same time, our age embarked on an adventure that it is still pursuing. And things moved faster than words. Language has its inertia, as has confidence. We know that in periods of inflation prices remain stable for a time while the currency falls: it is the same with words. This produced a new discrepancy from which everyone was to suffer, bankers and war veterans alike. Words chased vainly after their objects, but they had fallen too far behind. What, for example, did 'peace' mean? The Japanese were advancing with guns and tanks into the heart of China; yet they were at peace with the Chinese, since war was not declared. The Japanese and the Russians were fighting on the Manchurian front, yet peace was preserved, since the Japanese ambassador remained in Moscow and the Soviet ambassador in Tokyo. And if two countries are at war and a third keeps out of the operations, can I say it is at peace? Yes, if it remains neutral. But what is neutrality? If it supplies one of the warring parties, is it neutral? If it suffers blockade, is it neutral? Is armed neutrality still neutrality? And what of prebelligerence? Or intervention? And if we stop defining war as armed conflict, shall we say *the inter-war period* was wartime or peacetime? Everyone is entitled to their own opinion. Blockades, industrial rivalries, class struggles—aren't these enough for us to speak of war? Yet can I not legitimately look back nostalgically to the peacetime of '39? There are people who say that, since 1914, there has been no end to war—and they provide evidence. But others also prove that the war dates from September 1939. So was there a period of peace between two wars or one single war? Who knows?

Perhaps there was a single period of peace? Who will decide? I am put in mind here of the uncertainties of biology, whose terms were devised to designate clearly defined species and which suddenly discovered the continuity of living forms. Should we leave words to rot where they stand? 'Our age,' writes Camus, commenting on Parain, 'seems in need of a dictionary.' But Parain would reply that a dictionary presupposes a degree of discontinuity and of stability of meanings; it is, therefore, impossible to establish one today.

> In an age which, like ours, is one of deep social transformations, in which social values disappear without having been replaced yet by others and, by analogy, in any age, since there is no moment that is not undergoing transformation at a greater or lesser rate, no one can know precisely what other people's words mean—nor even their own.[21]

It is at this point, when all is lost, that Parain believes he has found a solution *in extremis*. There are people who have given up trying to understand the world and merely want to change it. Marx writes:

> The question whether objective truth can be attributed to human thinking is not a

question of theory but is a practical question. Man must prove the truth, i.e. the reality and power, the this-sidedness of his thinking in practice . . . The philosophers have only *interpreted* the world, in various ways; the point is to *change* it.[22]

Wasn't this what Parain was after when, returning from the war, he wrote:

Not being able to convey exactness, because I do not have the time (and even if I had, where would I find the talent to give an exhaustive chronological description of myself?), not being able to confront someone with the entirety of my personality, with everything in the still effective past and in my intentions that determines it . . . , being a particular human being—that is to say, different from anyone else and incapable by nature of defining within me what might be communicable with precision or, in other words, what in me is identical to something in everyone—I chose to express myself in a role. Giving up on making myself known, I am trying to make myself loved.'[23]

The man who gives up in this way on using words as instruments of knowledge is very close to accepting, out of despair, an anti-rationalist theory of language. That theory existed. And it was more than just a theory; it was a practice:

> Lenin did not believe in a universal value of reason and language; he did not believe in exact communication through language. Life in his view took place below and beyond language: watchwords for him were mere forms given body by activity and given life by personality—if not in individual, then at least in collective terms.[24]

With Lenin, words become watchwords, slogans. It would be pointless to hope for them to have pre-established meanings; they have only the meaning you want to give them; their value is strictly historical and practical. They are the words of the leader, of the dominant class. They are true if they are confirmed or, in other words, if they are obeyed and have consequences. This activist conception of language will represent the great temptation for Parain. When you are battling against a closed door, there comes a point when the desire to break it down gets the better of you. Parain's adherence to the activist doctrine appears to be as much a product of anger as of resignation. To him, the word remains an intermediary, but its function is now clearer: it interposes itself between the desire and its realization. 'What guides man at every moment, what musters him and orders him is what he says of himself, of his needs, his desires and his means. These are his watchwords.'[25] This is to recognize a primacy of desire and affectivity. Language is an instrument of realization. With this, reason is reduced to a more modest role.

> Reason is nothing but intelligence, which is itself nothing but the power to build a system of signs to be tested, that is to say the power to frame a hypothesis . . . Reason . . . is the endeavour man pursues . . . to present his desires with an exact, effective means of satisfaction . . . Its subservient role is very precise . . . The desires need to control it frequently, the way one takes an idling workman to task.[26]

With this, the scandal of language becomes clearer: if there is pressure to force Parain to adopt the language of the banker, that is because the banker is in command. For a poor demobbed soldier, the point is neither to strive to understand a language that is not made for him—which would lead him into servitude—nor to invent for himself a system of signs that is valid for him alone—which would lead him straight to madness. He has to find a community of the oppressed that are eager to take power and impose their language, a language forged in the silent solidarity of work and suffering. Parain can now say, modifying Marx's thesis slightly, 'We do not wish to understand words, we wish to change them.' But if it comes to re-inventing a language, you have to opt for a rigorous, precise one; the wobble in the handle or the 'play' in the gears has to be eliminated. For the order to be obeyed, it has to be understood down to its last details. And conversely, to understand is to act. You have to tighten the drive belts and the screws. Since you cannot be silent—that is to say, accede directly and immediately to being—you have at least to control the intermediaries strictly. Parain admits that his youth was buffeted between two dreams:

> Symbols lead us to believe that by eliminating all transmissions we can be said to be eliminating all hitches and to believe too,

conversely, that by perfecting that whole machinery, the mechanisms would function smoothly and accidents would become impossible.[27]

When that first dream, that of the 'idiot', the man on leave wandering around the crowded streets, of the 'frantic, half-mad' demobilized soldier, turned out to be unattainable, Parain threw himself body and soul into the other one, the dream of an authoritarian community of work, in which language is expressly reduced to its subordinate role as intermediary between desire and action, between the leaders and their men, in which everyone understands because everyone obeys, in which the elimination of social barriers also eliminates the 'play' in the gears:

> Thus, after having already experienced an already rigorous social order—war—but one that had still seemed to me to admit of many exceptions and privileges since its mystique was too fragile to gain total sway over us, I came to conceive and desire an even more rigorous social order, the most rigorous that could be achieved.[28]

We have reached the extreme point of Parain's journey. He went no further and the rest is a return.

Up to this point, he has merely developed the consequences of his original intuition. Here he is now,
adhering ultimately to a pragmatic, relativistic author-
itarianism, in which the words 'love' and 'hope' would
be given distinct, controlled meanings, as in the case
of mathematical symbols. He will come to recognize
this revolutionary impulse as a cunning attempt to
destroy language:

> If language derives its meaning only from
> the operations it designates and if it is these
> operations that constitute the object of our
> thought, not essences and their naming, then
> it must ultimately appear useless and even
> dangerous: useless because we accept that
> our thoughts all conform to the same pattern
> of action, which commands us of itself,
> without language playing a decisive role and
> that they develop spontaneously in parallel,
> and hence harmonious, directions; danger-
> ous because it then serves only to provide
> pretexts for the negligence and ill-will of the
> inferiors, who discuss instead of obeying.[29]

And so Parain, despite having abandoned the pursuit
of what I shall term 'infra-silence', that silence that
may be said to coincide with some sort of 'state of

nature' and to *precede* language, has still not given up on the project of falling silent. The silence he comes to at this point extends over the whole domain of language; it is identical with language itself; it is abuzz with murmurs, orders and solicitations. It is obtained in this instance not by the impossible destruction of words, but by their radical *devaluation*. He will later say, passing judgement on his own endeavour,

> Bolshevism was at that point an absolutely anti-rationalist attitude that completed the ideological destruction of the individual by a destruction, carried to the point of heroism, of the word that did not end in total sacrifice.[30]

He was not alone in pursuing these desperate endeavours. In these magnificent post-war years, there were many other young people in revolt against the human condition and, in particular, against the language that expressed it. The obsession with intuitive knowledge or, in other words, with a knowledge without intermediaries, which, as we have seen, first motivated Parain, was initially a driving force of Surrealism, as was that profound distrust of discourse Paulhan has dubbed 'terrorism'. But since one has, in the end to speak, since, whatever one does, the word

324

intercalates itself between the intuition and its object, our terrorists were ejected, like Parain himself, from silence and, throughout the postwar period, we can see an attempt to destroy words with words going on—and an attempt to destroy painting with painting, and art with art. There can be no doubt that this Surrealist destruction should be subjected to existential analysis. We need to know, in fact, what it means to *destroy*. But it is certain that this destruction limited itself, as in Parain's case, to the Word. This is proved to a great extent by Max Ernst's famous definition, 'Surrealism is the encounter, on a dissecting table, between a sewing-machine and an umbrella.'[31] And, indeed, just try to *effect* that encounter. There is nothing in it to stimulate the mind: an umbrella, a sewing-machine and a dissecting table are sad, neutral objects, instruments of human misery that in no sense clash; they merely form a little reasonable, resigned pile of objects that smack of hospitals and wage labour. It is the words that clash, not the things—the words with their sonority and their repercussions. And this leads on to automatic writing and its subsequent variants, efforts made by *talkers* to set up destructive short-circuits between terms. 'Poetry,' said Léon-Paul Fargue, 'is words burning up.' But he was happy merely to see them sizzle; the Surrealist wants to turn them to ashes. And Bataille will define poetry as 'a holocaust of words' in the same way that Parain defined Bolshevism as 'a destruction of the word'. The last on the list, M. Blanchot, reveals the secret of this endeavour, when he explains that the writer must speak *in order to* say *nothing*. If words annihilate each other, if they crumble into dust, won't a silent reality at last emerge behind them? The hesitation evident here is significant; it is Parain's own hesitation: is this suddenly emergent reality waiting for us, unnamed, behind the words or is it, in fact, *our* creation? If I speak, as Bataille does, of a 'butter horse', I destroy the word 'horse' and the word 'butter', but there is something there—the butter horse. What is it? A *nothing*, obviously. But a nothing I create or one that I disclose? The Surrealist makes no choice between these two contradictory hypotheses and, from his point of view, the choice may be unimportant: whether there is some secret underside to things or whether I create that underside, I am nonetheless an absolute, and the bonfire of words is an absolute event. Hence the Surrealists' flirtation with Bolshevism: they saw it as an effort, on the part of man, to forge his destiny in absolute terms. It is in this respect that they resemble the Parain of 1925, for does he not write:

> Words must be replaced by a more direct, more effective mode of action, by an immediate mode of action that occurs without intermediaries and abandons nothing of the anxiety from which it issues.[32]

This is because he, like the Surrealists, is driven by the mighty metaphysical pride that was the spirit of the post-war years. By following him, we have arrived at the limit point of the human condition, at that point of tension where the human being attempts to see himself as though he were an inhuman witness to himself. After 1930, the rising generation will register the failure of this endeavour, though some survivors, such as Leiris and Aragon, will go on in their various ways to evaluate it. Let us now follow Parain on the paths back towards his starting point.

II. EXPERIENCE

When Parain learned that 'the most rigorous social orders taught history, philosophy and literature', he must have felt a little of the stupour experienced by the Pythagoreans at the incommensurability of the sides of a right-angled triangle. If a society philosophizes, this means there is 'play in the gears' and a place for individual dreams, for each person's fantasy, for questioning and incomprehension. That means, then, ultimately, that there is no perfectly rigorous social order, for Parain saw philosophy and literature as the absurd dreams of an imperfect language. However, this purely external experience counts for little in my view, since one can still, in the end, decide to perfect the most imperfect of social orders. Will it *never* be rigorous? Or is it just not rigorous *yet*? The facts do not speak for themselves; it is for everyone to decide. Parain's decision seems, rather, to have been dictated to him by a deeper, more inward experience, a self-testing that is similar in more than one respect to what Rauh termed 'moral experience'. Parain the peasant had set out upon the paths of pride, the ways of the town and the proletariat, as a result of a misunderstanding.

It would be easy to show how the communal disciplines to which he had recently subscribed were at odds with his thoroughgoing individualism. And

Parain no doubt felt these contradictions from the first day. But these are conflicts that can be resolved, provided the original wellspring of the individualism is the will to power. It is always easy to obey if one can dream of commanding. Parain wants neither to command nor to obey. His individualism is anything but Nietzschean: it is neither the appetite of a captain of industry, nor the avidity of the urban oppressed, obsessed by the silky, ice-cold mirage of the city shops, but, quite simply, the stubborn, humble claim of the small farmer who wants to remain master on his own land. It isn't so much his individualism as the nature of that individualism that helps to separate Parain from his revolutionary friends. It is up on the plateaux that language is burned, on the plateaux that the great edifices of the capitalist order are set on fire. Parain is a man of the valleys. All these destroyers he followed for a short while are possessed, one way or another, by a demiurgic pride. They are all Nietzscheans in believing in the plasticity of human nature. If they burn the old Man, they do so to hasten the coming of a new one. There is Surrealist man, Gidean man and Marxist man, all awaiting us on the horizon. They have at once to be revealed and shaped.

In a sense, the future is empty, no one can predict it; in another sense, the future exists more than the present. The frenzied aim of all these destroyers is to construct a world they don't know and that they won't even recognize when they have built it. This is the joy of risk, the joy of not *knowing* what one is doing, the bitter joy of telling oneself one will lead men to the threshold of the promised land, but will oneself remain on the threshold, watching them recede into the distance. These sentiments are wholly alien to Parain. He has no eyes for the future, he doesn't believe in it. If he speaks of it, it is to represent a world that is unravelling, human beings who are going astray. All in all, his theory of language ought to lead him, and did for a moment lead him, to the idea of human plasticity: change words and you will change human beings. But, in reality, nothing is further from his deepest thinking. The image that lies deepest in his memory is that of the natural order. The return of the seasons and the birds, the growth of plants and children, the fixed order of the stars and planets. It is this order that he secretly set against the artificial order of discourse. The beasts of the field are subject to that order and so is man, that speaking beast. We have seen

that, in Parain's mind, words interpose themselves between desires and action. The conclusion should be
that the word forges the desire. To give these stirrings,
torpors and sudden bursts of anger the name 'love' is
to yoke them together by force, to impose a destiny
on them from the outside. But Parain sees suddenly
that he is reluctant to draw that ultimate consequence.
If man *were* what language *makes* him, there would be
no problem. But Parain maintains a distance between
what I am and what I call myself: man *is* something
outside of discourse. There is a pre-established
human order, the humble, silent order of needs. Take,
for instance, what he says of mothers in *Essai sur la
Misère humaine*:

> There isn't a woman—even when they don't
> admit it right away—who doesn't want to
> have children . . . [C]alculation speaks against
> it. They will be unhappy; they will be expen-
> sive; they may perhaps die . . . the risk is total.
> Yet . . . their energy is directed elsewhere. For
> social experience and historical truth are ar-
> guments; they are not their own experience
> and truth . . . When they reflect, they have
> something to reflect on and, behind their

reflections their existences are committed and their confidence remains; they are creative in their bodies, their muscles and their glands; *they do not flee from struggle for the sake of words, which are cowardly* . . . What has just been said of children could as well be said of anything else: love, honesty, manual labour, sleep, cash payment—all the things that civilization has left behind and is seeking to rediscover . . . In this way, we can compare what the brain declares impossible and the flesh maintains. What emerges is that it is the role of language to register difficulties as they appear . . . whilst the work of human beings in their bodies and their appetite for life is to deny those difficulties beforehand, so as never to lose the courage to confront them. This is the secret of simple people, of those who, above and beyond civilization, have retained the same simplicity; it lies in this stubborn determination of the body to love and to beget children, to transmit one's enthusiasm and one's joy.[33]

There is, then, an order of the body. But, manifestly, that order isn't purely biological. It was produced without words, against words; and yet it cannot be blind. Parain knows this well, explaining that we couldn't say, 'I am hungry' without saying something more—and something different from—what we mean. In order that, beyond vague impressions, women can, without naming their desire, know it and pursue its satisfaction entirely securely, there must be something other than the decree of uterine secretions: a design is needed—a plan. I see that plan—which is herself and yet is neither her language nor her thinking nor exactly her body, but a kind of intention and, ultimately, an entelechy—as something like Grace in the most religious sense of the term. And just as the harmonious course of the stars and the ordered succession of the seasons disclosed the designs of the divinity to the Stoic peasant of Latium, so it seems the encounter within us of this pre-established act discloses for the first time to Parain the fact of religion.

How far we are from the radical post-war experiments! For what Parain doesn't say is that this order of the body naturally involves a social extension; the society that is to correspond to it is one that is properly termed 'conservative'. The point now is not to change man, but to take the measures necessary to ensure that this balance of needs is *conserved*. There can be no new man because there is a natural man. Parain will probably not like me comparing him to Rousseau. But, in the end, isn't the peasant who is exposing himself in his 'rugged honesty' to the deceptions of language the noble savage and Natural man? Beneath this radical pessimism, there is an optimism of simplicity.

But I see immediately the ways Parain differs from Rousseau. For the Protestant, though the return to the state of nature is an impossible undertaking, the individual can at least achieve an equilibrium for himself more or less alone. Parain isn't so sure of himself. And then he bears the Catholic imprint upon him; he lacks Genevan pride. What he writes, in the belief that he is defining man, depicts only himself: 'Man is an animal who needs assurance . . . The whole history of man is his effort to establish and impose upon himself a mediating system of coordinates, to place himself in the hands of mediating powers . . .'[34] 'Man cannot do without mediating powers, as the earth cannot do without sun; everyone needs a task, a fatherland, children, a hope.'[35]

Nothing, then, is further from him than the great stripping-down process to which his comrades of 1925 invited him. Surrealists, Gideans and Communists all surrounded him then, whispering, 'Leave hold!' To leave hold and abandon himself, to abandon all orders, all coordinates and find himself at last alone and naked, a stranger to himself, like Philoctetes after he has surrendered his bow, like Dimitri Karamazov in prison, like the addict who takes drugs for amusement, like the young man who abandons his class, family and home to place himself alone and naked in the hands of the Party. If he gives all, then he will receive a thousandfold—that is what these sirens murmur to him. And it is, no doubt, a myth. But Parain doesn't leave hold. On the contrary, he clings on tighter, he lashes himself to the mast. Everyone knows the deep-seated resistance that suddenly reveals itself when one is in danger of coming to grief. Everyone knows too the stunned sense of remorse, the unquenched curiosity and the mulish anger that visits those who survive. Parain didn't come to grief. He didn't want to live without limits. The fields in the countryside have their limits. And roads, major and minor, have their marker posts, their milestones. Why would he lose himself? And what did he ask for? A few acres of land, an honourable wife, children, the humble freedom of the craftsman at work or the peasant in the fields—in a word, happiness. Did he need to lose himself to achieve all that? He never really wanted to launch himself into some great endeavour, and who can criticize him for that? He merely wanted a fairer, almost paternal form of organization to assign him a place on the earth and, by defining him within rigorous coordinates, to rid him of the need for security, of the 'worry that threatened to suffocate him'.[36]

> A man needs a *personal* god. When he isn't sleeping or has lost hope, along with confidence in his own strength, when he is defeated, he really has to turn to something stronger than himself for protection, he really has to find some security somewhere.[37]

So worry is there at the outset, for him as it is for everyone. Worry, anxiety—whatever we want to call it. And then came the need to choose. And some chose precisely this anxiety, but Parain chose security. Is he right or wrong? Who could judge him? And then, isn't the choice of anxiety sometimes a way of choosing security? We can only record that he is what he chose. Humble and assured, clinging to a few sad, simple truths, scanning the high plateaux with an impudent modesty and, perhaps, a secret discontent.

But suddenly the reign of the mediating powers returns. And the reign of language, first among the intermediaries. Admittedly, the earth would be better. 'For a peasant, the earth is that intermediary . . . that serves him as a norm both common and objective.'[38] But there are peasants without land as there are kings without kingdoms. And Parain is one of these; he is rootless. In one corner of his mind, there will remain, nostalgically, the totalitarian myth of an accord binding earthly and human powers, much as a tree's roots merge into the earth that feeds them; beneath his grumpy headmaster's air, he will retain the timid, shamefaced naturalism of the Danubian peasant, that other uprooted individual. But when he has to define himself and settle who he is, he will turn back not to the earth, but to language. It is a question of *being*. And for Parain, as for all post-Kantian philosophy, being is synonymous with stability and objectivity. The planet *is* because its paths across the heavens are set, the tree *is* because it grows according to set laws and doesn't move about. But, from the inside, man is as runny as a soft cheese; he *is* not. He will *be* only if he knows himself. And 'to know oneself' here doesn't mean to discover the truth lodged in everyone's heart: there is no heart and no truth, just a monotonous haemorrhage. To know oneself is to wilfully effect a transference of being: I set myself limits, I set up a system of markers and then I suddenly declare that I *am* these limits and these markers. I *am* a private soldier. I *am* French, I *am* a graduate of the École normale who has passed the *agrégation*. This means that I choose to define myself after the fashion of the sociologist: by means of frames. So, Halbwachs would say, this man being shown into this drawing-room is the gynaecologist, a former Paris hospital houseman and a medical officer during the 1914-18 war.[39] Take away the doctor and the medical officer, nothing remains but a bit of dirty water swirling off down a drain. It's language that makes the doctor or the magistrate:[40] 'He is asked to express what man has that is most intimately impersonal, most intimately similar to others.'[41] The voluntary aspect of language is neglected, namely its transcendence.

This enables us to grasp the dialectical movement that brought Parain back to his starting point. Like everyone, he was convinced at the outset of *being*, deep down, a certain given reality, an individual essence, and he called upon language to formulate that essence. But he realized that he couldn't slip into the socialized forms of speech. He didn't recognize his reflection in the mirror of words. It was at this point that a dual movement revealed a twofold fluidity to him: if he placed himself amid words, in town or city, he saw them melt and flow away, losing their meaning as they passed from one group to another, becoming increasingly abstract, and he set against them the myth of a natural ordering of human needs (love, work, motherhood, etc.). And if words could no longer express these needs, this was precisely because the changeable cannot convey that which stays the same, because made-up terms cannot apply to nature, because the town cannot speak of the countryside. At that point, language seemed to him a destructive force, separating man from himself. But if, deserting words, he wanted to recover his silence, the fixed order of desires he believed he would rediscover immediately vanished, revealing a memory-less, inconsistent fluidity, the shifting, disordered image of the void. Seen from within this fluidity, by contrast, words seemed as fixed as stars: when you are plunged into this little morass we know as love, when you feel tossed about by uncertain emotions, how fine the word 'love' seems, with all the ceremony of affection, desire and jealousy it implies: how you would like to *be* what it *bespeaks*. Parain attempted, then, to hold on simultaneously to these two fleeting entities; this was his expressionist, revolutionary period: language *is* not, it has to be made; the individual *is* not; he has to be named. Only, in the face of these endless, dizzying swirlings, he lost heart, gave up the struggle, clung to what seemed firm. And then, this universal fluidity rendered every solution contradictory: if the individual were to find sufficient coherence and strength in himself to recreate language, he would have to be something fixed and static; in a word, he would have first to be named. And so expressionism is a vicious circle: 'Action [is not] the measure of our language . . . Does it not, rather, presuppose an order that gives rise to it, and hence speech? Can its movement come to it of itself?'[42] And so we see Parain wandering once again from one side to the other: in *Essai sur la Misère humaine* he criticizes language from the standpoint of the order of needs; in *Retour à la France* words are, rather, fixed and restored to their intercessory function; it is we who are boundlessly fluid. But the solution is already forming: an attempt at a modest, positive synthesis and, at the same time, the recourse to God. This solution, which will become clearer in *Recherches*, can be summed up, I believe, in four points:

1. Having a bundle of experiences to put into order, Parain deliberately selects one of them and decides to make it *his* original experience. He constructs his history this way. It is this experience he will define in these terms: 'Man can no more do without language than he can direct it.'

2. It is this experience too that he will cash in through his theory of objectivity. It is the act of naming that divides up the universal fluidity of sensations and stabilizes it into 'things':

> The insect no doubt moves around in its universe of actions and reactions without representing the external world to itself as an object independent of that universe, which thus remains homogeneous. Would we not be equally ignorant if we did not have

> language? . . . I note the distinctness with
> which an object detaches itself from me as
> soon as I have named it. From that moment
> on, I can no longer deny it the status of ob-
> ject. The philosophers have observed that
> every perception is constituted by a judge-
> ment. But have they stressed sufficiently that
> it is naming that is the first judgement
> and that naming is the decisive moment of
> perception?[43]

Words are ideas. This means that man doesn't create ideas, but assembles them. We have been told for a very long time that man isn't God and can create nothing in the universe. He arranges and orders. But the coal, the oil and the marble are there. At least he still had his thoughts, which he produced—so the story went—as a sort of emanation. Parain takes them from him—they are lodged in words. And with that, I am suddenly *situated in language*.[44] But, as a result, words now become things. Admittedly, Parain tells us that language is 'neither subject nor object, belonging to neither the one nor the other. Subject when I speak, object when I listen to myself . . . and yet distinct from other beings, and distinct, similarly, from the self.' But, despite this caution, he has to recognize that language, as foundation of objectivity, is itself objective: 'Subject when I speak, object when I listen to myself.' But I never speak without listening to myself, as is proved by those deaf mutes who are mute because they are deaf. And how would Parain really accept that words are 'subjects'? How could they confer objectivity if they didn't already possess it? If words seem subjects when I speak, this is because I slip myself into my words; in this sense, the hammer or the spoon are subjects too when I use them and they aren't distinct from my action. And objects the moment afterwards, when I have put them back on the table and am contemplating them. So, having rejected the *chosisme* of perception and reduced the sun, walls and tables to fleeting, subjective arrangements of sensations, Parain deliberately accepts a *chosisme* of language. The word is that strange being: an idea-thing. It has both the impenetrability of the thing and the transparency of the idea, the inertia of the thing and the active force of the idea; we can take it as a thing between our fingers and carry it here or there; but it slips away, betrays us, suddenly regains its independence, and arranges itself with other words of its own accord, obeying affinites

that escape our control; individual and dated like
things, like ideas it never expresses anything but the
universal. We stand in the same relation to the word
as the sorceror's apprentice to his master's broom: we
can set it in motion, but not guide it or stop it. We are,
in one sense, entirely responsible, because we speak,
but, in another, we are wholly innocent, because we
don't know what we are saying. We are as incapable
of lying as of telling the truth, since it is words that
teach us what we mean by words. And I refer pur-
posely to the sorceror's apprentice here. Didn't Alain
say that magic 'is spirit loitering among things'?
Parain's language is the reign of magic. Ideas blinded,
blocked by matter; matter possessed by spirit and in
revolt against spirit. Not Descartes's 'evil daemon', but
a topsy-turvy one.

3. However, Parain hasn't resolved to abandon his
expressionist attitude entirely. Language is, no doubt,
in a sense, that magical, capricious anti-reason that at
times puts itself in the service of man and at times escapes him. It is, no doubt, *the reverse side of an unknown
being's reason*. But Parain cannot ignore the historical life
of words; he asserts, as in the past, that words change
meaning depending on the group using them. How

can this objectivity be reconciled with that relativity? Are there fixed, transcendent meanings or is it the social act that gives its meaning to words? Neither. The fact is that words, for him, have open significations in the sense in which Bergson speaks of 'open' societies. Words are both 'germs of being' and promises.

> Any sign is concrete which, in isolation or within its system, ends in complete accomplishment, as is any promise that is scrupulously kept . . . Man must no longer regard his language as a mere notation of facts and laws . . . but as a *de facto* engagement in the life he sustains and re-creates at every moment.[45]

In a way, the meaning of words lies before them, 'to be filled out'. But if they are to be 'filled out', they are like the empty form which the town-hall clerk or hotelier hands us. One part is variable and one part fixed. It is our action that concretizes them, but the abstract pattern and general outlines of that action are given in advance in every word:

> I tell a woman I love her . . . Have I not simply made a promise? Is it not merely understood between us that this word shall have

the meaning we shall give it by living together? We are going to recreate it and that is
a great undertaking. Has the word been waiting for us to have this meaning we shall give
it? And if it is our intention to give it a meaning, then we are going to work for it, not for
ourselves. This means it is our master.[46]

This situation has moral consequences that are
impossible to assess: if words are promises, if their
meanings are to be constructed, then the ambitious
pursuit of *truth*, that is to say, of a deeply buried treasure that is to be extracted, loses all meaning. There is
nothing anywhere, on earth or beneath it, that awaits
us; nothing with which we can compare the sentences
we form. But if the outlines of my promise are already registered in words, if words are like impersonal
registration forms that I have to fill up with my life,
my work, my blood, then the deep, discreet virtue that
lay hidden in our love of truth isn't lost; *honesty* isn't
lost. With the expressionist 'watchword', honesty gave
way to arbitrary powers of invention and of lawless
action—in a word, to force. Truth was measured by
success and success was merely a matter of chance.
By according a powder charge and a potential to

words, by permitting them to hypothecate the future, Parain intends to reserve a role in the world for human beings. He also banishes the marvellous, contradictory power to see the absolute in silence—and the crazed inventiveness that tosses words around haphazardly like pebbles. In exchange, he preserves for man the power to establish a human order: commitments, work, fidelity—these are the things restored to us. And it isn't enough just to be honest, once the promise has been made. We have also to be scrupulous in choosing our promises and to promise little so that we can be sure to keep them. There are wild-eyed, drunken, outlandish words we must be careful to shun. And there are also simple words, such as work, love and family. Parain retained his trust in these and his affection for them even at the height of his crisis. They are human-scale words. It is by them that I should allow myself to be defined, it being understood that that definition isn't the consecration of a factual state, but the announcement of a new duty. If I keep my promises, if I 'fulfil' my commitments, if, having asserted that I love, I carry that undertaking through, then I *shall be* what I *say*.

The identity of man and of his expression through language . . . is not given at birth. It is the work of the individual who, in achieving it, cannot do without the contribution of society. Much as a man may believe naively in it in his mature years, an adolescent is nonetheless forced to deny it . . . That identity is our task, our need for honesty. It is the happiness and faith we arrive at, but only after long meanderings.

When we express ourselves, we always say more than we want to, because we believe we are expressing something individual and we are saying something universal:

I'm hungry. I am the one saying 'I'm hungry', but I am not the one who is heard. Between these two moments of my speech, I have disappeared. As soon as I pronounced the words, all that remains of me is the man who is hungry and this man belongs to everyone . . . I have entered the ranks of the impersonal or, in other words, entered on the path of the universal.[47]

Since to speak, however, is to commit oneself, the sense of this morality is clear: as in Kant's system, the aim is to achieve the universal with one's own flesh. But the universal isn't given at the outset, as in *The Critique of Practical Reason*, nor is it the universal that first defines man. I am 'situated' in language, I cannot remain silent; by speaking, I throw myself into this unknown, alien order and I suddenly become responsible for it: I have to *become* universal. To bring into being, with humility and caution, and by means of my own flesh, the universality into which I first threw myself heedlessly—this is the only possibility open to me, the only command I must obey. I have said that I love; the promise is made. I now have to make sacrifices so that the word 'love' assumes meaning through me, so that there is love on Earth. As reward, at the end of this long undertaking, it will fall to my lot to be *the one who loves* or, in other words, to deserve the name I have given myself. To distrust words and their magical powers; to cling only to some of them, the simplest and most familiar; to speak little; to name things cautiously; to say nothing of myself that I'm not sure I can uphold; to apply myself my whole life long to keeping my promises—this is what Parain's morality offers me. It will seem austere and, so to speak, fearful: he is quite aware of this. The fact is that it occupies a place between an original disquiet and a terminal sense of resignation. It has always been Parain's concern to 'preserve the initial disquiet';[48] it is his conviction that 'man achieves fulfilment with a certain resignation.'[49] It will prove easy to recognize the successive forms of this troubled soul: this perpetual oscillation between the individual and the universal, the historical and the eternal; these perpetual disappointments that suddenly lead us to discover the universal in the heart of the individual and, conversely, reveal the ruse and illusoriness of history to those who believe themselves ensconced in the bosom of the eternal; this contradictory, harrowing wish for a rigorous social order that will nonetheless preserve the dignity of the individual and, lastly, this resigned affirmation that the individual finds accomplishment in the sacrifice in which he destroys himself so that the universal may exist: what is this but that desperate dialectic Hegel laid before us in the Unhappy Consciousness? I am as nothing when confronted with the compact immobility of words. The point is *to be*. But who will first decide on the meaning of being? Everyone. And everyone will choose himself precisely insofar as he will have made his choice of the nature and meaning of being in general. For Parain, *to be* means fixity, dense fullness, universality. This is the ideal which, from the outset and of his own free choice, he assigned to his existence. But how can the nothingness *be*?

4. We have abandoned everything; we confine our ambition to adapting ourselves progressively to words we have not made. Yet this resignation cannot save us. If words move around, then it is all up with this equilibrium we have acquired with such difficulty. And they do move around. There are quakings of words more dangerous than earthquakes. We are pitched, then, into a universal changeability, since we hook up the restless, living slippages of our individual lives to the slower, more massive slippages of language. From this peril there is only one relief: God. If words come from society, then they are born and die with it and we are their dupes. Happily, 'the arguments ordinarily employed to prove that language cannot have been invented by man are irrefutable.'[50] If it doesn't come from man, then it comes from God:

> Man can no more do without language than
> he can direct it. He can only accord it his
> trust, attempting, through his resources as a

human being and the seriousness of his
individual experience, not to abuse it. This
law of our thought is the best proof of the
existence of God, parallel to all the proofs
the theologians have, by turns, advanced, but
situated in a narrower domain and perhaps,
as a result, more impregnable.[51]

Parain doesn't formulate this proof. Perhaps he is saving it for another book. We can glimpse it nonetheless.
In it God appears as both the author and the guarantor
of language. He is its author: that is to say, the order
that shows through, despite everything, in discourse
cannot come from man. In this regard, the proof is
akin to the physico-theological argument: it is the order
seen in the course of words or in the course of the
stars that compels us to deduce the existence of some
transcendent purpose. But since, in another sense, that
order is postulated more than perceived, since it is a
question, above all, of rescuing man from despair by
letting him hope for a hidden fixity in the shifting life
of words, it may seem too that we have here the so-
called moral proof, which deduces the existence of
God from the great need we have of Him. It is, in fact,
both moral and teleological. Both demand and entreaty

at one and the same time. Descartes had limited his ambitions to thinking in clear, distinct ideas; and yet there had to be some guarantor of those ideas. In his work, God appears, then, as a necessary function. Similarly for Parain, who confines himself to thinking in simple words, to 'making language serve only ends for which its inexactitude presents the least danger,' something must stand surety for these simple words. Not for their truth, since that is still to be made and it is up to us to make it. Nor for their absolute fixity, since they live and die. But rather for a certain stability preserved in the heart of their very mobility. Hegel says somewhere of law that it is the still image of movement: and it is laws that Parain demands of God. It matters little that everything changes, so long as words, the germs of being, have a regulated course to them; so long as there is somewhere a still, silent image of their fluidity. And it has to be that way or else everything will sink into absurdity: things, which don't exist if they aren't named; speech, which will crumble away randomly; and our human condition, since 'we are not beings of silence, but logical creatures.' And just as there is a God for Descartes, because we cannot be mistaken when our will, in spite of itself, is induced to pass an opinion, so there is a God for Parain because we are animals whose main function is to speak.

A strange God, indeed, closer to Kafka's and Kierkegaard's than to the god of Saint Thomas Aquinas. He suffers from a thoroughly modern impotence. The messages he sends to men are scrambled—or, rather, they reach us the wrong way round. Starting out from the bosom of silence and from the unity of a thought governing matter, we receive them as a plurality of noises and it is matter that has subjugated the meanings in them to itself. This God doesn't speak to man, he suggests His silence to him by means of sounds and words. He reminds me of Kafka's emperors, who are omnipotent and yet incapable of communicating with their subjects. Moreover, God too is a word; God is *also* a word. As such, as promise and germ of being, 'God must be . . . applied in terms of the demand that language carries within it and conveys to us.'[52] This perhaps is Parain's theology at its clearest: there is the *word* of God, which suggests to us and at the same time conceals from us the *fact* of God. And we have honestly, by faith and works, to re-create the meaning of that word. Thus, having started out from silence, Parain returns to silence. But it isn't the same

silence. His starting point was an infra-silence, a violent
mutism of the moment that drove holes in language:

> When I take a walk, there are times when I
> do not speak. Do not speak to myself, I
> mean. There are times when, as I look at the
> mist over the Seine, suddenly timorous, I am
> struck by the discovery in the sky of some-
> thing like a policeman's uniform, a jovial fel-
> low or a beautiful woman. Such moments of
> emotion constitute the only circumstances in
> which we feel ourselves existing.[53]

But he understood that this silence had meaning only
through the language that names and underpins it.[54]
Since words are the basis of objectivity, then if I
discover a policeman's uniform or a jovial fellow in
the sky, this is because I have at my disposal, in the
background, the words 'fellow', 'uniform', 'policeman'
and 'jovial'. To be silent is to understand certain
implied words; that is all there is to it. Yet the love of
silence in Parain is such that he discovers another silence, an ultra-silence, that gathers to itself and runs
through the whole of language, in the same way as
the Heideggerian nothingness embraces the world or
non-knowledge in Blanchot and Bataille envelops

knowledge and underpins it. This is merely one of those many surprises that *totalization* keeps in store for us. To contest is, in fact, to totalize. The totality of knowledge is non-knowledge because it appears to a point of view that transcends knowledge. And the totality of language is silence, since one has to be situated in the midst of language to speak. Except that, in the case that concerns us here, totalization is impossible *for man*, since it would be achieved through words. And Parain's silence is merely a great optimistic myth—a myth which he has, if I am not mistaken, now entirely left behind.[55]

Shall I present a critique of these arguments? I have known Parain for ten years. I have often held discussions with him. I have watched each of the moves made by his honest, rigorous thinking and have often admired his knowledge and the efficacy of his dialectic. To avoid misunderstanding, I shall forewarn the reader, then, that my objections seem to me like a stage in a long, friendly dialogue we have been conducting over many years. He will no doubt respond to my criticism another day, and I shall make other objections to which he will, further, respond. In the meanwhile, his thinking will have followed its course.

He will have changed his position and probably I will
too. We shall have moved closer together or farther
apart; another Parain and another Sartre will carry on
the discussion. But since the function of the critic is
to criticize—that is to say, to commit himself for or
against and to situate himself as he situates his object,
I shall say quite bluntly that I accept the greater part
of Parain's analyses: I merely contest their scope and
their place. What is at issue between us, as has so often
been the case in the history of philosophy, is the question of the beginning. Perhaps Parain will be criticized
for not starting out from the psychology of the speaking human being. But that isn't my view. Being enough
of a Comtian to be deeply mistrustful of psychology,
Parain on no account wishes to get into analyses of
those 'verbal images' or 'verbo-motor' processes with
which the psychologists lethally assailed us in the early
years of the twentieth century. He is right: if there are
wordless thoughts, as the subjects of Messer and Büh-
ler discovered within themselves around 1905, what
concern is that to us? For it would have to be proved
that these wordless thoughts aren't framed, limited or
conditioned by the whole of language. And the empirical transition from idea to word may very well be

described, but what does it teach us? We would have to be sure that the idea isn't simply the dawning of a word. Parain boasts of reconstructing the whole of a man with needs and with words. And if we are talking of the empirical man that psychology claims to grasp, perhaps he isn't wrong. The sociologists argued that the physiological and social facts were enough to make up the human order. We shall perhaps grant them that: it all depends on the definition of the social and the physiological. But is there no other beginning than introspective psychology?

Someone is talking to me. And now the word 'hail' strikes my ears. We have here something precisely located in time and space—in a word, an individual event. Looked at strictly, it isn't *the* word hail that I hear; it's a certain highly particular sound, pronounced in a gentle or husky voice, swept away in a whirlwind, amid light that penetrates it, odours impregnating it and a sadness or gaiety colouring it. Three hours pass and now I am myself pronouncing the word 'hail'. Can we say that I hear myself? Not entirely, since, if you record my voice, I won't recognize it. What we have at this point is a quasi-hearing, which we needn't describe here. And if the word I am *chewing on*, the word that fills my mouth with its substance, resembles the one I heard not so long ago, it does so only insofar as both are individual events. Let us take another individual event: I'm looking at a page in a book, a page glazed by the light of a cold sun; a mouldy cellary smell rises from the page to my nose and, among so many singularities, I see some singular strokes traced on a line: 'hail'. Now I ask Parain, where is the *word* 'hail'? Where is that timeless, dimensionless reality that is, at one and the same time, on the page of the book, in the vibration of the air and in that moist mouthful I taste and which resists absorption by any of these singular phenomena. Where is *this* word, which *was not* either yesterday or the day before yesterday, which *is not* today and *will not be* tomorrow, but which manifests itself yesterday, today and tomorrow, in such a way that each time I hear it, I grasp the auditory phenomenon as one of its incarnations and not as an absolute event? In a word, if language is the ground of objectivity, what is it that grounds the objectivity of language? I see this cockchafer grub and, according to Parain, I need the words 'cockchafer grub' to confer a certain permanency on it, to give it a future, a past, qualities and relations with the other objects in the world. But when

I open this book on atmospheric phenomena, I see these little black, spidery marks that make up the word 'hail' in precisely the same way as I see the cockchafer bug. If it's true that this latter, unless it is named, is merely a labile grouping of sensations, then the former cannot exist any differently. Do we, then, need a word to name the word 'hail'? But who will name this word in its turn? We find ourselves, curiously, in an infinite regress; this means that the simple act of naming— and hence of speaking—has become impossible. This is the Third Man argument which was employed by Aristotle in his day against Plato. It isn't unanswerable when applied to pure Ideas, since Plato referred to it himself with some degree of irony in the *Parmenides*. But this is because ideas have no need of ideas to make themselves understood. They are nothing but the act of pure intellection. By contrast, when I consider a word, I see that it has a body and reveals itself to me through that body, amid a host of other bodies. Whence, then, its privileged character? Shall we say it comes from God or from society? But this is a lazy solution. Or rather, we are at a level here where neither God nor society can play a part.

Let us assume, in fact, that, by some divine grace, the word 'hail' is preserved, endowed with a kind of permanence, and that it is the *same word* that struck me yesterday and strikes me again today. After all, it is the same ink bottle I saw a moment ago and see again now; it is the same desk, the same tree. Well, we must confess, then, that even in this unachievable conjecture, the *external* identity of the word 'hail' would be of no use to me; for, however identical it were physically, I would still have to *recognize* it, that is to say, carve it out and stabilize it in the flow of phenomena, relate it to its appearances from yesterday and the day before yesterday, and establish a synthetic site of identification between these various different moments. What matter, in fact, that this ink bottle is the same outside of me? If I have no memory, I shall say there are ten inkbottles, a hundred or as many as there are appearances of inkbottles. Or, rather, I shan't even say there is an inkbottle; I shall say nothing at all. Similarly, where the word 'hail' is concerned, knowledge and communication are possible only if there is *one* word 'hail'. But even if the word existed in the heart of God, I would have to produce it by the operation termed 'synthesis of identification'.[56] And I now understand that the word wasn't privileged, since I have also to make the table and the tree and the cockchafer bug exist as permanent syntheses of relatively stable properties. It isn't by naming them that I confer objectivity on them, but I cannot name them unless I have already constituted them as independent units or, in other words, unless I objectify both the thing and the word in a single synthetic act that names it. I hope no one will imagine replying with the argument that God maintains the identity of the word *within us*, for if God thinks in me, then I vanish; God alone remains. And Parain surely wouldn't go that far. No, it is I, whether listening or speaking, who constitute the word as one of the elements of my experience. Before discussing language, Parain should have asked himself how experience is possible, since there is an experience of language. He has meditated on Descartes, Leibniz and Hegel: all well and good; but he says nothing of Kant. And this enormous lacuna in the *Recherches* doesn't occur by chance: it indicates quite simply that Parain has erred in the order of his thinking. For, ultimately, if I constitute my experience and the words within that experience, it isn't at the level of language, but at the level of the synthesis of identification that the universal appears. When I say, 'I am hungry', then clearly the word universalizes; but, in order to universalize, it must first be the case that *I* individualize it, that is to say, that I extract the word 'hungry' from the disordered confusion of my current impressions.

But we have to go back even further than this. Parain wasn't averse to reproducing a lamentable analysis of the *cogito* that he found in *The Will to Power*. It is well-known that Nietzsche was no philosopher. But why does Parain, as a professional philosopher, rely on this nonsense? Does he really believe he can get away with it? But it matters little what Descartes *says* of the *cogito*. What counts is that, when I understand a word, it is clearly necessary that I am aware of understanding it. Otherwise, the word and the understanding plunge into darkness. Language, says Parain, interposes itself between me and the knowledge I have of myself, though perhaps on condition that knowledge and language are equated, on condition that the relation I have with myself is made to begin with knowledge. But when I am aware of understanding a word, no word interposes itself between me and myself: the word, the sole word in question is there *before* me as *that which is understood*. And where, indeed, would you put it? In my consciousness? You might just as well put a tree in there or a wall that would cut it off from itself. And yet it has to be understood or else it is mere empty noise. After that, it matters little to me that there is such endless discussion over the 'I' of the cogito: that has to do with syntax, grammar and, perhaps, logic. But the efficacy, the eternal nature of the *cogito* is precisely that it reveals a type of existence defined as presence to oneself without intermediary. Words interpose themselves between my love and me, between my cowardice or my courage and me, but not between my understanding and my consciousness of understanding. For the consciousness of understanding is the law of being of understanding. I shall call this the silence of consciousness. And, with this, we are a long way from that flow of sensory impressions to which Parain wants to reduce us. Yet I know what his reply will be: have it your way on your consciousness, but as soon as you try to *express* what you are, you get bogged down in language. I am still in agreement: only I know what I want to express, because I *am* that thing without any intermediary. Language may resist me, may lead me astray, but I shall be deceived by it only if I allow myself to be so, for I always have the possibility of returning to what I am, to that void, that silence that I am, by which, however, there is a language and there is a world. The *cogito* escapes Parain's clutches, as does the synthesis of identification, as does the universal. And that was the commencement.

The fact remains that the *Other* is there, understanding my words, as he wishes, or able to refuse to understand them. But it seems to me precisely that the Other isn't present enough in Parain's work. He intervenes at times, but I don't know where he comes from. Now, this is also a commencement problem. Which is first, the Other or language? If it is language, the Other vanishes. If the Other is to appear to me only when he is named, then it is words that create the Other, as they create the cockchafer grub or hail. And it is also words that can take him away; I cannot escape solipsism: among the flow of my sensations, the word *Other* carves out a certain whole which it endows with a certain universal meaning. This cannot be a privileged experience. But then I speak wholly alone. The alleged interventions of the Other are merely reactions of my language on my language. If, on the other hand, as soon as I speak, I have the agonizing certainty that words slip beyond my grasp, that, outside of me, they are going to assume unsuspected aspects and unforeseen meanings, isn't it then part of the very structure of language that it is to be understood by a freedom that isn't mine? In a word, isn't it the Other who makes language; isn't it the Other that comes first? Parain grudgingly agrees on this point, since he resorts to that Other—that quintessence of otherness—that is God. But why, then, is God needed here? To explain the origin of language? But there is no problem unless man exists first, alone, naked, silent and complete, and speaks *afterwards*. Then one might, indeed, ask how he took it into his head to speak. But if I exist originally only by and for the Other; if, as soon as I appear, I am thrown before the Other's gaze; and if the Other is a thing as certain to me as I am myself, then I am language, for language is merely existence in the presence of someone else. Take this still, hateful, perspicacious woman staring at me silently, as I come and go in the bedroom. All my gestures are immediately alienated, stolen from me; they form, over there, into a horrible package of which I know nothing. Over there I am clumsy and

ridiculous. Over there, in the heat of that stern gaze.
I pull myself together and battle against this alien
ponderousness that suddenly inhabits me. And I become, over there, too jaunty, too conceited—ridiculous again. Here we have the whole of language: it is
this dumb, despairing dialogue. Language is being-for-
others. What need do we have of God? The Other—
any other—is enough. He comes in and I no longer
belong to myself; He interposes Himself between me
and myself. Not in the silent privacy of the *cogito*, but
between me and everything I am on Earth—happy,
unhappy, handsome, ugly, mean or magnanimous: for
the Other must play a part before I can be any of
those things. But if it is true that to speak is to act
under the gaze of the Other, there is every danger that
the famous problems of language will merely be a re-
gional instance of the major ontological problem of
the existence of others. If the Other doesn't understand me, is that because I am speaking or because he
is other? And if language plays me false, is this the
product of some malignancy specific to it or is it not,
rather, because it is the mere surface of contact between me and the Other. In a word, for there to be a
problem of language, the Other must first be given.

367

Against Parain, then, we must maintain the priority of the *cogito*, of universalizing syntheses,[57] and of immediate experience of the Other. In this way we restore language to its true place. However, if its power is thereby limited from above, it is, as I see it, also limited from below; not only by human reality that names and comprehends, but by the objects that are named.

> When, feeling certain inner disturbances, I declare that I am hungry, I am not conveying my sensations to the people I am speaking to, but merely indicating to them that I want to eat or, rather, that I believe I need to eat. I have thought, in fact, that my unease would be settled if I took some food. In doing so, I have put forward a hypothesis concerning my state. But I may be wrong. Amputees actually feel cold in the leg that has been removed.[58]

The fact is that Parain is still under the influence of nineteenth-century psychology, which admits of purely experienced affective states, to which we attach meanings from the outside, out of habit. Isn't this a little premature? And shouldn't he first have taken a

stance on the phenomenological conception of affectivity, which regards each desire as an intentional
Erlebnis, that is to say, as directly bearing on its object.
I knew a young woman suffering from a stomach
ulcer. When she had gone a long time without food,
she would feel a sharp pain and know at that point
that she had to eat. In this case, we are certainly dealing with 'affective states' or 'sensations', as postulated
by Parain. Only the young woman didn't say she was
hungry. Nor did she think it: she presumed that the
pain she suffered would disappear if she fed herself.
To be hungry, on the other hand, is to be aware of
being hungry; it is to be pitched into the world of
hunger, to see loaves or meat lit by a painful gleam in
shop windows, to catch oneself dreaming of chicken.
'The doctor,' writes Parain, 'would perhaps reject my
diagnosis.' But there is no diagnosis—that is to say, no
groping induction tending to interpret mute data—
and the doctor cannot help us here. He may explain
to me that I shouldn't eat, that there is something suspicious about this hunger, that it corresponds to a certain bodily state far removed from lack of nourishment.
But he cannot deny my desire. What would a joy, a
pain or a sexual desire be that needed language to

assure them of what they are? Language will doubtless extend their scope dangerously, indicating them to me as 'universal desires' and suggesting lines of conduct that could satisfy them. But a desire that didn't give itself out as desire would be in no way different from indifference or resignation. When I have a headache, I *assume* that an aspirin will ease my pain; but my headache is, in no sense, a desire for aspirin. By contrast, when I desire a woman, my desire doesn't want to be eased, but to be satisfied and I don't need to advance an hypothesis as to how I might satisfy it. The desire is there, for those arms and that bosom; either it is a desire for that particular woman or no desire at all.

But, it will be objected, the external object re-mains: the tree, the table, this darkness. Here we shall not demur; language forms a constitutive stratum of the thing. But it isn't language that gives it its cohesion, shape or permanence. In this case too, it seems to me that Parain's psychological presuppositions are a little dated. Why speak here of sensations? The sensation was consigned to the lumber room a long time ago; it is a fantasy of psychology; for the moment, it is merely a word. The experiments of *Gestalttheorie* reveal, rather, a formal cohesion of objects, laws of structure, dynamic and static relations that surprise the observer, bewilder him and have no regard for whether they are named or not. At night, a gleaming spot on a bicycle wheel seems to me to describe a cycloid; in daylight, the movement of this same spot seems circular. Words cannot affect this; something quite different is in play. The fly doesn't speak, says Parain, and so 'the sensations of flies remain in a rudimentary state.'[59] I find this rather audacious. What does Parain know of the fly? He asserts what actually needs to be proved. In fact, the Gestaltists' experiments tend to show that the least evolved animals behave according to the perception of *relations*, not in terms of alleged sensations. A chicken, a bee or a chimpanzee interprets the *lightest* colour as a signal, not this or that particular shade of grey or green.[60] Does Parain contest the findings of these experiments? If so, he ought at least to say so. The fact is that his knowledge is that of his generation: either he knows nothing of the German psychologists and philosophers of today or he doesn't understand them. He knows very little of Hegel; he is unaware of Kant's unpublished writings; recent work on aphasia by Gelb and Goldstein has passed him by. As a result, he is, without realizing it, thrashing about among outdated problems. He is drawing conclusions that ensue from the movement in French philosophy that runs from Ribot[61] to Brunschvicg[62] by way of Bergson.[63] He is settling accounts and making a final reckoning. For us, these names are all dead and gone, and our accounts with them were long since painlessly and noiselessly settled: we were schooled differently.

Language is situated between stable, concrete objects that didn't await its appearance to reveal themselves (intentional desires, forms of external perception) and human realities that are eloquent in their very nature and, for that very reason, lie outside speech, for they are in direct contact with each other and thrust against each other without intermediary. As a result, language can lie, deceive, distort and make unwarranted generalizations: the questions it raises are technical, political, aesthetic and moral. On that terrain, Parain's analyses retain their relevance. But there is no metaphysical problem of language. And I see flowing from Parain's pen all the theories that encapsulate the attitudes man has assumed in the modern world in respect of himself and his destiny. I find

Descartes and rationalism, Leibniz, Hegel, Nietzsche and pragmatism. But there is a constant source of annoyance here, as it seems to me that Parain does much more than interpret them. In fact, he translates them into his own language. Descartes trusts in clear, distinct ideas and Parain translates this as trusting in words. Nietzsche attempts a *logical* critique of the *cogito* and Parain writes that he 'poses the problem of language perfectly, while *believing that he is posing* only the problem of logic'. Modern pragmatism takes as its watchword, Faust's '*Im Anfang war der Tat*' and Parain translates, 'Action is the measure of our language.' The Platonic *logos* becomes discourse and so on. But isn't this a biased view? Isn't this forcing the truth? Has the Greek term *logos* only one meaning? And can't I have some fun myself *translating* Parain's thought? Can't I say that this man, after despairing of knowledge and reason, after having for a time subscribed— in an age when man was trying to forge a destiny for himself—to a kind of radical pragmatism, has returned, with his contemporaries, to a trust in a transcendent order that can assuage his anxiety? What has language got to do with any of that? And if he translates me, I shall translate his translation: and it will be never-ending. Isn't it better to leave each person to say what he meant to say? 'No, sir,' said André Breton to a commentator on Saint-Pol Roux.[64] 'If Saint-Pol Roux had *meant to say* "carafe", that is what he would have said.' Doesn't the same apply to Descartes or Hegel?

It is in our hearts that Parain's books are most deeply resonant. It is when he writes, for example, 'I feel I am responsible for a world I did not create,'[65] that we subscribe to what he says wholeheartedly. Parain is a man for whom man exists. Man, not that ready-made reality human *nature*, but man *in situ*, that being who derives his being from his very limits. We love this resigned, but activistic wisdom, this serious-ness, this resolve to look things in the eye, this proud, courageous honesty and, above all, this great charity. Perhaps the theoretical principles underlying his work seem a little old-fashioned to us, but in his morality he is akin to the youngest among us. I am thinking, in particular, of Camus. For him, man's response to the absurdity of his condition doesn't lie in some great Romantic rebellion, but in daily application. To see clearly, keep one's word and do one's job—this is our *true* revolt, since there is no reason why I should be faithful, sincere and brave and it is *for that very reason* that I must show myself to be so. Parain asks nothing more nor less of us. He gives us a glimpse, no doubt, of some divine sanction, but his God is too distant to trouble us. Will the young people of these difficult times be satisfied with this morality or is it merely a necessary stage in the exploration of the limits of the human condition? Are Parain himself and Camus satisfied with it? Parain readily agrees that the preference for scrupulous honesty in the choice of words leads the novelist easily into populism. For the words 'bread', 'factory', 'piece-work', 'plough' and 'school' are more familiar to us than 'love' and 'hatred', 'freedom' or 'destiny'. And yet he detests this grey, spineless, horizonless world. Similarly, Camus seems, as a person, to exceed the confines of his doctrine in every way. What will they do? We shall have to wait and see. What Schlumberger says somewhere of Corneille applies admirably to the post-war world, even though he claims to despise it, as well as to the return that followed it and perhaps to what will follow that return:

> There is no great movement that does not start out from some creation . . . with all the harshness, perfunctoriness and, if you will,

artifice such a thing implies; nor is there any movement which,—after living on these new models for varying periods of time—isn't succeeded by the need for a more minute focus, for a 'return to nature' or, in other words, to average models. Alternation between the two disciplines is necessary. What a relief when a humbly truthful work puts the great exalted figures back in their place, those figures that have with time become little more than vacuous marionettes! But what a burst of energy we see when a decisive affirmation produces a new start in a stagnant age of increasingly meticulous, refined and pedestrian analysis, when a man once again sets about that lofty task, the invention of man.[66]

Notes

1   On Brice Parain, *Recherches sur la nature et les fonctions du langage* (Paris: Gallimard, 1942). Parain (1897–1971), a great friend of Albert Camus, was an essayist whose work was so characterized by a deep concern for the particularities of language

that the critic Charles Blanchard dubbed him 'the Sherlock Holmes of language'. Parain was a committed Communist and lived for a time in the USSR after World War I; he was no longer so when he wrote *Retour à la France*. [Trans.]

2 Jean Schlumberger (1877–1968): a French author and publisher, and one of the founders, with Gide among others, of the *Nouvelle Revue Française*. [Trans.]

3 Julien Sorel is the central character in Stendhal's 1830 novel, *Le Rouge et le Noir* (variously translated as *The Red and the Black*, *The Scarlet and the Black*, etc.). [Trans.]

4 Armand-Marcel Petitjean (1913–2003): son of the founder of the Lancôme perfume company, he had some success as an avant-garde writer and essayist in the 1930s. Though an anti-fascist in the pre-war period, Petitjean went over to Marshal Pétain's 'National Revolution' during the Occupation. [Trans.]

5 Louis Aragon (1897–1982): one of the greatest French poets and novelists of the twentieth century. [Trans.]

6 Roger de la Fresnaye (1885–1925): a French painter associated successively with the Section

d'Or and Puteaux groups of artists. He moved away from the Cubist style decisively after World War I, though by then his health was failing badly. [Trans.]

7 Brice Parain, *Retour à la France* (Paris: Grasset, 1936). Sartre gives no page number. [Trans.]

8 Henri Daniel-Rops (1901–65): French novelist, social theorist and historian.[Trans.]

9 Brice Parain, *Essai sur la misère humaine* (Paris: Grasset, 1934). Sartre again gives no page number. [Trans.]

10 Upublished manuscript of November 1922.

11 Parain, *Essai sur la misère humaine*, pp. 157–8.

12 Ibid., p. 99.

13 See '*Aminadab*: Or the Fantastic Considered as Language', p. 218, NOTE 16. [Trans.]

14 From an unpublished essay of 1923.

15 Parain, *Essai sur la Misère humaine*, p. 238.

16 Ibid., p. 205.

17 Ibid., p. 217.

18 Ibid., p. 226.

19 Parain, *Recherches sur le langage*, p. 170.

20 See '*The Outsider* Explained', p. 182, NOTE 15.

21 Parain, *Essai sur la misère humaine*, p. 206.

22 This passage, from Marx's 'Theses on Feuerbach', is cited by Parain, *Recherches sur le langage*, p. 121. For the original text, see Karl Marx, *Early Writings* (Harmondsworth: Penguin, 1975), pp. 421–3. [Trans.]

23 Unpublished essay of 1922.

24 Parain, *Essai sur la misère humaine*, p. 208.

25 Ibid., p. 169.

26 Ibid., p. 167.

27 Parain, *Retour à la France*, p. 186.

28 Ibid., p. 182.

29 Parain, *Recherches sur le langage*, p. 119.

30 Sartre provides no source for this quotation. [Trans.]

31 Ernst is following Lautréamont.

32 Sartre provides no source for this quotation from Parain. [Trans.]

33 Parain, *Essai sur la Misère humaine*, pp. 64, 66, 73–4.

34 Parain, *Retour à la France*, p. 31.

35 Ibid., pp. 37–8.

36 Ibid., p. 22.

37 Ibid., p. 105.

38 Parain, *Essai sur la Misère humaine*, p. 99.

39 Maurice Halbwachs (1877–1944): a student of Bergson and Durkheim, was a close collaborator of Marcel Mauss and the editor of *Annales de Sociologie*. [Trans.]

40 Sartre's reference to magistrates here is a nod towards the saying '*l'habit fait le magistrat*': clothes maketh the man. [Trans.]

41 Parain, *Recherches sur le langage*, p. 173.

42 Ibid., p. 121.

43 Ibid., pp. 22–3.

44 Ibid., p. 183.

45 Parain, *Essai sur la Misère humaine*, pp. 238–92.

46 Parain, *Recherches sur le langage*, p. 177.

47 Ibid., p. 172.

48 Parain, *Retour à la France*, p. 23.

49 Parain, *Essai sur la Misère humaine*, p. 123.

50 Parain, *Recherches sur le langage*, p. 175.

51 Parain, *Retour à la France*, p. 16.

52 Ibid., p. 17.

53 Unpublished manuscript, 1923.

54 Compare what Bataille says of the *word* silence in *Inner Experience*. [J.-P. S.] See Georges Bataille, *Inner*

Experience (Albany: State University of New York Press, 1988), p. 16. [Trans.]

55 He was already tempted by this equation of linguistic totality with silence when discussing Tolstoy's last works with me. These could be equated, he told me, with an 'old man's great silence'. A writer is God insofar as he creates his language; and we can totalize his words and speak of the language of Plato or of Shakespeare. As a result, it is beyond his words that he discloses himself and his work can be equated with silence. At this point we are back with Blanchot.

56 A reference to Husserl's concept, *Identifikationssynthese*. [Trans.]

57 I have simplified the problem of the syntheses by presenting it in its Kantian form. Perhaps we should speak of 'passive syntheses' as Husserl does or show that, by temporalizing itself, human reality makes use of already *synthesized* complexes. In any event, the argument remains the same: what holds for language holds also for any object, for language is also an object.

58 Parain, *Recherches sur le langage*, p. 25.

59 Ibid., p. 22.

60 See Paul Guillaume, *Psychologie de la forme* (Paris: Flammarion, 1937).

61 Théodule Ribot (1839–1916): French philosopher and psychologist. [Trans.]

62 See 'A Fundamental Idea of Husserl's Phenemenology: Intentionality', p. 46, NOTE 1.

63 Henri Bergson (1859–1941): one of the foremost French philosophers of his day. [Trans.]

64 Saint-Pol Roux (1861–1940): a French Symbolist poet, much of whose work was destroyed when his manor house was burned down by invading German troops in 1940. [Trans.]

65 Parain, *Recherches sur le langage*, p. 183.

66 Jean Schlumberger, 'Corneille', in *Tableau de la littérature française. XVIIe et XVIIIe siècles. De Corneille à Chénier* (Paris: Gallimard/nrf, 1939).

Man and Things

If we come at the published work of Francis Ponge without preconceived notions, we are tempted at first to think that, out of a singular affection for 'things', he has undertaken to describe them with the resources to hand. That is to say, he has set about describing them with words, with all the words that there are, with worn-out, overused, eroded words, such as present themselves to the naive writer, a mere assortment of colours on a palette. But if we read attentively, we are quickly disconcerted. Ponge's language seems bewitched or enchanted. As the words disclose a new aspect of the named object to us, it seems they also elude our grasp; they are no longer precisely the docile, commonplace tools of everyday life and they reveal new aspects of themselves. As a result, reading *Le Parti pris des choses* often seems like a worried oscillation between word and thing, as though in the end we are no longer quite sure whether the word is the object or the object the word.

Ponge's original concern is *with naming*. He isn't—or at least he isn't primarily—a philosopher and it isn't his aim to convey things at all costs. But the first thing he does is speak—and write. He has entitled one of his books *La Rage de l'expression* and he refers to himself, in *Le Mimosa*, as an ex-martyr of language.[1] He is a man of 45 who has been writing since 1919, which shows well enough that he came to things by way of reflection on the spoken word.

Let's be clear about this, however. You shouldn't believe that he talks for the sake of it, that the objects of his descriptions are themes to which he is indifferent, or even that it was his troubles with words that led him to his awareness of the existence of things. He himself says, in *Le Mimosa*:

> I have deep down an idea [of the mimosa] that I have to get out . . . I wonder whether it might not be the mimosa that first aroused my sensuality . . . I floated in ecstasy on the powerful waves of its scent. So that each time the mimosa appears now in my interior or around me, it reminds me of all that and fades immediately . . . Since I write, it would be unacceptable for there not to be a piece by me about mimosas.[2]

That he doesn't come to things by chance couldn't be more clearly put. Those he speaks about are chosen. They have lived in him for many a year; they inhabit his being; they carpet his memory. They were present in him long before he had his troubles with words, long before he opted to write about them; they already scented him with their secret meanings. And his current effort is directed much more at fishing these teeming monsters from the depths of his being and at *conveying* them, than at determining their qualities after scrupulous observations. It is said that Flaubert told Maupassant, 'Stand in front of a tree and describe it.' The advice, if it were actually given, is absurd. The observer can take measurements—and that is all. The thing will always refuse to yield its meaning—and its being—to him. Ponge no doubt looks at mimosas; he looks at them attentively and at length. But he already knows what he is looking for. Pebbles, the rain, the wind and the sea are already within him as complexes—and it is these complexes he wants to bring to light. And if we wish to know why, instead of the commonplace Oedipus complex or inferiority complex—or perhaps *alongside* the inferiority complex—he defines himself by the pebble-complex, the shellfish-complex or the moss-complex, the answer must be that this is the way it is for each of us and that this is the secret of his personality.

And yet he was one of those whose literary vocation is characterized by a furious wrestling with language. Though he began by assimilating and digesting the world of things, it was the great flat space of words that he discovered first. Man is language, he says. And he adds elsewhere with a kind of despair, 'All is words.' We shall better understand the meaning of this sentence in a moment. For the present, let us simply note this bias towards considering man from the outside, as the behaviourists do. Nowhere in his work will there be any question of *thought*. What distinguishes man from other species is this objective act we name speech, this original way of striking the air and constructing a sound object around himself. Ponge will even *naturalize* speech by making it a secretion of the human animal, a slime comparable to the snail's. 'The true secretion common to the human mollusc man . . . : I mean LANGUAGE.'[3] Or, elsewhere, 'Shapeless molluscs . . . millions of ants . . . your only dwelling is the common vapour of your true blood: speech.'[4]

Ponge regards speech as a real shell that enwraps us and protects our nudity, a shell we have secreted that suits the softness of our bodies. In his view, the tissue of words is a real, perceptible existence: he sees words around him, around us. But this rigorously objectivist conception of discourse, this materialist conception, so to speak, is at the same time an unreserved commitment to language. Ponge is a humanist. Since to speak is to be a man, he speaks to serve the human by speaking. Such is the avowed origin of his vocation as a writer.

> Instead of those gigantic monuments that testify only to the grotesque disparity between his imagination and his person, . . .

> I wish that man applied himself through the
> ages to creating a shelter not much larger
> than his body, one involving all his imagina-
> tion and reason, that he put his genius to
> work on appropriate scale rather than dispro-
> portion . . . In that light, I particularly admire
> certain restrained writers or composers, . . .
> above all the writers, because their monu-
> ment is made from the true secretion com-
> mon to the human mollusc.[5]

It is well and good to serve the human by speaking,
but that still requires words that must lend themselves
to the task. Ponge is of the same generation as Parain;
he shares with him that materialist conception of lan-
gauge that refuses to distinguish the Idea from the
Word; like him, in the aftermath of 1918, he experienced that sudden distrust of discourse, that same bitter disillusionment. I have tried to give the reasons for
this elsewhere. It seems generally agreed there was a
'crisis of language' later on in the period 1918–30.
The experimentation of the symbolists, the famous
'crisis of science', the theory of 'scientific nominalism' it inspired and Bergsonian critique had laid the
ground for it. But the young people of the post-war

years had need of more solid motives. There was the violent discontent of the demobilized, their maladaptedness to civilian life; there was the Russian revolution and the revolutionary agitation that spread almost everywhere throughout Europe; and, with the appearance of new, ambiguous realities that were neither flesh nor fowl, there was the dizzying devaluation of the old words that couldn't quite name these new realities, even though the very ambiguity of these forms of existence prevented new names being found for them. However this may be, not all the malcontents chose to level their anger at language. To do so, one first had to have accorded remarkable value to it. This was the case with Ponge and Parain. Those who believed they could unstick ideas from words were none too troubled, or applied their revolutionary energies in other directions. But Ponge and Parain had, from the outset, defined man by speech. They were caught like rats in a trap, because speech was now worthless. We can truly say in this case that they were in despair: their position denied them the slightest hope. We know that Parain, haunted by a silence that constantly eluded him, went first to the extremes of terrorism before returning to a nuanced rhetoric. Ponge's path was more tortuous.

His objection to language is, first and foremost, that it is the reflection of a social organization he abhors. 'Our first motive was probably disgust with what we are compelled to think and say.' In this sense, his despair was less total than Parain's. Whereas Parain thought he saw an original defect in language, there was a naturalistic optimism about Ponge that made him see words as vitiated by our form of society.

> With all due deference to *words* themselves, *given the habits they have contracted in so many obnoxious mouths*, it takes quite some courage to make the decision not merely to write, but even to speak.[6]

And:

> These stampedes of cars and lorries, these districts where no people reside, but only goods or the files of the companies that transport them . . . these governments of hucksters and traders, *we'd say nothing about it* if they didn't force us to take part . . . Alas, horror of horrors, the same sordid order speaks *inside ourselves*, because we don't have other words or other big words (or phrases, that is to say, other ideas) than those that

daily usage in this coarse world has prostituted from time immemorial.[7]

As we can see, Ponge's objection isn't really to language, but to language 'as it is spoken'. Hence he has never seriously considered remaining silent. As a poet, he sees poetry as a general enterprise of *cleaning up* language, just as the revolutionary may, in a way, look to clean up society. Moreover, for Ponge, the two are the same: 'I shall only ever bounce back in the pose of the *revolutionary* or the *poet*.'[8]

But, though he doesn't find the theoretical impossibility or formal contradiction in language that Parain saw in it, his position is scarcely more enviable at the beginning. For in short, since he wants nothing of silence—because silence is a word, an empty word, and perhaps a trap—all that he has with which to make himself heard are words that he abhors. What is he to do? Ponge first adopts the negative solution offered to him by the Surrealists of destroying words with words. 'Let us make words ridiculous through catastrophe,' he writes, 'the simple abuse of words.'[9] He has in mind a radical devaluation; this is a scorched earth policy. But what can it produce? Is it true we shall construct a silence in this way? This is doubtless speaking 'so as to say nothing'. But is it, ultimately, words we are destroying? Aren't we simply continuing the movement begun by the 'obnoxious mouths' we detest? Aren't we hounding the proper meanings out of words, only to find ourselves later with all names rendered equivalent, forced, amid the disaster, to go on speaking nonetheless? And indeed Francis Ponge didn't press on with this experiment. His particular genius led him elsewhere. The point for him was, rather, to wrest words from those who misuse them and to attempt to develop a new trust in words. As early as 1919 he glimpses a solution, which might be said to be based on the imperfection of the Word:

> Divine necessity of imperfection, divine presence, in written texts, of the imperfect, of defects[10] and of death, bring me your help too! May the *impropriety* of terms make possible a new induction of the human among signs that are already too detached from it, and too dry, pretentious and swaggering. May all abstractions be consumed from within and, as it were, melted by this secret heat of vice, caused by time, death and the flaws of genius.[11]

His objection to words is that they adhere too closely to their most commonplace signification, that they are both exact and impoverished. But, looking more closely, he distinguishes turgidities, accidental detachments and adventitious meanings in them—an entire secret, useless dimension produced by their history and the blunderings of those who have used them. Aren't there the elements, in this neglected depth, of a rejuvenation of terms? It isn't so much a question of emphasizing their etymological sense to refresh them, as Valéry does, or discovering a subjective side to them by which to appropriate them the more surely: we should, rather, see them with the eyes that Rimbaud turned on the 'absurd pictures',[12] grasp them at the very moment when man's creations warp and buckle and escape him by the secret chemistries of their significations. In short, we should catch at them and seize them at the point when they are becoming *things*. Or, rather, since the most human and most constantly handled of words is always, from a certain angle, a thing, we should strive to grasp all words—with their meanings—in their strange materiality, with the signifying humus, dregs or residue that fill them. To this very day he remains obsessed with the materiality of the word:

> Oh human traces, at arm's length, Oh original sounds, monuments of art's infancy . . . mysterious objects and characters preceptible by two senses only . . . I want to have you loved for yourselves rather than for your meaning. To raise you at last to a nobler condition than that of mere designations.[13]

He wrote these words in 1919. And, in *Le parti pris des choses*, his most recent work, returning to this assimilation of words to a shell secreted by human beings, he delights in imagining these shells emptied, after the disappearance of our species, in the hands of other species that would view them as we view the shells on the seashore.

> Oh Louvre of the written word, which may perhaps after the demise of this race be inhabited by other proprietors—monkeys, for instance, or birds, or some superior being— just as the crustacean takes the place of the mollusc in the periwinkle shell.[14]

Escaping, in this way, man who produced it, the word becomes an absolute. And Ponge's ideal is for his works, built out of word-things that will survive his age and perhaps his species, to become things in their turn. Should we see this merely as the consequence of a resolutely materialist attitude? I don't believe so. But it seems to me that I find in Ponge a desire shared by many writers and painters of his generation: that their creation should be a *thing*, solely and precisely inasmuch as it was their creation.

This effort to shift the meaning of terms remained pure revolt still, so long as the half-petrified significations discovered beneath the superficial crust of common sense were not directed towards objects specific to them. This was still a pure effort of negation. Did Ponge understand that a genuine revolutionary had to be constructive? Did he understand that, if it too was not used to *designate* things, the 'semantic density' of words was in danger of remaining up in the air? He wanted to 'offer everyone the opening of inner trap-doors, a journey into the density of (words) . . . a subversion comparable to that effected by plough or spade, when suddenly and for the first time millions of particles of earth, seeds, roots, worms and little insects are turned up that have previously been buried.'[15]

But—and this is perhaps the most important turning-point of his thought—Ponge realized that one couldn't go on for long burrowing into words *without any purchase on things*; he turned away from the great Surrealist prattling which, in many cases, consisted merely in banging objectless words against one another. He could renew the meaning of words and fully appropriate their deep resources only by employing them to name *other things*. So, if it is to be complete, the revolution of language has to be accompanied by a re-routing of attention: discourse has to be wrested from its commonplace usage, our gazes turned towards new objects, and we have to render 'the infinite resources of the density of things . . . with the infinite resources of the semantic density of words.'[16]

What, then, will these new objects be? The title of Ponge's collection tells us. Things exist. We have to come to terms with this; we have to come round to their terms. We shall, then, abandon all-too-human discourse and set about speaking of things, of taking their side.[17] Of things: that is to say, of the inhuman. However, the term inhuman has two meanings. If I thumb through Ponge's book, I see he has written about pebbles and moss, which I clearly recognize as things, but also of the cigarette, a very human requisite, and of the young mother, who is a woman—and the gymnast, who is a man—and of the Restaurant Lemeunier, which is a social institution. If, however, I read the passages relating to these latter objects, I see that the gymnast,

> Rosier than nature, less agile than an ape, . . . lunges at the apparatus, driven by sheer zeal. Then with the top of his body held fast in the knotted rope, he interrogates the air like a worm half out of its mound.
>
> For a finish, he sometimes plummets from the rigging like a caterpillar, only to bounce back on his feet . . .[18]

The thing I immediately note is Ponge's effort to eliminate the privileged status accorded to the *head*, the human being's most human organ. For the rest of us, it is the soul of a person, or a little image of the soul perched atop the collar, and a separate entity. But Ponge restores it to the body; he no longer calls it head or face or countenance—these words are too fraught with human meaning, loaded as they are with smiles, tears or knittings of the brow—but 'the top of his body'. And if he compares the gymnast's body to a worm, he does so in order to eliminate the differentiation of the organs, by forcing upon us the image of the smoothest, least differentiated of creatures, so that the head becomes a mere questioning movement on top of an annelid. However, the trick of this description lies, mainly, in Ponge showing us the gymnast as the representative of an animal species. He describes him the way Buffon did the horse or the giraffe. What has been acquired by effort, he presents to us as a congenital property of the species. 'Less agile than an ape', he says—and these words are enough to transform this acquired skill into a kind of innate gift. In the end, he breaks down the artist's 'performance' into a series of behaviour patterns fixed by heredity, succeeding each other in a monotonous, meaningless order.

And now let us take the 'young mother':

Her face, often bent over her chest, grows slightly longer.

Her eyes, attentively peering down at a nearby object, occasionally look up, faintly distracted. Their gaze is filled with confidence, but seeking continuation. Her arms and hands bend together in a crescent, mutually sustaining. Her legs, grown thin and weakened, are gladly seated, knees drawn up

high. The distended belly, livid, still very
tender; the abdomen readjusts to rest, to
nights under covers.

. . . But soon up and about, the tall body
moves in cramped fashion . . .[19]

In this case, the organs are separated out from
each other and lead a slow-motion life, each in their
turn. The human unity has vanished and we have
before us not so much a woman as a polypary. And
then, in the last lines, everything is gathered together.
And the result is not a person, but a great, blind body.

Here, then, we have a mother and a trapeze artist
turned to stone. They are *things*. All it took to achieve
this result was to look at them without that human bias
that freights human faces and actions with signs. There
has been a refusal to stick the traditional labels of 'high'
and 'low' on their backs, to presume that they have consciousness, to regard them, in short, as witch dolls. In
a word, they have been seen through the eyes of behaviourists. And, with that, they are suddenly part of
Nature once more; the gymnast, somewhere between
ape and squirrel, becomes a *natural* product; the young
mother is a higher mammal who has given birth.

We have now understood that any kind of object will appear as a thing as soon as we have taken care to divest it of the all too human significations initially bestowed upon it. The project may actually seem an ambitious one: how am I, who am a man, to catch sight of a Nature without human beings? I once knew a little girl who would stamp noisily out of her garden and then tiptoe back in 'to see what it looked like when she wasn't there'. But Ponge isn't so naive as that: he is fully aware that his plan of getting down to the bare thing is merely an ideal.

> It is to the mimosa itself (sweet illusion!) that we now must come; if you like, to the mimosa without me . . .[20]

He writes elsewhere that he would like, 'to describe things from their own point of view, but this is, as end-point or perfection, impossible. There is always *some* relation to human beings . . . It is not things that speak among themselves, but human beings who speak among themselves about things, and it is not in any way possible to step outside the human.'[21]

We shall have to limit ourselves, then, to better and better approximations. And what we are entitled to do immediately is to divest things of their *practical* significations. Speaking of the pebble, Ponge writes:

> Compared to the finest gravel, one can say that given the place where it is found, and because man is not in the habit of putting it to practical use, the pebble is rock still in the wild, or at any rate not domesticated.

> For the few remaining days it still lacks meaning in any practical order of the world, let us profit from its virtues.[22]

What in fact are these 'practical' meanings but the reflection on to things of that social order Ponge detests? Gravel refers us on to the grass of the lawn, the lawn to the villa, and the villa to the town and here we have, once again, 'All these crude lorries that move *within us*, these factories, workshops, theatres and public monuments that make up *much more* than the backdrop to our lives.'[23]

There is, then, first in Ponge a rejection of collusion. He finds *within himself* words that are soiled and 'ready-made' and *outside himself* objects that are domesticated and abased. He will attempt in one and the same movement to de-humanize words by seeking out their 'semantic density' beneath their surface meaning and to de-humanize things by scratching away their veneer of utilitarian meanings. This means that one has to come at the thing when one has eliminated within oneself what Bataille calls the *project*. And this attempt depends on a philosophical assumption which I shall confine myself, for the moment, to revealing: in the Heideggerian world, the existent is, first, *Zeug* or item of equipment. To see it as *das Ding*, the temporo-spatial *thing*, the proper course is to 'neutralize' oneself. One stops, forms the project of suspending any project, and then remains in the attitude of *'nur verweilen bei'* (merely tarrying with). It is at this point that the thing emerges, being, all in all, merely a secondary aspect of the item of equipment—an aspect grounded in the last resort in equipmentality [*das Zeughafte*]—and Nature appears as a collection of inert things. Ponge's movement is the opposite: it is the thing that exists first for him in its inhuman solitude; man is the thing that transforms things into instruments. One merely has, then, to muzzle this social, practical voice inside oneself for the thing to disclose itself in its eternal, instantaneous truth. Ponge reveals himself here an anti-pragmatist, because he rejects the idea that, by his action, man confers its meaning upon the real in an *a priori* fashion. His primal intuition is of a *given* universe. He writes,

> I must first confess to an absolutely charming, longstanding, characteristic temptation that my mind finds irresistible:
>
> It is to assign to the world, to the set of things I see or imagine seeing not—as most philosophers do and *as is, no doubt, reasonable*[24]—the shape of a large sphere, a big, soft, nebulous and, as it were, misty pearl or, conversely a limpid, crystalline one, in which the centre would, as one of them once said, be everywhere and the circumference nowhere . . . but rather, arbitrarily and by turns, the shape of the most peculiar, most asymmetrical, reputedly contingent things— and not just the shape, but all the characteristics . . . such as, for example, a lilac branch or a prawn.[25]

If he loves each flower and animal enough to give its shape and being to the universe by turns, then at least the existence of that universe is in no doubt for him; he at least considers it 'reasonable' to conceive it in the terms that dogmatic realism has lent it for twenty centuries. And in this solid universe, whether it be lilac, prawn or sphere of mist, man finds himself a thing among other things. In this almost naive conception, let us find, then, the affirmation of scientific materialism: that the object is preeminent over the subject. Being pre-exists knowing; Ponge's initial postulate is the same as the initial postulate of science. Like many artists and writers of his generation, Ponge began with methodical doubt; but he refused to challenge science. Perhaps this omission will come back to haunt him later.

But for the moment we have discovered our object. It is, in the end, the universe, with man in it. 'I would like to write a kind of *De rerum natura*. You can see the difference from contemporary poets: it isn't *poems* I would like to write, but one single cosmogony.'

Why does this cosmogony present itself today in discontinuous fragments? This is because you have to build up an alphabet:

> The wealth of propositions contained in the slightest object is so great that I cannot yet conceive of anything but the simplest: a

stone, a blade of grass, fire, a piece of wood,
a piece of meat.[26]

So, for the moment, it isn't so much a question
of writing a Cosmogony as of producing a kind of
Compendium of Characteristics by the designation
of elementary entities that can be combined to reproduce more complicated existents. There is, then, in
Ponge's eyes, an absolute simplicity and an absolute
complication; the idea doesn't cross his mind that
everything is perfectly simple or infinitely complicated
depending on the standpoint one adopts. A man lighting a cigarette is a perfectly simple thing, provided,
however, that I regard this man with his cigarette as a
single, signifying totality—that is to say, provided that
I register the emergence of a *Gestalt*. But if I am wilfully blind to this synthetic form, then here I am with
so much meat, bones and nerves on my hands, and
amongst all this butcher's meat, I shall have to choose
relatively simple 'pieces' susceptible of description.
This is what Ponge does. But my question to him is:
why does he grant the unity that he denies to the
smoker to his femur or his biceps? We shall come
back to this point later.

So here we are, then, in the countryside. The countryside has insinuated itself even into the city centre. A cabbage in a garden, a pebble on the strand, a lorry on the square, a cigarette in the ashtray or stuck in a mouth—these are all the same, because we have stripped out the *project*. Things are there, waiting for us. And what we notice first is that they call out for expression: 'the mute insistence [things] make that we speak them, as they deserve and for themselves—outside of their usual meaning-value—without choice and yet in measured tones. But what a measure: their own.'[27]

We have to take this passage literally. This isn't a poet's formula for characterizing the calls that the most obscure, most deeply buried of our memories make to us. It is a direct intuition of Ponge's, as untheoretical as possible. He comes back to it insistently in *Le Parti pris des choses*, particularly in the admirable pages he devotes to vegetation.

> [T]rees . . . let fly with their words, a flood of them, an eruption of green. They try to achieve a complete leafing out of words . . . They fling out words at random, or so they believe, fling out twigs on which to hang still

more words . . . Believing they can say everything, blanket the whole world with a full
range of words, they say only 'trees' . . . Ever
the same leaf, ever the same way of unfolding, the same limits, forever identical leaves
hung identically! . . . Ultimately, nothing
could ever stop them but this sudden observation: 'There's no getting away from trees
by way of trees.'[28]

He explains this further on in the following
terms:

They are nothing but a will to express. Holding nothing back for themselves, they cannot
keep one idea secret, they lay themselves
completely open, candidly, without reserva-
tion . . . [A]ll drive to express themselves is
unavailing, except toward developing their
bodies, as though for us each desire required
us thereafter to nourish and sustain an additional limb. An infernal increase of substance prompted by every idea![29]

I don't believe anyone has ever gone further in
grasping the being of things. Materialism and idealism
aren't the issue here. We are a very long way from
theories; we are at the heart of things themselves; and

we see them suddenly like thoughts fleshed out by their own objects. As though this idea that had set out to become the idea of a chair suddenly solidified from one end to the other and *became* chair. If we look at Nature *from the standpoint of the Idea*, we cannot escape this obsession with the absence of distinction between the possible and the real, which we find to a lesser degree in dreams and which is characteristic of Being-in-itself. The assertion is, in fact, always an assertion *of* something; in other words, the act of asserting is distinct from the thing asserted. But if we suppose the existence of an assertion in which what is asserted fills up the asserter and merges with him, then this assertion can no longer be asserted, for reasons of excessive plenitude and the immediate inherence of the container in the content. In this way, the entity is opaque to itself precisely because it is filled with itself. If it wishes to take a reflexive view of itself, then that view—leaf or branch—itself grows dense: it is a *thing*. This is the aspect of Nature we apprehend when we view it in silence: it is a petrified language. Hence the duty Ponge feels towards it: to make it manifest. For it is just this that is at issue: making something manifest. But Ponge's efforts differ profoundly from Gidean 'manifestation'. In 'making manifest', Gide is aiming to stitch Nature back together, to tighten its weft and at last make it exist on the plane of aesthetic perfection, so as to verify Wilde's paradoxical statement that 'nature imitates art.' Gidean 'manifestation' stands in the same relation to its object as the geometrical circle does to the 'rings' found in Nature. Ponge merely wants to lend his language to all these bogged-down, clogged-up words emerging all around him from earth, air and water. How can he do this? First he must go back to that naive attitude dear to all philosophical radicalisms—to Descartes, Bergson and Husserl: 'Let me pretend that I know nothing.'

> I look over the current state of the sciences: whole libraries on every part of each one of them . . . Should I begin, then, by reading and learning them? Several lifetimes would not suffice. Amid the enormous extent and quantity of knowledge acquired by each science, we are lost. The best option, then, is to regard everything as unknown and to stroll or recline in the woods or on the grass and start everything over again from the beginning.[30]

In this way Ponge is unwittingly applying the axiom at the origin of all Phenomenology: 'To the things themselves.'[31] His method will be love, a love that involves neither desire, fervour nor passion, but is total approval and total respect, 'extreme diligence in not troubling the object', such a perfect and detailed adaptation 'that your words forever treat everyone as this object treats them by the place it occupies, by what it resembles and by its qualities . . .' In short, it isn't so much about observing the pebble as settling into its heart and seeing the world with its eyes, the way the novelist, to depict his protagonists, slips into their minds and describes people and things as they appear to those protagonists. This stance enables us to see why Ponge calls his work a cosmogony rather than a cosmology. Because it isn't a matter of *describing*. You will find very little in him of those brilliant snapshots by which a Virginia Woolf or a Colette exactly render the *appearance* of an object. He speaks of the cigarette without saying a word about the white paper that surrounds it, of the butterfly almost without mentioning the designs mottling its wings: he isn't concerned with *qualities* but with *being*. And the being of each thing seems to him a project, an effort at expression, at a *certain* expression of a certain nuance of dryness, stupour, generosity or stillness. To get inside this effort, beyond the phenomenal aspect of the thing, is to have reached into its being. Hence the following discourse on method:

> The entire secret of the contemplator's happiness lies in his refusal to regard the invasion of his personality by things *as an evil.* To avoid this veering off into mysticism, one must 1) be precisely, that is to say expressly, aware of each of the things one has made the object of one's contemplation; 2) change objects of contemplation quite often and, overall, retain a degree of moderation. But the most important thing for the contemplator's health is the *naming,* as he goes along, of all the qualities he discovers; the qualities that 'carry him away' must not carry him further than their exact, measured expression.[32]

This brings us back, then, to naming, which is where we started. It now appears as the practice of a Hellenic virtue of moderation. And yet let us be clear: in Ponge's eyes, if man names, he doesn't do so merely to fix as a notion something that is always in danger of degenerating into *ekstasis,* but because, ultimately, everything begins and ends for him with words; in naming, he fulfils his duties as a man: 'The Word is God; there is only the Word; I am the Word.'[33]

Consequently, the bestowing of names assumes the status of a religious ceremony. First, because it corresponds to the moment of renewal; through this renewal, man, diluted into the thing, withdraws, gathers himself and reassumes his human function. Second—and foremost—because the thing, as we have seen, awaits being named with all the ardour of its aborted expressiveness. As a result, naming is a metaphysical act of absolute value; it is the solid, definitive union of man and thing, because the *raison d'être* of the thing is to require a name and the function of man is to speak in order to give it one. This is why Ponge can write of the 'modification of things by the word':[34]

> Into a . . . wave, into a shapeless ensemble that fills up its content, or at least espouses its form to a certain degree—through waiting or through an accommodation, a kind of attention that is of this same nature—may enter that which will effect its modification: the word.

For the things of the spirit, the word might be said then to be their state of rigour, their way of holding steady outside of their containers. Once this has been made understood, one will have the time to study their specifiable qualities calmly, minutely and diligently, and the pleasure of doing so.

The most remarkable thing, striking one immediately, is a kind of growth, a sort of increase in volume of the ice in relation to the wave, and the breaking, by the ice itself, of the container, a previously indispensable form.[35]

This means that, by the very act that gives the thing its name, the idea becomes thing and makes its entry into the field of objective spirit. Equally, it isn't just a question of naming but of *making a poem*. By this, Ponge means a work of a quite particular sort that strictly excludes lyricism: after the fumblings and approximations that yielded the nouns and adjectives to him that will match the thing, these have to be gathered into a synthetic totality and this has to be done in such a way that the very organization of the Word in this totality exactly renders the emergence of the thing into the world and its inner articulation. It is precisely this which he terms a poem. Doubtless it isn't entirely the thing itself, as we have seen, and it preserves something of the relationship with man: 'Otherwise, each poem would please each and every individual, would please all of them all the time, as the objects of the sensations themselves please us and strike us.' But 'at least, by a kneading, a primordial disrespect of words etc., one will have to give the impression of a new idiom that will produce the effect of surprise and novelty of the objects of sensation themselves.'

And this poem, precisely because of the profound unity of the words in it, because of its synthetic structure and the agglutination of all its parts, will not be a mere copy of the thing but the thing itself.

> The poet must never offer a thought but an object. That is to say that he must even make thought assume the stance of an object.

> The poem is an object of delight offered to man, made and put in place especially for him.[36]

We meet up here once again with that trend common to the literature and painting of the twentieth century, which sees a painting, for example, not so much as an—albeit free—translation of nature, but as a nature in and of itself. But we must understand this clearly. It is the form itself, in its opacity, that is a thing here. The content remains the deep movement of the thing named. However this may be, when the poem is finished, the unity of the world is restored. In a sense, everything is actually expression, since things tend of themselves towards the Word, in the same way as Aristotelian Nature tends towards God; everything is expression, self-expression or an attempt at expression; and naming, which is the most human of acts, is also man's communion with the universe. But, in another sense, everything is *a thing*, since poetic naming has itself turned into stone. In Ponge's world, it is as though a subtle materialization seized meanings themselves from behind; or, rather, as though things and thoughts congealed. Thus the universe, which is for a moment pierced by thought, closes up and encloses thingly thought within itself, together with the things that have been thought. All is full: the Word has embodied itself and 'there is only Word.'[37]

That moment of *ek-stasis* in which he installs himself, outside of himself, in the heart of the thing

Ponge terms 'contemplation' and we have seen that love, as he defines it, is itself rather Platonic, since it is not accompanied by true possession. Yet we should not imagine that this intuition falls foul of the criticism normally made of strictly contemplative attitudes. This is because it is of a very particular kind. First, I shall happily term it 'active contemplation', for, far from suspending all dealings with the object, it presupposes, on the contrary, that one will adapt to it by a range of efforts whose only limitation is that they mustn't be utilitarian. Ponge tells us, for example, that, in order to bring out the singular qualities of the washing boiler:

> It isn't sufficient to have sat on a chair and contemplated it on many an occasion.
>
> Complainingly, you have to have lifted it, filled with its load of filthy fabrics, to put it on the fire, to which you have, in a way, to drag it, and then you have to set it down just on the edging of the fireplace.
>
> You have to have stirred the wood into flames beneath it to get it going gradually; to have tested often the temperature of its—

tepid or boiling—sides; then to have listened
to the deep inner rustling and lifted the cover
several times to check it is operating freely
and evenly.

And you have, finally, to have put your
arms around its boiling form once again, to
set it back on the ground.

Perhaps by then you will have discovered it.[38]

It goes without saying that when Ponge executes
these various forms of hard labour, doubtless to help
his wife or some female relative, he strips them—to
the great detriment of the washing, perhaps—of all
practical significance. He sees in them merely an op-
portunity to form a closer contact with the boiler, to
appreciate its weight, to gauge its circumference with
his arms, to warm himself through with its heat. With
other objects, his dealings will be even more disinter-
ested. He opens doors for the pleasure of opening
them: '. . . The joy of grabbing one of those tall barriers to a room by the porcelain knob in its middle;[39]
he scalps their moss from 'the old austere rocks'. And
there is, admittedly, no one who hasn't opened a door,

dragged a boiler on to the range, scraped away a layer of moss or plunged their arm into the sea. The essential question is to know what you put into these things.

But, above all, Ponge hasn't let go for a moment of his revolutionary bias. His contemplation is active because it dashes from things the social order that is reflected in them. It stands opposed to any vain escapism: 'Against any desire for escape set contemplation and its resources. No use leaving: transfer oneself to things.'[40] Inasmuch as it is de-humanizing, his intuition contributes to closing the material world over our heads, leaving us lost, like things, within it; it is little short of pantheistic. Let us call it a pantheism brought to a timely halt. We see, then, that his intuition operates as much *against* as *with*. However, its ultimate goal is the substitution of a true human order for the social order it dismantles. The bias towards things [*parti pris des choses*] leads to the object-lesson. The fact is that 'millions of feelings, as different from the little catalogue of those currently experienced by the most sensitive of people, are still to be known and experienced.' And it is amid things that we discover them. The aim, then, is to lay hold of them and bring them about in ourselves:

For my part, I'd like to say that I am something very different and, for example, apart from all the qualities I share with the rat, the lion and the net, I aspire to that of the diamond and I feel total solidarity . . . with both the sea and the cliff that it attacks and also with the pebble thereby created . . . without prejudice to all the qualities that I expect to become aware of and gain effective enjoyment from subsequently, through the contemplation and naming of extremely different objects.[41]

This may perhaps be thought to display a naive animism, incompatible with the materialism Ponge was just professing: but it is, in fact, the opposite. When Ponge wishes to benefit from sentiments he sees as being enclosed in the heart of objects—and wishes others to benefit from them—he isn't, in any sense, regarding things as little silent people, but rather seeing people deliberately as things. He doubtless attributes 'ways-of-behaving' to inanimate objects. But this is precisely because he remains entirely behaviouristic and doesn't believe our 'behaviours' to be, *a priori*, of a different nature from theirs. In every thing there is a material effort, a striving and a project that makes up its unity and permanence. But we are constituted no differently. In his view, our unity is the unity of our muscles, tendons and nerves and that physiological striving that keeps the whole together until we die. Far from there being a humanization of the pebble here, there is a de-humanization of man, reaching even as far as his feelings. And if my very feelings are things, are particular orders that impose themselves on my innards, can we not speak of the feelings of stones? If I can fuel my anger, can I not maintain in myself, at least as an affective pattern, a certain type of sober, lofty dessication that will, for example, be the mark of the pebble. It isn't yet time to attempt to determine whether Ponge is right or wrong and how he may be right—perhaps in spite of himself. We are merely setting out his doctrine. The fact remains that this attempt to conquer virgin territories for our sensibilities seems to him a highly moral task. In achieving it, he will thus not merely have done the work of a painter, but genuinely fulfilled his mission as a man, since, as he has it, the proper notion of man is 'the word and morality: humanism.'

So what has he done? And has he succeeded? The moment has at last come to examine his works. And since he himself regards them as objects, let us examine them *as things*, which is how he himself sees cigarettes or snails, teasing out their meaning and internal articulation with no regard for the stated intentions of their author. We shall see then whether their 'way-of-behaving' corresponds in every particular to the theories we have just outlined.

II

Ponge's poems present themselves as chamfered constructions, each facet of which is a paragraph. Through each facet, we see the total object. But from a different point of view each time. The organic unit is, therefore, the paragraph: it is sufficient unto itself. Seldom is any transition effected between paragraphs. They are separated by a certain density of void. We don't move from one facet to the next, but one has to rotate the entire construct to bring a new facet before our eyes. Neither Ponge nor the reader benefits from any acquired impetus; there is, each time, a new beginning. Thus, the inner structure of the poem is, manifestly, juxtaposition. It isn't possible, however, for memory to prevent itself from conserving the past paragraphs and bringing them to bear upon those I am currently reading. This is also because, through this mosaic, a single idea is developing. Often, as with *Le Mimosa*, the poem takes the form of a series of approximations and each approximation is a paragraph. *Le Mimosa* presents the aspect of a theme followed by variations: all motifs are indicated first—or almost all; and each paragraph presents itself as a fresh combination of these motifs with the introduction of very few new elements. Each of these variations is then rejected as imperfect, as transcended or buried by a new combination that starts again from scratch. Yet it remains there, if only as the image of what has already been done and is no longer to be done. And the final 'poem' will merge all these trial runs into a 'definitive version'. In this way, each paragraph is present, in spite of everything, to the next paragraph. But not in the style of that 'multiplicity of interpenetration' that Bergson speaks of,[42] nor like the elapsed notes of a melody that are still audible in the next note, colouring it and lending it its meaning: the past paragraph *haunts* the present one and seeks to merge into it. But it cannot: the other repels it with all its density.

The organic unit being the paragraph, each sentence takes on a differentiated function within that totality. We can no longer speak here of juxtaposition: there is movement, transition, ascent, re-descent, slippage, vection, beginning and end. I read the first lines of 'Sea Shores': the initial sentence is an unconditioned assertion. The second, beginning with a 'but', corrects it. The third, opening with a 'This . . . is why' draws the conclusion from the first two, and the fourth, beginning with 'For' brings ultimate justification to the whole. Here, then, is movement and a highly developed division of labour—the very image of life; we are no longer dealing with a polypary, but with an evolved organism. Yet a kind of rather complex unease gives me pause. This bustling, teeming life has something suspicious about it. I open Pascal's *Pensées* at random:

> Let man then contemplate the whole of nature in its full and lofty majesty, let him avert his view from the lowly objects around him. Let him behold that brilliant light set like an eternal lamp to illuminate the universe, let the earth seem to him like a point in comparison with the vast orbit described by that

star and let him be amazed that this vast orbit is itself but a very small point in comparison with the one described by the stars rolling around the firmament. But if our gaze stops here, let our imagination pass beyond; it will sooner tire of conceiving things than nature of producing them. This whole visible world is only an imperceptible trace in the ample bosom of nature. No idea approaches it. However much we may inflate our conceptions etc. . . .[43]

See how, in Pascal, the full stop represents a sigh, not a pause. It has been put between the first two sentences for considerations of breathing and visual pleasure rather than meaning, since, in both the first and the second sentence, we find similar exhortations separated by mere commas. The result is a flow that runs from one sentence to the next and a deep unity beneath these superficial divisions; and the second sentence benefits so greatly from the impetus imparted by the first that it doesn't even trouble to name its subject: it is the same 'man' who inhabits both. After this strong opening, the third sentence can catch its breath and vary slightly the mode of presentation of the same exhortation; the beginning was so violent that this sentence is playing on velvet; the mind puts it together, in spite of itself, with the two preceding ones. There is a move here now from exhortation to statement. But see what wariness there is: it is within the third sentence, after the frail barrier of a semi-colon, that this transition occurs. With the result that this central sentence is the pivot of the paragraph: in it the initial movement dies; in it this stirring of calm, concentric waves begins that will carry us to the end. Here is a genuine melodic unity. Melodic to the point of setting our teeth on edge somewhat.

By contrasting it with this, we can understand the structure of Ponge's paragraphs better: his sentences clearly beckon to each other, essay transitions, attempt to build bridges. But each is so dense, so definitive and its internal cohesion is such that, as we saw just now with his paragraphs, there are gaps and emptiness between them. The entire life of the poem lies between two full stops; and the full stops here assume their maximum value: that of a tiny annihilation of the world, which takes shape again a few moments later. Hence the disconcerting savour of the object:

the sentences are constructed as a function of one an-other. With hooks and 'eyes'; they are hook-shaped and should be able to catch, but an imperceptible dis-tance means the hooks fall off without grasping on to anything. The unity of the paragraph is set before us, but it is a semantic unity, too immaterial, too much a thing of intelligibility to be tasted. It is a ghostly unity, present everywhere, but nowhere tangible. And the 'Fors', the 'Buts' and the 'Howevers' take on an am-biguous, rather solemn dimension as a result, because they were made for connecting and for effecting tran-sitions, and suddenly they are elevated to the dignity of first beginnings. At which they are as surprised as anyone (I might say if I wanted to ape Ponge's style).

There are, admittedly, many possible explanations for this aspect of *Le Parti pris des choses*. Ponge has warned us himself that he worked in a discontinuous fashion. He has a job that takes all his attention for ten hours a day. He writes in the evening and only for short periods. Each evening everything has to be begun again, without any existing momentum or springboard. Each evening he has to get back into the presence of things—and of paper. Each evening he has to discover a new facet and write a new paragraph.

But he forewarns us himself against this excessively
material explanation:

> Moreover, even if I had the time, it doesn't
> seem to me that I'd have the inclination to
> work at length, and several times, on the
> same subject. What counts for me is to seize
> almost every evening on a new object and
> derive pleasure and instruction from it.[44]

There is something like a bias towards the discontinuous here that amounts to an original choice. We
ought perhaps to show—it wouldn't be difficult but
would take us too far from our purpose—why the
'lovers of souls', like Barrès, are on the side of continuity and the 'lovers of things' prefer the discrete, as
Renard and Ponge do. The important thing here for
us is to define the effect—whether consciously obtained or not—of these discontinuities. It represents
perhaps the most immediate attractions of Ponge's
works—and one that is most difficult to explain. It
seems to me that, in their relationship with each other,
his sentences are like those solid bodies you see in the
paintings of Braque and Juan Gris; between them the
eye has to establish a hundred different unities, a thousand relations and correspondences, to make them

eventually into a *single* picture; these objects are, however, ringed with lines so thick and dark and are so
deeply centred on themselves, that the eye bounces
perpetually from the continuous to the discontinuous,
attempting to fuse together different splashes of the
same violet and running up, at every turn, against the
impenetrability of the mandolin and the water jug. But
in Ponge's work this flitting about seems to me to have
a very particular meaning: it constitutes the poem itself in its intuitive form as a perpetually evanescent
synthesis of living unity and inorganic dispersion. Let
us not forget that the poem is a *thing* here and that, as
a thing, it claims a certain type of existence which the
ordering of sentences and paragraphs necessarily
confers upon it. Now, it seems to me this type of
existence could be defined as that of an enchanted
statue; we are dealing with marble figures haunted by
life. These paragraphs perpetually visited by the memory of other paragraphs that are incapable of articu-
lating themselves with them; these sentences which,
in their inorganic solitude, are abuzz with calls to
other sentences they cannot join—doesn't all this
resemble an abortive effort on the part of stone to
achieve organized existence? We find here an intuitive

image, provided by the style and the writing, of the way Ponge wants us to envisage 'things'. We shall have to come back to this point.

Ponge's sentences, suspended as they are like this in the void by a subtle breakdown of the links between them, are enormously affirmative. The author's own taste is the first reason for this: he wants to leave 'proverbs' behind him. By proverbs, I mean sentences already petrified and laden with meaning, whose power of assertion is such that a whole society takes them as its own. We therefore understand this severe economy of words that he wants to achieve everywhere—that the conjunction 'and' has been practically eliminated from his work, for example, or appears in it only as a ceremonial exordium—and that subordinate clauses, weighted with this omnipresent affirmation, sometimes stand up on their own, without any main clause, between two full stops, looking rather like preliminary provisions in a legal decree:

> But since each caterpillar head was left blinded and blackened, each torso emaciated by the veritable explosion which sent flaring up symmetrical wings,

> The erratic butterfly alights simply at the
> whim of its haphazard flight, or so it seems.[45]

But it is the primary function of the act of assertion, with all its pomp, to imitate the categorical bursting-forth of the thing. Let us not forget that it isn't Ponge's aim to describe the undulation of appearances, but the internal substance of the object at the precise point where that substance determines itself. His sentence consequently reproduces this generative movement. It is, first and foremost, genetic and synthetic. Ponge's problem connects here with Renard's: how is one to get the greatest possible number of ideas into a single sentence? But whereas Renard was pursuing the impossible ideal of silence, Ponge aims to reproduce the thing at a single stroke. The words have to crystallize as the eye moves over them and the sentence has, at the end, to have reproduced the emergence of something. But, since this emergence has the stubbornness of things, not the flexibility of life, since it isn't so much a birth as a kind of fixed apparition, then instead of being propagated softly from sentence to sentence like a wave, the generative movement has to dash against the buffer of the full stop and stop dead in its tracks. Hence the frequent sentence

structure of a rapid, liquid world of appositions at the
beginning, followed suddenly by a halt in the form of
a short, pithy main clause: the thing 'has congealed'
and is suddenly bounded. Here, for example, is the
butterfly: 'Miniature sailboat of the skies, ill-treated
by the winds as a petal superfluity, footloose it goes
breezing about the garden.'[46]

Ponge's sentence is, in itself, a world articulated
in minute detail, where the place of every word is cal-
culated, where it is the function of enjambments and
inversions to present the facts in their true order, but
also to figure as a distant memory of symbolism and
the syntactic inventions of Mallarmé. Sometimes, in
this world in fusion, there are sudden solidifications,
the formation of lumps—mostly of adverbs—and
then entire members of sentences bulking large as
sticky masses and manifesting a kind of independence. This is because Ponge feels compelled hurriedly
to describe, within his sentences themselves, the elements that make up the 'thing' being studied and their
genesis. And so there are things within the thing and
geneses within the genesis. This is the rain:

> Moulding to *the entire surface of a small tin roof*
> *that's visible below*

it trickles in a thin skim moiréd *in eddies*
from the imperceptible bumps and ripples of the
    metal sheet.
In the adjoining gutter
it sluices along *with all the application of a shallow*
    rivulet gently pitched
then plunges abruptly
an absolutely vertical strand rather loosely tressed
straight to the ground where it shatters
and dashes up *in glittering bead-tipped needles.*[47]

There remain the words, whose 'semantic density' has to convey the richness of things. This is, in fact, the least striking aspect. We undoubtedly find a happy levity towards language in Ponge's work, a certain way of manhandling it, of making puns, of inventing, where need be, words like 'gloriolous' or 'floribund', but in him this is more like a smile of deliverance. 'As an ex-martyr of language, you'll grant me the right not to take it seriously every day.'[48] And doubtless too he lingers more than anyone else over the correspondences between words and the things to which they refer: '. . . what makes my work so difficult is that the name of the mimosa is already perfect. Knowing both the plant and the name of the mimosa, it becomes difficult to find a better word to define the thing than the name itself.'[49]

But what counts, above all, is a sensual affection for names, a way of squeezing them to make them yield up all their meaning. Take, for example, 'it goes breezing about the garden,' which has its full impact only if we juxtapose the idea of wandering over un-defined areas contained in the word 'breezing' with the confined, carefully polished, perfect quality in the word 'garden'. In this regard, Ponge should be read attentively, word by word; and re-read. There is pro-fundity in his choice of words and it is this profundity that dictates the cascading rhythm in which they should be read. But seldom are they chosen with that concerted impropriety he initially had in mind. And, though we must first register that his desire to pro-duce thing-poems has been almost entirely fulfilled, we should also acknowledge that he failed in his attempt to give, 'the impression—by a kneading of words and a primordial disrespect for them—of a new idiom that will produce the effect of surprise and novelty made by the sensory objects themselves.'

It is time to move on now to examine content. But not without having noted that these sentences that are so sturdy and could easily veer towards solemnity are lightened and, as it were, hollowed out by a kind of innocent playfulness that gets everywhere. Eventually Ponge himself steps from the shadows and speaks about himself. Not as the character he normally affects to be, whom I imagine to be more sombre, but as a kind of ironic, gossipy, naive entomologist, reminiscent of one of Fabre's charming caricatures. This is because he conceives his poems in a happy state, when he is at his best. They are no doubt, as we have seen, revolutionary acts. But in the act itself he finds his deliverance and his pleasure:

> One ought to be able to give this title to all poems: Reasons to live happily. At least where I am concerned, those that I write are each like the note I try to take when a moment of meditation or contemplation lights the fuse within my body of a few words that give it new vigour and persuade it to live a few more days.[50]

* * *

As we have seen, Ponge doesn't observe or describe. He neither seeks after nor captures the qualities of the object. Nor do things seem to him, as they do to Kant, a pole X, something on which to hang sensory qualities. Things have *meanings*. Everything must be subordinated to grasping and establishing these meanings, these 'reasons in the raw or natural state when they have just been discovered amid the unique circumstances that surround them at that same second'.[51] Reasons, meanings, ways-of-behaving: it is all the same. Yet it needs a special kind of lighting to see them. This is why the angle of approach varies from object to object. The mimosa is seen from the front, at the point when its yellow balls, its 'gloriolous chicks' 'cheep with gold', whilst its palms are already giving out signs of discouragement. With the shrimp, by contrast, we are going to try to catch it at the moment when 'a translucence as effective as the creature's darting motions ultimately removes, even when seen immobile, all semblance of continuity from its presence.'[52] The books teach that the butterfly is born from the caterpillar. Yet it isn't at the point of its metamorphosis that we shall look for it, but in the garden, when it seems suddenly to arise in droves, newborn from the earth: this is its true genesis. The pebble, on the other hand, demands to be understood on the basis of the rocks and the sea that give birth to it: we shall come to it after a long preamble on stones.

Concerned to allow every thing its real dimensions—rather than the dimensions it assumes in our eyes, which depends on our measurement—we shall see the sea shell on the beach as an object 'out of all proportion' or as an 'enormous monument'.[53] And it will seem to us then that we are viewing some Dalí painting in which a giant oyster, capable of gobbling up three men at a single go, is lying on an infinitely monotonous stretch of white sand.

In appearance, then, we are exemplarily docile, and it is our aim merely to grasp the dialectic of the object and submit ourselves to it. And, with each reality that comes before us, we shall try to 'leav[e] it to enter on its own the coils of circumlocution . . . and ultimately to grasp through words at the dialectic point dictated by its form and environment, its mute condition, and the pursuit of its own true profession.'[54]

Yet is this how Ponge really proceeds? Does the impression that his poems leave us match his declared method? Didn't he come to things with preconceived ideas? We must examine this closely.

I note first that a large part of the charming mystery surrounding Ponge's productions derives from the fact that there is constant mention of man's relationships with the thing in question, but these are stripped of all human meaning. Let us take the oyster:

> It is a world categorically closed in upon itself. And yet it can be opened: that takes gripping it in a folded rag, plying a nicked and dull-edged knife, chipping away at it over and over. Probing fingers get cut on it, nails get broken. It's a rough job.[55]

This is a universe peopled by human beings and yet bereft of them. Which is the more oyster, the oyster itself or that strange, stubborn indeterminate being, who seems to come straight from a Kafka novel, torturing it with a 'nicked' knife, without our being able to guess the reasons for such zeal, given that we haven't been told that the oyster is edible? And now this being itself—half-divinity and half-violent outburst that it is—disappears and gives way to these probing fingers that are not unlike those of the rapping hands in Fra Angelico's frescoes. A strange world, in which man is present through his undertakings, but absent as spirit or project. A closed world, that one can neither enter nor leave, but which calls most specifically for a human witness: for the writer of *Le Parti pris des choses* and its reader. The inhumanity of things throws me back on myself; in this way, consciousness, extricating itself from the object, finds itself in the Hegelian dialectic. Yet consciousness, in Ponge's view, is itself a thing.

Where does the unity of the object derive from? This is Ponge's pebble:

> . . . smaller day by day but ever certain of its form, blind, secure, and dry within, by nature it would sooner be reduced by the seas than blended in. So when stone, vanquished, is turned at last to sand, water still can't penetrate as it does with dust.[56]

I see Ponge as affirming here—*against science*—the unity of the stone that offers itself as such to his perception. But when he extends this unity as far as the scattered fragments of the pebble, as far as that pebble dust, I would argue that he is relying neither on science nor on sensory intuition, but solely on his human capacity for unification. For perception certainly provides him with the unity of the pebble, but not the unity of pebble and sand. And science definitely teaches him that sand comes, largely, from broken pebbles; but it adds that—Nature being exteriority—there never was any unity in stones, but simply a collection of molecules obeying various different types of motion. Judgement and decision are needed to carry over on to these metamorphoses, which geology reconstitutes, the unity that perception vouchsafes to us. Yet man is absent; the object precedes—and crushes—the subject. The unity of the pebble comes from the pebble itself and imparts itself to its tiniest particles—to that stone in smithereens—by way of an inner force that corresponds to its original project and must probably be termed *magical*. The cigarette, the orange, bread, fire and meat can all be seen in this same light. All these entities have a cohesion that is carefully distinct from life, which nonetheless accompanies them through all their various transformations. This is a curious frozen spontaneity, bearing some similarity with the intentness on its part that maintains the circle as a circle, when, from another standpoint, it breaks down

439

perpetually into an infinity of juxtaposed points: these objects are bewitched.

Let us get closer to them. I can no longer distinguish now between the gymnast—that *man* Ponge was describing a moment ago—and the crate or cigarette he is describing now. The fact is that he downgrades the one while elevating the status of the others. We have seen that he reduced the *acts* of this athlete to being the mere *properties* of a species. But, conversely, he endows inanimate things with specific properties. Of the gymnast, he says: 'To top it off, he sometimes plummets from the rigging like a caterpillar, only to bounce back on his feet.'[57] And of the cigarette: '. . . the atmosphere, hazy yet dry, wispy, with the cigarette always placed right in the thick of it, once engaged in its continuous creation'.[58] Or of water: '. . . water endlessly ravels in upon itself, constantly refuses to assume any form, tends only to self-humiliation, prostrating itself, all but a corpse.'[59] This isn't about the states into which an external cause (for example, gravity) has put the thing, but about the shared habits of a species, and this assumes that each object is to some degree independent of its environment and attributes a specific internal necessity to it. The outcome is that this 'Cosmogony' takes on the features of a natural history. In the end, human beings, animals, plants and minerals are all put on an equal footing. It isn't that all entities have been raised—or lowered— to the pure form of life, but the same close cohesion has been bestowed upon each by—to use Hegelian language—projecting interiority on to exteriority. What gives the things in Ponge's lapidary their ambiguous originality is the very fact that they are not *animate*. They retain their inertia, their fragmentation, their 'stupefaction', that perpetual tendency to collapse that Leibniz called their stupidity. Ponge does more than merely maintain these qualities; he proclaims them. But they are gathered together and linked up by 'properties' or even feelings that metamorphose as they touch them and, imparting to them a little of their inner tension, both are petrified and disintegrate at one and the same time. Look at the stone, it is alive. Look at life, it is stone. Anthropomorphic comparisons abound, but at the same time as they cast—a relatively dubious—light on things, their effect is mainly to abase the human, to 'tangle it up', as our author has it. Let's take another look at water:

> Water is colourless and glistening, formless
> and cool, passive and determined in its single
> vice: gravity. With exceptional means at its
> disposal to gratify the vice: circumvention,
> perforation, infiltration, erosion.[60]

Isn't this like a description of a family of plants?
But Ponge goes on:

> The vice plays an inner role as well: water
> endlessly ravels in upon itself, constantly
> refuses to assume any form, tends only to
> self-humiliation, prostrating itself, all but a
> corpse.[61]

This inner collapse brings us back abruptly to the
inorganic. The unity of water vanishes almost entirely.
We hesitate to go down a path that would lead us to
one of those fantastical limp, boneless characters of
folk tale, who are always ready to fall flat and whom
one lifts by an ear, but who immediately throw themselves flat on their faces again; or to take that other
path that shows us all the particles of water coming
unstuck, its very essence being pulverized, affirming
against any attempt at unification the omnipotence of
inertia and passivity. And just as we are at the crossroads, in that state of indecision the Ponge reader

never escapes, the poet suddenly adds: 'You might almost say that water is insane.'[62] Who cannot see that in this passage it isn't water having a new character attributed to it, but madness which undergoes a secret metamorphosis, which *transforms into water* because it has touched its surface, which becomes, both within and outside man, an inorganic behaviour? I contend the same of all the passions Ponge bestows upon his things. They are so many meanings that he takes from man, so many techniques to maintain this subtle state of disequilibrium he wants to put us into.

What are the relations between the object thus described and its environment? They cannot be relations of pure exteriority. Very often, what belongs to the external world and settles on the object for a moment is incorporated into the object by Ponge and made one of its properties: it is the pebble that 'dissipates' the sea water that flows over it, not the sun; gravity is a 'vice' of water, not an external demand upon it. This, we may say, is what happens with observation: I see a gas-filled balloon rising and I speak of its 'uplift' or I say, with Aristotle, that its natural place is on high. What could be more natural for Ponge, since he has decided to show things as he sees them?

Indeed he has. And this would be perfect if he refrained, as he promised to do, from any recourse to science. But we see that, by a deliberate new ambiguity, Ponge has made this universe of pure observation *also* and *at the same time* a universe of science. It is his scientific knowledge that constantly lights his way and guides him, enabling him to question his object the more precisely. Leaves are 'taken aback by slow oxidation',[63] plants 'exhale carbon dioxide by the chlorophyll function, like a sigh lasting night after night.'[64] In writing of the pebble, Ponge describes the birth and cooling of the earth, doing so magnificently in fact. His images are, at times, merely metaphors intended to give more agreeable expression to a scientific law. He writes, for example, that the sun 'forces water into a perpetual cycle, treating it like a caged squirrel on its wheel'.[65] The magical universe of observation enables us to glimpse—from beneath—the world of science and its determinism:

> To the mind casting about for ideas which has first been nourished on images such as these, nature in respect to stone will ultimately seem, too simplistically perhaps, like a clock whose mechanism is made up of

cogwheels revolving at very different rates,
though driven by a single motor.[66]

And this mechanistic vision is so strong in him that it
causes in his book a kind of disappearance of liquid-
ity. Water is defined by its collapse, rain is compared
to a 'rather loosely tressed . . . strand', to peas, marbles
and needles; it is explained by a 'mechanism . . . like
clockwork'.[67] The sea is, at times, a 'pseudo-organic
accumulation of veils strewn evenly across three quar-
ters of the globe' and, at times, a 'voluminous marine
tome' riffled and turned down at the corners by the
wind.[68] These transmutations of elements are, admittedly, the province of poet and painter; it was such
effects that Proust admired in Elstir.[69] But Elstir also
transmuted the earth into water. Here we feel that
things have a *solid* base. 'LIQUID is what seeks to
obey gravity rather than maintain its form, forgoes all
form to obey its gravity.'[70] We notice, then, that liq-
uidity is a function of matter—and that *there is*,
ultimately, a matter. It is this perpetual flitting from
interiority to exteriority that gives Ponge's poems their
originality and power; it is these little collapses within
a single object that reveal *states* beneath its *properties*,
and then it is the sudden recoveries that all at once

unify states into *behaviours* and even feelings; it is this disposition of mind he awakens in the reader, this sense of never feeling at rest anywhere, of doubting whether matter isn't animated and if the soul's stirrings aren't quakings of matter; it is these perpetual exchanges that make him show man as the little bit of meat around a few bones and, conversely, meat as a 'sort of factory . . . Tubing, blast furnaces, vats, traffic with trip hammers, grease tubs',[71] this way of unifying the mechanical systems of science with the formulas of magic and, suddenly, of showing the universal determinism beneath the magic. But in the end the solid predominates. The solid and science, which has the last word.

Ponge has, in this way, written some admirable poems that are entirely original in tone, and created a material nature all his own. We can ask no more of him. We must add that his project is, by the ideas behind it, one of the most curious and perhaps one of the most important of our day. But if we want to bring out its importance, we have to prevail upon its author to throw over certain contradictions that mask and mar it.

First, he hasn't been faithful to his original intention: he came to things not, as he claimed, with naive wonderment, but with a materialist bias. In fact, with Ponge it isn't so much a question of having a preconceived philosophical system as of having made an original choice of his selfhood. For his work is aimed as much at expressing this as at rendering the objects on which he is focussing. That choice is quite difficult to define. Rimbaud said:

> If I have any taste, it is hardly for anything but earth and stones.[72]

And he dreamed of enormous massacres that would deliver the earth of its populations, fauna and flora. Ponge isn't so bloodthirsty. He is a 'vanilla' Rimbaud. And *Le Parti pris des choses* might well be called 'geology without massacres'. He even seems, on the face of it, to love flowers, animals and even people. And no doubt he does so. A great deal. But on condition that they are first petrified. He has a passion, a vice, for the inanimate, material *thing*. For the solid. Everything is solid in his work: from his sentences to the deepest foundations of his universe. If he ascribes human behaviour to mineral objects, it is in order to mineralize human beings. If he borrows ways of being from things, it is in order to mineralize himself. Perhaps we are justified in glimpsing a great necrological dream behind his revolutionary undertaking: the dream of enwrapping everything living—and man in particular—in the the shroud of matter. Everything that comes from his hands is a *thing*, including, most especially, his poems. And his ultimate desire is that this whole civilization, together with his books, should one day appear as an immense necropolis of sea-shells to some higher ape, itself a thing, that will leaf abstractedly through these remnants of our glory. He has a premonition of this ape's gaze; he can already sense it upon himself: beneath these petrifying eyes, he feels his humours solidifying, he is turning into a statue; it is all over, he is one with the rock and the pebble, the stupefaction of stone paralyses his arms and legs. It is for this inoffensive, radical catastrophe that his writings aim to prepare. For this disaster that he needs the services of science and a materialist philosophy. And I see this first as a way of eliminating at a stroke all the sources of his suffering—the abuse, the injustice, the rotten disorder of the society into which he has been cast. But, even more than this, it seems he has opted for a quick path to symbolically fulfilling our shared desire *to exist after the manner of the 'in-itself'*. What fascinates him in the thing is its mode of existence, its total adherence to self, its stillness. Anxious flight, anger and anguish are banished in the insensible imperturbability of the pebble. I have observed elsewhere that the desire of all of us is to exist *with complete consciousness* in the mode of being of things: to be entirely a consciousness and, at the same time, entirely a stone. Materialism provides a theoretical satisfaction of this dream since it tells human beings they are merely mechanisms. I thus have the dismal pleasure of *feeling* myself think and *knowing* myself to be a material system. Ponge, it seems to me, isn't content with this pure theoretical knowledge; he it is who has made the most radical effort to have this purely theoretical knowledge descend into intuition. If he were to be able to unite the two, he would in fact have done the trick. And this flitting between interiority and exteriority which I mentioned a moment ago has a precise function: for want of a *real* fusion between consciousness and thing, Ponge has us oscillate between the two at very great velocity, hoping to achieve fusion at the upper limit of the oscillation.

But this isn't possible. He can have us flit between the two as quickly as he likes, but it is always *he* who is sending us from the one extreme to the other. He may close the world over himself with all that is in it, but he still ends up on the outside, staring in at things, all alone. We have already encountered this effort to see oneself through the eyes of an alien species, to rest from the painful duty of being a subject; we have seen it a hundred times, in different forms, in Bataille, Blanchot and the Surrealists. It represents the meaning of modern fantastic literature and also that of the highly individual materialism of our author.[73] On each occasion it has come to nothing. This is because the person making the effort, by the very fact of making it, becomes lost to himself and projects himself to a point beyond where his strivings were located. Like Hegel, not being able, whatever he does, to get inside Hegelianism. Ponge's endeavour is doomed to failure like all others of the same kind.

And yet it has had an unexpected outcome. Ponge has locked up everything in the world, including himself insofar as he is a thing; all that remains is his contemplative consciousness which, precisely because it is consciousness *of* the world, finds itself necessarily *outside of* the world: a naked, almost impersonal consciousness. What has he done but effect the 'phenomenological reduction'? And doesn't this consist, in fact, in 'bracketing out' the world in order to rid oneself of all preconceived ideas? The world is no longer either representation or transcendent reality then. Neither matter nor spirit. It is simply there—and I am conscious of it. What an excellent starting point, if Ponge were to accept it, for approaching 'things themselves' without the slightest prejudice! Science would be in the world, but bracketed out. Ponge would only have to say truly what he saw—and we know how powerfully he sees. Nothing would be lost—except perhaps this bias towards treating human beings as stuffed dummies. For they would have to be accepted with their human meanings, instead of setting out from a theoretical materialism forcibly to reduce them to the status of automatons. This slight change would be no bad thing, since Ponge's *only* bad writings—and they are very bad—are 'R. C. Seine No.' and 'Le restaurant Lemeunier', which are about human communities.[74] The *meaning* of things and their 'ways-of-behaving' would shine out all the more brightly, for, in the end, in Ponge's strange materialism, if everything may be said to be matter, on the other hand, everything is thought, since everything is expression. We have to continue to agree with him that things can teach us ways of being: I want him to be a lion, a pebble, a rat, a sea, and I want to be one with him. I shall refuse to believe, just as he does, that it is our psychological experience that enables physical matter to be shaped symbolically. But shall I conclude, as he does, that the object precedes the subject here? That isn't necessary. I have written elsewhere, if I may be permitted to quote myself:

> The slimy does not symbolize any psychic attitude *a priori*; it manifests a certain relation of being with itself and this relation has originally a psychic quality because I have discovered it in a plan of appropriation and because the sliminess has returned my image to me. Thus I am enriched from my first contact with the slimy, by an ontological pattern that is valid, beyond the distinction between psychic and non-psychic, for interpreting the ontological meaning of all the existents of a certain category, this category arising, moreover, like an empty skeletal

framework *before* the experience with different kinds of sliminess. I have projected it
into the world by my original project when
faced with the slimy; it is an objective structure of the world . . . What we say concern-
ing the slimy is valid for all the objects which
surround the child. The simple revelation of
their matter extends his horizon to the extreme limits of being and thereby bestows
upon him a collection of *clues* for deciphering the being of all human facts.[75]

Given this, I don't, however, think that 'by transferring
ourselves to things', as Ponge wants us to do, we find
in them previously unknown ways of feeling, nor that
we have then to borrow these from things in order to
enrich ourselves with them. What we find everywhere—in the inkwell, on the phonograph needle or
on the honey on a sandwich—is ourselves, always ourselves. And this range of indistinct, obscure feelings
that we bring into being are something we had already—or, rather, we *were* those feelings. Only they
couldn't be seen, they were hidden in the bushes, between stones, almost uselessly. For man isn't rolled up
inside himself, but is outside, always outside, between

earth and sky. The pebble has an interior, man does not: but he does lose himself so that the pebble may exist. And all these 'rotten' human beings Ponge wants to get away from or be rid of are also 'rats, lions, nets and diamonds'. They are so, precisely because they 'are-in-the-world'. Only they don't notice that they are. It is something that has to be revealed to them. The point, then, in my opinion, isn't so much to acquire new feelings as to plumb the human condition more deeply.

What seems really important to me is that, at the point when Gaston Bachelard is attempting, through psychoanalysis, to identify the meanings our 'material imagination' lends to air, water, fire and earth, Ponge, for his part, is attempting to reconstruct them synthetically. There is in this encounter something like a promise to take the inventory as far as possible. And the only evidence I need that Ponge has succeeded fully wherever he has tried his hand at this are the multiple resonances evoked within me by his most successful passages. I shall cite at random the following lines on the snail:

> Snails . . . are fond of humid earth. Go on, they advance at full length, adhering to it all the way. They lug some along, they eat some,

excrete some. They traverse it. It traverses them. This is interpenetration in the best of taste, tone on tone you might say—with one passive element, one active, the passive nourishing as it bathes the active . . .[76]

These lines put me in mind irresistibly of a fine, grim passage from Malraux describing a dead woman at Toledo:

Ten yards below a woman lay on the slope, one arm extended and the other clasping her head; he could clearly see the crisp, dark curls. She might have been asleep (but her head was pointing towards the bottom of the valley), were not the body under the flimsy dress flatter than any living woman's, and welded to the soil by the peculiar earthward impulse of the dead.[77]

Beyond the dead woman and the snail here, I sense a sort of relationship with the earth, a certain sense of fusion, of flattening, a relation of everything to death, to a mineralization of corpses. Everything is there in Ponge, superimposed.

Admittedly, you have to be careful not to *put* into the thing what you will subsequently claim to have *found* in it. Ponge hasn't always avoided this error. It is for this reason that I am less fond of his Washing Boiler. In that poem, he writes:

> Admittedly, I will not go so far as to claim that the example or lesson of the washing boiler should genuinely galvanize my reader—but I would no doubt feel a little contempt for him if he didn't take it seriously.[78]

In short, this is that lesson:

> The washing boiler is designed in such a way that, when filled with a pile of filthy fabrics, the inner emotion and boiling indignation it feels at them, channelled toward the upper part of its being, falls back down as rain on this pile of filthy fabrics that sickens it—quasi-perpetually—and this leads to a purification.[79]

I fear I may be one of those contemptible readers who don't take the lesson at all seriously. How can we but see that what we have here is purely and simply a metaphor? Do we need a washing boiler to give body to this schema of purification that is present in everyone's mind and whose origins go back much further and are much more deeply rooted in us? And then the comparison is inexact, even from the standpoint of simple observation: it isn't the presence of dirty linen that heats up the water in the boiler. Without the heat from the hearth, that water would remain inert and would gradually grow dirty without effectively washing the clothes. And Ponge ought to know this better than anyone, since he was the one who put the boiler on the fire.

But there are so many other passages in which Ponge reveals to us both the behaviour of things and, at the same time, our own behaviour, that his art seems to us, as is usually the case, to go further than his thought. For Ponge the thinker is a materialist[80] and Ponge the poet—if we leave aside the regrettable intrusions of science—has laid the foundations of a Phenomenology of Nature.

December 1944

Notes

1   Francis Ponge, 'Le Mimosa', in *La rage de l'expression* (Paris: Gallimard, 1976), p. 80.

2   Ibid., pp. 76–7.

3   Francis Ponge, 'Notes for a Sea Shell', in *The Nature of Things* (Lee Fahnestock trans.) (New York: Red Dust, 2000), p. 48. I have generally opted to use this translation, which, though its title is somewhat at variance with Ponge's, captures the tone of the collection well. [Trans.]

4   Francis Ponge, 'Des raisons d'écrire', in *Le Parti pris des choses, précédé de douze petits écrits et suivi de* Proêmes (Paris: Gallimard/nrf, 1972), pp. 162–3.

5   Ponge, *The Nature of Things*, pp. 47–8 (spelling anglicized).

6   Ponge, 'Des raisons d'écrire', in *Le Parti pris des choses*, p. 163.

7   Francis Ponge, 'Les Écuries d'Augias', in ibid., pp. 155–6.

8   Francis Ponge, 'A chat perché', in ibid., p. 159.

9   Francis Ponge, 'Justification nihiliste de l'art', in ibid., p. 124.

10 Sartre's published text has 'vide' here rather than the 'vice' of Ponge's text. I have reverted to Ponge's original, on the assumption that Sartre's version is merely a misprint or mistranscription. [Trans.]

11 Francis Ponge, 'La Promenade dans nos serres', in ibid., pp. 127–8.

12 Arthur Rimbaud, *A Season in Hell* (Oliver Bernard trans.) (London: Penguin, 1995), p. 33.

13 Ponge, 'La Promenade dans nos serres', in *Le Parti pris des choses*, p. 128.

14 Ponge, 'Notes for a Sea Shell', in *The Nature of Things*, p. 48.

15 Francis Ponge, 'Introduction au galet', in *Le Parti pris des choses*, p. 176.

16 Ibid.

17 The undifferentiated triple meaning of Ponge's title—*le Parti pris des choses*—shows us how Ponge intends to draw on the semantic density of words. That title implies '*prendre le parti des choses*' [taking the side of things] against human beings; *prendre son parti de* [coming to terms with] their existence (against the idealism that reduces the world to representations); and making an aesthetic *parti pris* [bias or prejudice] of them.

18 Francis Ponge, 'The Gymnast', in *The Nature of Things*, p. 39 (translation modified).

19 Francis Ponge, 'The Young Mother', in ibid., p. 40 (translation modified).

20 Ponge, 'Le Mimosa', in *La rage de l'expression*, p. 77.

21 Francis Ponge, 'Raisons de vivre heureux', in *Le Parti pris des choses*, p. 167.

22 Francis Ponge, 'The Pebble', in *The Nature of Things,* p. 65.

23 Ponge, 'Des raisons d'écrire', in *Le Parti pris des choses*, p. 162.

24 My emphasis. [J.-P. S.]

25 Francis Ponge, 'La forme du monde', in ibid., p. 115.

26 Ponge, 'Introduction au galet', in ibid., p. 175.

27 Francis Ponge, 'Les façons du regard', in ibid., p. 120.

28 Francis Ponge, 'The Cycle of Seasons', in *The Nature of Things*, p. 25.

29 Francis Ponge, 'Fauna and Flora', in ibid., pp. 51–3.

30 Ponge, 'Introduction au galet', in *Le parti pris des choses*, p. 177.

31 '*Aux choses mêmes*', '*An die Sache selbst*'.

32 Ibid., p. 175–6.

33 This is at variance with the most recent editions of Ponge, which have: 'The Word is God; I am the Word; there is only the Word.' See Francis

Ponge, 'La dérive du sage', in *Le Parti pris des choses*, p. 139. [Trans.]

34 Francis Ponge, 'De la modification des choses par la parole', in ibid., p. 122.

35 Ibid., pp. 122–3.

36 Francis Ponge, 'Natare piscem doces', in ibid., p. 130.

37 *'Il n'y a que du Verbe.'* This is presumably an allusion to the phrase *'Il n'y a que le Verbe'* (there is only the Word) cited above. [Trans.]

38 Francis Ponge, 'La lessiveuse', in *Pièces* (Paris: Gallimard, 1962), p. 73.

39 Francis Ponge, 'The Pleasures of a Door', in *The Nature of Things*, p. 23. 'Knob' here translates Ponge's *'noeud'*, which means 'knot' and hence suggests 'navel'. [Trans.]

40 Ponge, 'Introduction au galet', in *Le Parti Pris des Choses*, p. 174.

41 Ibid.

42 Henri Bergson, *Time and Free Will* (authorized translation from the French of *Essai sur les données immédiates de la conscience* by F. L. Pogson) (New York: Harper and Brothers, 1960), p. 75.

43 Blaise Pascal, *Pensées* (Roger Ariew ed. and trans.)

(Indianapolis: Hackett Publishing Company, 2005), p. 58 (translation modified). For obvious reasons, I have restored Pascal's original French punctuation, but I have also reinserted Pascal's reference to the 'ample bosom' (*l'ample sein*) of nature, which Ariew renders merely as 'amplitude'. [Trans.] Francis Ponge, 'Préface aux Sapates', in *Le Parti Pris des Choses*, p. 111.

44 Ibid., p. 111.

45 Francis Ponge, 'The Butterfly', in *The Nature of Things*, p. 32.

46 Ibid.

47 Francis Ponge, 'Rain', in ibid., p. 13. I have italicized the phrases that stand in isolation. Note the mimetic nature of the sentence that actually ends at 'shatters' and bounces up again weakly like rain.

48 Ponge, 'Le mimosa', in *La rage de l'expression*, p. 80.

49 Ibid., p. 78.

50 Ponge, 'Raisons de vivre heureux', in *Le Parti pris des choses*, p. 166.

51 Ibid. Ponge's 1948 text of this poem has 'reason' in the singular. Sartre may be referring to an earlier version (Ponge dates the original poem '1928–29'). [Trans.]

52 Francis Ponge, 'The Shrimp', in *The Nature of Things*, pp. 56–7.

53 Ponge, 'Notes for a Sea Shell', in ibid., p. 46.

54 Ponge, 'The Shrimp', in ibid., p. 56.

55 Francis Ponge, 'The Oyster', in ibid., p. 22.

56 Ponge, 'The Pebble', in ibid., p. 67.

57 Ponge, 'The Gymnast', in ibid., p. 39.

58 Francis Ponge, 'The Cigarette', in ibid., p. 20.

59 Francis Ponge, 'Water', in ibid., p. 37.

60 Ibid.

61 Ibid.

62 Ibid.

63 Francis Ponge, 'Trees coming undone within a sphere of fog', in ibid., p. 23.

64 Francis Ponge, 'Faune et flore', in *Le Parti pris des choses*, p. 85. In *The Nature of Things*, Fahnestock is working here from a different edition of the text. [Trans.]

65 Ponge, 'Water', in *The Nature of Things*, p. 38.

66 Ponge, 'The Pebble', in ibid., p. 64.

67 Ponge, 'Rain', in ibid., p. 13.

68 Francis Ponge, 'Sea Shores', in ibid., pp. 36, 33.

69 Elstir is a fictional impressionist painter in Proust's *A la recherche du temps perdu*. [Trans.]

70 Ponge, 'Water', in ibid., p. 37.

71 Francis Ponge, 'The Cut of Meat', in ibid., p. 39.

72 Rimbaud, *A Season in Hell*, p. 41.

73 It is one of the consequences of the Death of God. So long as God lived, man was at ease: he knew he was being looked at. Today, when man is the only God and it is beneath his gaze that everything flourishes, he twists his neck round to try to see himself.

74 Ponge, *The Nature of Things*, pp. 41–5.

75 Jean-Paul Sartre, *Being and Nothingness* (Hazel E. Barnes trans.) (London: Methuen and Co Ltd, 1976), pp. 611–12, translation modified (Barnes renders '*le sens d'être de tous les existants d'une certaine catégorie*' as 'the meaning *of being and of* all the existents of a certain category' [p. 611, my emphasis], which clearly cannot be correct). [Trans.]

76 Francis Ponge, 'Snails', in *The Nature of Things*, p. 27. (I have ignored the misprint in Sartre's original French transcription of this poem [Trans.]).

77 André Malraux, *Days of Hope* (Stuart Gilbert and Alastair MacDonald trans.) (Harmondsworth: Penguin, 1970), pp. 122–3.

78 Francis Ponge, 'La lessiveuse', in *Pièces*, p. 75.

79 Ibid.

80 But a genuine materialist will never write *Le Parti pris des choses*, since he will have recourse to Science and Science calls, *a priori*, for radical exteriority or, in other words, for the dissolution of all individuality. Now, what Ponge needs to petrify are, precisely, the countless significant individualities he finds around him. In short, he wants the world, as it is, to be eternalized.

Man Bound Hand and Foot:
Notes on Jules Renard's Journal

He created the literature of silence. We know how it has prospered since. We have had the theatre of silence and also those enormous bonfires of words that were the Surrealists' poems: the curtain of words went up in flames; behind this veil of fire we were allowed to glimpse a great mute presence: Spirit. Today Blanchot strives to construct peculiar precision machines (that we might call 'silencers', after the devices that make pistols deliver their bullets without a sound) in which the words are carefully chosen to cancel each other out and which resemble those complicated algebraic operations, the product of which has to equal zero. Exquisite forms of terrorism. But Jules Renard isn't a terrorist. He isn't aiming to conquer an unknown silence beyond words; his aim isn't to *invent* silence. He imagines he possesses silence from the outset. It is in him, it is *him*. It is a thing. All that is needed is to pin it down on paper, to copy it with words. This is a realism of silence.

He has generations of mutism behind him. His mother spoke in short peasant sentences, full but few and far between. His father was one of those village eccentrics, as was my paternal grandfather, who, having been disappointed by his marriage contract, never spoke three words to my grandmother in forty-five years—she called him 'my lodger'. He spent his childhood among peasants who, each in their different ways, proclaimed the uselessness of speech. 'When he gets home,' he writes, 'the peasant moves no more than the three-toed sloth or the tardigrade. He loves the darkness, not only out of thrift, but as a preference. His burning eyes can rest.'[1] Take the portrait of old Bulot. A new servant comes to the house:

'The first day, she asked, "What am I going to cook you for your tea, then?"

"Potato soup."

The next day she asked, "What am I going to cook you?"

"I told you: potato soup."

So she got the message and from that point on, every day, off her own bat, she made him his potato soup.'

There was something gnarled and solitary that made him like old Bulot: a real villager's misanthropy. As a country doctor or magistrate or village mayor, he would have adapted perfectly to his functions; perhaps he would have been happy. But this taciturn individual had a taste for writing; he came to Paris to *play* the eccentric, he sought out company to show his loneliness in it; his demanding silence was feared in the circles he frequented; he came to Paris to be silent in writing.

He wanted to shine by works which, amid the loquacious books of the time, were like he was among the salon gossips. Today, such a desire would have led him to seek out a formula for the self-destruction of language. That idea wasn't around in his age.

He thought that brevity in speech came closest to silence and that the most silent sentence was the one that achieved the greatest economy. He believed all his life that style was the art of being brief. And it is no doubt true that the most concise expression is usually the best, though, we must add: concise relative to the idea one is expressing. Thus, a number of the long sentences of Descartes or Proust are extremely short, because one couldn't express in fewer words what they are saying. But Renard wasn't content with this relative conciseness, which tests the sentence against its meaning. He wanted absolute concision: before he had the idea, he set the number of words that were to express it. The only problem to concern him was the one Janet calls the problem of the basket, which he formulates in the following terms: 'How to carry the most bricks in a single basket?' Renard claims he lost all taste for poetry because, he says, 'a line of poetry is still too long.' In novels, what interests him are 'sylistic curiosities'. And it is there they are to be found least, for, in a novel, style remains in the background. But Renard didn't like novels.

Renard's sentence is round and full, with the minimum of internal organization; it resembles those solid, rudimentary animals that have a single hole which serves them as mouth and meatus. There are none of those subordinate clauses that are like dorsal spines or arteries or, sometimes, nerve ganglions. Everything that isn't part of the main proposition seems suspicious in his eyes: it is chatter, useless restrictions, otiose adjunctions, reservations. His beef is really with syntax itself; to this peasant it resembles the refinement of an idler. It was the earthy, people's sentence, the single-cell sentence of old Bulot, he made his own. Words alone are assigned the mission of rendering the nuances and complexity of the idea. Rich words in a poor sentence. This was necessarily his goal: the word is closer to silence than the sentence. The ideal would be for the word itself to be a sentence. In that way, discourse and silence would be united in it, as time and eternity are united in the Kierkegaardian moment. But since we cannot have the word-sentence, let us put into the sentence the fewest, most meaningful words. Let them not restrict themselves to expressing the idea in its nakedness, but let them, by the play of their different meanings—etymological, demotic and scholarly—give us a glimpse of a harmonic 'beyond' of the idea.

What a fine role Malherbe could play at this time:

'Of a word put in its place [he could teach]
the power'[2]

And throw into the rubbish bin all the other
words that are limp as jellyfish.[3]

The sentence is, then, a super-saturated silence.
It never refers on to another: why say in two sentences
what could be expressed in one? We are getting to the
essential point here: the person who writes by paragraphs or books is, when he traces out a sentence on
paper, referred by that sentence to the whole of language. He doesn't dominate language, he is *making* it;
these words I write imply all those that came before
them and all those I will write afterwards and, moving
from one to the next, they imply all words; I need the
whole language to understand what is merely an incomplete moment of the language. In this case, silence
exists now only as a word within language and *I* situate
myself in language, in this to-ing and fro-ing of meanings, none of which is complete and each of which
requires all the others. But if, like Renard, I think in
brusque sentences that hem the total idea between
two boundary markers, each sentence, referring to no
other, is itself the *whole* language. And I who read it,

who write it, condense it with a viewpoint; before it and after it there is emptiness; I decipher it and understand it *from the standpoint of* silence. And the sentence itself, hanging in silence, becomes silence, in the same way as knowledge, when contemplated by Blanchot or Bataille, from the standpoint of non-knowledge—that is to say, of a 'beyond' of knowledge—becomes non-knowledge. For language isn't this loose-limbed sound that sputters for a moment at the height of silence, but a total undertaking on the part of humanity.

It happens, however, that Renard reverses the order of expression in a curious way: his initial aim being silence, it is *in order to remain silent* that he seeks out the right sentence, a momentary drop of silence, and it is *for the sentence* that he seeks out the right idea: 'How empty an idea is: if I didn't have the sentence, I'd go to bed.'[4]

This is because he believes naively that the idea is contained in *one* sentence that expresses it. The sentence, between the two full stops that are its outer limits, seems to him the natural body of the idea. It has never occurred to him that an idea may be embodied in a chapter or a volume, and that it may too—in the sense in which Brunschvicg speaks of the 'critical idea'—be inexpressible and simply represent a method of approach to certain problems or, in other words, a rule of discourse.

The idea, for Renard, is an assertive formula in which a certain number of experiences is condensed; similarly, the sentence—which, in so many other writers, is a joint, a passage, a slide, a twist, a hub, a bridge or a rampart within that microcosm that is the paragraph—is merely for him the condensation of certain quantities of ideas. Idea and sentence, body and soul present themselves to him in the form of a maxim or paradox. For example: 'I would so enjoy being good.' This is because he has no ideas. His deliberate, studied, artistic silence masks a natural, helpless silence: he has nothing to say. He thinks in order the better to be silent; this means that 'he speaks to say nothing.'

For, in the end, this preference for dumbness brings him back to chattering. You can chatter in five words just as you can in a hundred lines. You merely have to prefer sentences to ideas. For then the reader encounters the sentence and the idea remains hidden.

Renard's *Journal* is a laconic chatter; his entire opus a pointillisme—and there is a rhetoric of this pointillisme, just as there is of the great, thought-out sentence of Louis Guez de Balzac.[5]

The reader will perhaps be surprised to hear that Renard had nothing to say. It will be asked why certain ages and certain human beings have no message to deliver, when one has only to depict oneself to be original. But perhaps the question is poorly framed. Hearing it, we might have the impression that human nature is fixed, together with the inner eye observing it, and that eye merely has to adapt itself to our darkness to distinguish some new truths. In fact, the eye prefigures and sorts what it sees; and that eye isn't given from the outset. Its way of seeing has to be invented; it is thus one determines *a priori* and by free choice what one sees. The empty ages are the ones that choose to look at themselves with already invented eyes. They can do nothing but refine others' discoveries, for those who provide the eyes at the same time provide the things seen. Throughout the whole of the second half of the French nineteenth century, we saw ourselves with the eyes of the London empiricists, with the eyes of John Stuart Mill and the spectacles of Spencer. The writer has only one method: observation; and only one instrument: analysis. One could already detect a certain unease by the time Flaubert and the Goncourt brothers had had their day. In his journal of 27 August 1870, Goncourt notes:

> Zola comes to lunch with me. He talks to me about a series of novels he wants to write, an epic in ten volumes, the natural and social history of a family . . . He tells me: after the analysis of infinitely fine matters of sentiment, as attempted by Flaubert in *Madame Bovary*; after the analysis of artistic, plastic, sinewy things, as done by yourself; after these *jewel-works*, these finely-chiselled volumes, there is no place now for the young. There is nothing more to be done. No constituting or constructing of characters or figures. It is only by quantity of volumes, by creative power that one can speak to the public.

This meeting must have been quite richly comic. But let us take it, in the end, for what it is. It proves to us that, already in 1870, a young writer felt himself obliged to become a wholesaler because there was too much competition in the retail trade. Well and good. But *what then*? After the 10-volume epics? What remained to be done? It is at this moment that Renard appears. He is in the latter ranks of that great literary movement that runs from Flaubert to Maupassant via Zola and the Goncourt brothers. All the exits are closed, all the paths blocked. He enters on his career with a desperate sense that everything has been said and that he has arrived too late. He is obsessed with a desire to be original and by the fear that he cannot possibly manage it. For want of having chosen a new way of seeing, he looks everywhere in vain for new sights. For us, finding as we do that all paths are open to us, believing that everything is still to be said and dizzied at times by these empty spaces stretching out before us, nothing is more alien than the complaints of these men bound hand and foot, restricted to a piece of overworked ground and anxiously on the lookout for a patch of virgin earth. Yet this is Renard's situation: he is scornful of Zola and his obsession with documentary evidence, but he acknowledges nonetheless that the writer must seek out *the truth*. Now, that truth is precisely the exact description of the physical and psychological appearance, as it presents itself to a supposedly impartial observer. So, for Renard, as for the naturalists, reality is appearance, as organized, filtered and sorted by positivist science, and this famous 'realism' to which he adheres is a pure and simple rendering of the phenomenon as such. But in that case, what is there to write about? The analysis of the major psychological or social types no longer needs doing: what new things are there to say about *the* financier, *the* miner, *the* kept woman? Zola has already ploughed that furrow. The study of general sentiments has been exhausted. There remains the detail, the individual, the things that Renard's elders neglected, for the very reason that they had higher ambitions. On 17 January 1889, Renard writes: 'Put at the beginning of the book: I did not see types, but individuals. The scientist generalizes, the artist individualizes.'

This formula may seem to offer something like a forestaste of the famous pages in which Gide calls for monographs.[6] But I believe we should see it rather as a confession of impotence. Gide is attracted by what he sees that is positive in the study of the individual. But for Renard and his contemporaries, the individual is what has been left to them by their elders. The proof of this is the uncertainty they are in regarding the nature of these singular realities. Admittedly, in 1889 Renard is cross with Dubus[7] because he 'has theories about woman. Still? Are we not finished with having theories about woman?' But this doesn't prevent him, in 1894, advising his son as follows: 'Fantec, as an author, study just one woman, but go deeply into her and you will know woman.'[8]

So the old dream of arriving at the typical hasn't disappeared. Except that a roundabout route will be adopted: if you scratch long enough at the individual, it crumbles and fades and, beneath the peeling varnish, the universal appears.

On the other hand, Renard seems at other moments to despair of ever being able to generalize his observations. But this is because he came, almost unwittingly, under the influence of a pluralistic, antifinalistic, pessimistic conception of truth that emerged, at around the same time, out of the collapse of positivism and the difficulties the sciences were beginning to encounter, after a triumphal beginning, in certain fields. He writes, for example, 'Our elders saw the character, the continuous type . . . We see the discontinuous type, with its periods of calm and its crises, its moments of goodness and of wickedness."[9]

Truth disappeared with Science. Sciences and truths remain. We must admit that this pluralism is still very fragile in Renard, since at the same time he accepts determinism. True pluralism can only be based on a partial indeterminacy of the universe and on human freedom. But Renard didn't go so far into this. And neither did Anatole France, who in *La Vie littéraire* in 1891 (the passage from Renard quoted above is from 1892) wrote:

> . . . It has been said that there are brains that are impermeably partitioned. The subtlest fluid that fills one of the compartments does not soak through to the others at all. And when, in the presence of M. Théodule Ribot, an ardent rationalist expressed astonishment that brains of this kind existed, the master of experimental philosophy replied, with a gentle smile: 'Nothing is less surprising. Is it not, rather, a highly spiritualistic conception that wishes to establish unity in a human intelligence? Why will you not allow a man to be double, triple or quadruple?[10]

This is a page we may treasure for its stupidity, since it shows us that experimental pluralism was directed expressly against spiritualist rationalism. This whole pessimistic current of thinking was to lead to Metchnikoff's *Disharmonies in the Nature of Man*.[11] And it was indeed a study of the 'disharmonies in nature' that Renard wanted to undertake. In this way he will provide a theoretical justification for his exclusive taste for snapshots: 'In pieces,' he exclaims, 'in little pieces, tiny pieces.'

This brings us back by another route, to which he refers pretentiously as his nihilism, to our starting point: pointillisme and the sentence conceived as a work of art sufficient unto itself. If human nature is, first and foremost, disorder and disharmony, it is consequently no longer possible to write novels. Renard never tires of repeating that the novel has had its day, since it requires a continuous development. If man is merely a chopped-up series of moments, it would be better to produce short stories: 'Produce a volume with shorter and shorter tales and entitle it *The Rolling Mill*.'

In the end we shall be back to the simple sentence. Renard, they said, would end up writing, 'The

hen lays.' And so the circle is closed: in this instantaneous universe, where nothing is true and nothing is
real but the instant, the only form of art possible is
notation. The sentence, which can be read in an instant
and is separated from other sentences by a twofold
void, has as its content the instantaneous impression
that I catch 'on the fly'. Hence, the whole of Renard's
psychology will be made up of notations. He examines himself, analyses himself, catches himself out—
but always on the fly. Which is just too bad: he notes
down his momentary jealousies, his puerile or petty
desires, the jokes he makes to amuse the maid; with
little effort, he acquires a reputation for fierceness. But
why should we be surprised: this is what he chose to
see, what he chose to be in his own eyes. And that
choice was dictated by aesthetic considerations, not
by a moral resolve. For, in the end, he was also a
constant and more or less faithful husband, a good
father and a zealous writer. In other words, he existed
on the level Kierkegaard refers to as the level 'of repetition' and Heidegger the level 'of project' . . . These
vague outbursts of egotism count so very little for the
person whose life is an enterprise. And, in a sense,
everyone's life is an enterprise. 'Swinish' psychology

is merely a littérateur's invention. By having been resolutely blind to the *composed* aspect of his existence,
the continuity of his designs, Renard failed to grasp
himself accurately and has left us an unfair picture of
himself: our moods have importance only if we pay
special heed to them. And we should not consider
him or judge him by his moods, but as a man who
chose to pay attention to his moods.

Besides, the study of the passions and the stirrings
of the soul never concerned him much. From his peasant childhood he had retained a liking for animals and
for country things; he likes to speak of them, to describe them. But, here again, he was too late. The writers of the preceding generation—Flaubert, Zola and
Dickens—had undertaken an enormous inventory of
the real: it was a matter of conquering new regions for
art and rendering literary language sufficiently supple
to describe such lowly objects as a machine, a garden
or a kitchen. In this regard, Flaubert's *Sentimental Edu-
cation* figured as a manifesto. Everything had come into
the novel: it had made the public house its own with
L'Assommoir, the mines with *Germinal* and the great department stores with *Au Bonheur des Dames*.[12] It was a
picture painted with broad brush strokes; more than

this, it was a classification. The only task left for Renard's contemporaries was one of refining. It could have been the starting point for a form of new art. And indeed, by contrast with his predecessors, who had been concerned above all to put everything in its place, to count out the kitchen utensils, to enumerate the flowers in the garden, and who experienced a simple delight in naming tools by their technical names, Renard, when faced with the individual object, feels the need to grasp it deeply, to get inside the stuff of it. He is no longer concerned with counting the glasses on the bar and the various drinks that are served in the bar; he no longer considers each object in its relation to others within a detailed inventory; and he knows nothing, either, of the descriptions of 'atmosphere' that Barrès will make fashionable some years later: to him the glass he is looking at seems severed from its ties to the rest of the world. It is a thing alone and closed in on itself like a sentence. And Renard's sole ambition is that his sentence shall convey more closely, precisely and profoundly the inner nature of the glass. In the very first pages of his *Journal* we see him bent upon sharpening the instrument that will cut into the material, a thing that shows up in these brief notes: 'the strong smell of dry faggots' or 'the quivering of the water beneath the ice'. One can only sympathize with these clumsy efforts to make things bleed. They are at the origin of many more modern endeavours. But Renard is hampered by his very realism: to arrive at this visionary communion with things, one would have to free oneself from Tainean metaphysics.[13] The object would have to have a heart of darkness; it would have to be something other than a pure sensory appearance, a collection of sensations. The profundity Renard senses and seeks in the tiniest pebble, in a spider or a dragonfly, is denied to these things by his timid, positive philosophy. You have to invent the heart of things if you want to discover it one day. Audiberti[14] tells us something about milk when he speaks of its 'secret blackness'. But, for Renard, milk is hopelessly white, since it is merely what it seems. Hence the essential character of his images. Admittedly, they are, first and foremost, a way of abbreviating. When he writes, 'This man of genius is an eagle stupid as a goose', we see immediately the brevity these words eagle and goose achieve. The image is, for Renard, among other things, a foreshortening of thinking. And, as a result, this scholarly style, this 'calligraphy' as Arène[15] calls it, is akin to the mythical, proverbial speech of the peasant; each of his sentences is a little fable. But this isn't the main thing. In Renard's writing, the image is a timid attempt at reconstruction. And the reconstruction always miscarries. The aim is, in fact, to penetrate the real. But in terms of Tainean metaphysics, the real is, primarily, something that is observed. That was the wisdom of the age, a literary version of empiricism. And the poor man observes as much as he can: it is on the 17th of *January* that he speaks of the quivering of the water beneath the ice, on the 13th of *May* that he speaks of lilies of the valley. He wouldn't take it into his head to speak of flowers in winter or of ice in midsummer. Yet, everyone today knows that you cannot penetrate reality by passive observation of it: the best of poets is either distracted or fascinated; at any rate, he isn't an observer. Moreover, it matters little that Renard is nihilistic and pessimistic: he believes obediently in the world of science; he is even convinced that the scientific world and the world he observes are one and the same. The sounds striking his ear are, he knows, vibrations of the air; the colours that meet his eyes are vibrations of the ether. And so he will find *nothing*: his universe is suffocating in the philosophical and scientific brace he has imposed on it. Observation yields it up to him in its commonplace outlines; the universe he *sees* is everyone's universe. And for what he doesn't see he trusts to science. In a word, the real he confronts is entirely constructed already by common sense *chosisme*. And so most of his notations are made up of two parts of a sentence, the first of which—solid, precise and definite—conveys the object as it appears to common sense, and the second of which, joined to the other by the words 'like' or 'as', is the image properly so-called. But precisely because all the information is assembled in the first part of the sentence, the second teaches us nothing; precisely because the object is pre-constituted, the image cannot reveal its structures to us. Take the following, for example: 'A spider slides along an invisible thread, as though it were swimming in the air.'

The animal is first named; its movement is described in precise terms and, beyond mere appearances, there is even a supposition about what we cannot see, for previous experience, together with specialist studies, teaches us that spiders move about on the end of a thread. Nothing could be more positive or reassuring than this first part of the sentence. The second part, with the word 'swimming', serves, conversely, to make the strange resistance the air seems to mount against the spider very different from the resistance it mounts, for example, against the bird or the fly. Only this part is cancelled out by the previous part. Since we are *informed* that the spider is sliding on the end of a thread, since the existence of that invisible thread is revealed to us, and since we are given to understand that this is the reality and the truth, then the image remains up in the air and has no solid basis. Even before we meet it, it is exposed as a mythic translation of a mere *semblance*, if not, indeed, as something wholly unreal—in a word, a fantasy of the author. In this way, the sentence is divided into strong and weak sections, since the first term stands solidly in a social and scientific universe the author takes seriously, while the second goes up in pleasant smoke. This is the warping that threatens all Renard's images and deflects them towards the comical; the 'graciousness' that makes them so many escapes from a tedious, perfectly known reality into an entirely imaginary world that can throw no light whatever on alleged reality.

In 1892, he writes: 'Replace the existing laws with non-existent ones.' And this is what he does in each of his similes, since he puts the real law, the scientific explanation, on the one side and the law he invents on the other. He will note that, 'to faint is to drown in the open air.' He will describe as 'delightful' Saint-Pol Roux's expression, 'The trees exchange birds, as they might exchange words.' He will eventually write: 'The bushes seemed drunken with sun, tossed about as though indisposed and spewed hawthorn, a white foam', which is positively horrendous and *means nothing* because the image develops under its own impetus. Note the 'seemed', aimed at reassuring the reader and Renard himself by warning them from the outset that they will remain in the realm of pure fantasy and that bushes don't spew anything. Note, too, the clumsy juxtaposition of real and imaginary: 'hawthorn, a white foam'. Though Renard compares this flowery froth to foam, he does so after first having named it and attached it to a family, a genus and a kingdom. And, by so doing, he cancels his image, renders it unreal. This is what he thought of as poetry: it was precisely the opposite; there is poetry only when one denies preeminence to the scientific interpretation of reality and treats all systems of interpretation as absolutely equivalent. And yet, at the source of this horrendous image we can sense something like an immediate apprehension of a certain nature. There is, in fact, something nauseating in the *existence* in full sunshine of bushes that are dusty and sticky with sap. These tepid plants are already herbal infusions, and yet all the white dusts of the summer coagulate on them. This is something a Francis Ponge would, in our day, convey admirably. By contrast, Renard's attempt miscarries before he has even realized what he was wanting to do, because it is tainted at its heart. What it needed was for Renard to lose himself, for him to confront the object alone. But Renard never loses himself. Just watch him running after the red ribbon[16] and weeping with emotion when he is finally awarded it: he may well be able to escape momentarily into the imagination, but he is a man who needs the protection of science and the whole social apparatus. If, like Rimbaud, he had rejected escape, if he had taken issue directly with alleged 'reality', if he had exploded its bourgeois, scientistic frames, he would perhaps have achieved the Proustian 'immediate' or the surrealism of the *Paysan de Paris*;[17] he would perhaps have divined that 'substance' behind things that Rilke or Hofmannsthal[18] were seeking. But he didn't even know what he was looking for; and if he is at the origin of modern literature, he is so because he had a vague presentiment of a field to which he forbade himself access.

The fact is also that Renard never lived alone. He was a member of an 'elite'; he regarded himself as an *artist*. This artist notion came from the Goncourt brothers. It bears their stamp of pretentious, vulgar stupidity. It is all that remains of the *poète maudit* of the heroic age: the Art for Art's sake movement took that course. What weighs on the heads of Renard and his friends is merely a comfortable, *embourgeoisé*, white-magic curse: no longer that of the solitary wizard, but a mark of election. You are cursed if you have a particularly friable 'brain' and refined nerves. And, in fact, this *'artist'* idea isn't just the debased relic of a great religious myth—that of the poet, the *vates*.[19] It is, above all, the prism through which a small group of prosperous, cultivated bourgeois—who write—conceive and recognize themselves as the elite of the Third Republic. It may surprise us today: Jules Romains or

André Malraux would probably agree that they are artists, since it is, after all, generally accepted that there is an *art* of writing. But it doesn't seem that they view themselves from this standpoint. A more thorough-going division of labour has come about in our day—particularly since the 1914–18 war. The contemporary writer is concerned, above all, to present his readers with a complete image of the human condition. In so doing, he 'commits himself'. Today a book that doesn't involve a commitment is something we rather scorn. As for beauty, it comes as something additional, when that is possible. It is the beauty and the pleasure of art that Jules Renard puts at the forefront of his concerns. The writer of 1895 is neither a prophet, nor a damned soul, nor a fighter: he is an initiate. He stands apart from the masses less by what he does than by the pleasure he takes in doing it. It is this aesthetic delight, the product of his 'exquisite', highly-strung nerves, that makes him an exceptional creature. And Renard is angered by the thought that an old violinist can claim to feel a more intense artistic pleasure than his own circle:

> Comparison between music and literature.
> These people would have us believe that

their emotions are more complete than ours
. . . I find it hard to believe that this little
man, who is barely alive, experiences greater
delight in art than Victor Hugo or Lamartine,
who didn't like music.

So here is Renard bound hand and foot: the fact
is that, despite a number of feeble denials, he is a realist. Now, the essence of the realist is that he doesn't
act. He contemplates, since he wishes to portray reality as it is or, in other words, as it appears to an impartial witness. He has—this is his duty as a literary
man—to *neutralize* himself. He is not, he must never
be 'a part of the action'. He floats above the parties,
above classes, and by that very fact asserts himself as
bourgeois, since the specific characteristic of the
bourgeois is to deny the existence of the bourgeois
class. His contemplation is of a particular kind: it is
an intuitive delight accompanied by aesthetic emotion.
Only, since the realist is pessimistic, he sees only disorder and ugliness in the world. His mission, then, is
to transpose real objects—just as they are—into sentences of a form capable of giving him aesthetic
pleasure. The realist finds his pleasure in *writing*, not
in looking, and what enables him to appreciate the

value of the sentence he writes is the delight that sentence affords him. In this way, this nihilistic realism leads Renard, like Flaubert before him, to an entirely formal conception of beauty. The material is grim and nasty, but these elite sensibilities thrill to the phrase that can deck it out magnificently. The aim is to dress up reality. Flaubert's fine oratorical period becomes, then, Renard's little instantaneous silence. But that silence, too, aspires to be a thing of marble. And so we are back, once more, at our starting point: a fine sentence, for Renard, is the one that can be carved on a stone. Beauty is economy of thought; it is a tiny silence, carved in stone or bronze, suspended amid the great silence of Nature.

He fell silent, he did nothing. His project was to destroy himself. Trussed up and gagged by his family, his age and his milieu, his bias towards psychological analysis and his marriage, sterilized by his *Journal*, he found resources only in dreams. His images that were at first to sink themselves like claws into the real, quickly became instant daydreams, at the margin of things. But he was too afraid of getting out of his depth to think of constructing a universe beyond the world that was personal to him. He very soon came back to objects, his friends, his decoration, and his most persistent dreams—because they were the least dangerous—confined themselves to toying with the idea of a pleasant little dull adultery that he seldom had the courage to commit. Similarly, his *Journal*, which had seemed set to become an exercise in clear-sighted severity, very quickly became a lukewarm, shady corner of shame-faced complicity with himself. This is the other side to the fearful family silences of Monsieur Lepic.[20] In it he lays himself bare, though that isn't immediately evident, since the style is formally dressed. He heaps abuse on his life; realism, in its death throes, chose him to die through. And yet—whether through this determined attempt to destroy himself, this systematic fragmentation of the great Flaubertian period, or his ever-deceived presentiment of individual concreteness beyond the abstract appearances of empiricism—this moribund character attests to a kind of catastrophe that afflicted the *fin-de-siècle* writers and is, directly or indirectly, at the origin of contemporary literature.

1945

Notes

1 Jules Renard, *Journal* (16 January 1889). There is a version of this passage in *The Journal of Jules Renard* (Louise Bogan and Elizabeth Roget eds) (Portland: Tin House Books, 2008), p. 25. Since translations into English of this work are only partial and there are various French editions, many of them consisting only of extracts, all references to Renard's *Journal* are made to the date of the entry, so far as I have been able to track it down. [Trans.]

2 This is one of the most famous lines of Boileau's work *Art Poétique*, celebrating the coming of Malherbe (1555–1628) in French literature. [Trans.]

3 Renard, *Journal* (9 August 1893).

4 Ibid. (1 December 1891).

5 Jean-Louis Guez de Balzac (1597–1654): widely credited with having introduced a major reform of French prose style, particularly through his *Lettres*. [Trans.]

6 André Gide tended to refer to his early works, such as *The Immoralist* or *Strait is the Gate*, as 'monographs', by contrast with his later novels, such as *The Counterfeiters*, in which multiple points of view are adopted. [Trans.]

7   Édouard Dubus (1863–95): a French symbolist poet. [Trans.]

8   Fantec was the pet name of Renard's son Pierre-François. [Trans.]

9   Renard, *Journal* (29 February 1892).

10 Anatole France, 'Blaise Pascal et M. Joseph Bertrand', in *La Vie littéraire. Quatrième série* (Paris: Calmann-Lévy, 1892).

11 The essay mentioned was published in English as Part One of Élie Metchnikoff (Ilya Mechnikov), *The Nature of Man: Studies in Optimistic Philosophy* (New York: Putnam, 1910), pp. 1–136. [Trans.]

12 These are all novels by Zola, dating from 1877, 1885 and 1883, respectively. [Trans.]

13 The reference is to the great French historian Hippolyte Taine (1828–93). [Trans.]

14 The reference is to the poem 'Du côté de Lariboisière' by Jacques Audiberti (1899–1965), in the collection *Race des Hommes* (Paris: Gallimard, 1937). [Trans.]

15 Paul-August Arène (1843–96): a poet and critic who wrote in both French and Provençal. [Trans.]

16 A reference to the red ribbon of the Légion d'honneur, the highest decoration available to

French citizens and awarded for excellent conduct in either the civil or military spheres. [Trans.]

17 *Le Paysan de Paris* is a work by Louis Aragon, serialized initially in the *Revue Européenne* (1924–25) and published in book form in 1926. [Trans.]

18 Rainer Maria Rilke (1875–1926): born in Prague, he was one of the greatest German-language poets of the twentieth century; Hugo von Hofmannsthal (1874–1929): another of the great writers of the Austro-Hungarian empire, he was a prolific novelist, poet, librettist and essayist. [Trans.]

19 *Vates*: implied is the poet as prophet, seer or soothsayer. [Trans.]

20 The central character of Renard's most famous work, *Poil de Carotte*. [Trans.]

Cartesian Freedom

Freedom is indivisible, but it manifests itself in different ways, depending on circumstances. To all the philosophers who set themselves up as its defenders, we may ask a preliminary question: in respect of what special *situation* have you experienced your freedom? It is one thing to feel you are free in the realm of action, of social or political activity or of creation in the arts, and another to experience it in the act of understanding and discovering. A Richelieu, a Vincent de

Paul or a Corneille would have had some things to say about freedom, had they been metaphysicians, because they seized it from the one end, at a point when it manifested itself through an absolute event, through the appearance of something new, whether a poem or an institution, in a world that neither called for nor rejected it. Descartes, who is a metaphysician first and foremost, comes at matters from the other end: his primary experience wasn't one of creative freedom *ex nihilo*, but of autonomous thought which, by its own power, discovers intelligible relationships between existing essences. This is why we Frenchmen, who have been living by Cartesian freedom for three centuries, implicitly understand 'free will' as the practice of independent thought rather than the production of a creative act, and, like Alain, our philosophers in the end equate freedom with the act of judging.

This is because, in the thrill of understanding, there is always the joy of feeling ourselves responsible for the truths we discover. Whoever the master may be, a moment comes when the disciple faces the mathematical problem all on his own; if he doesn't bring his mind to grasp the relationships, if he doesn't himself produce the conjectures and schemas which apply just like a grid to the figure in question and will reveal its principal structures and if he doesn't, lastly, bring about a decisive insight, then the words remain dead signs and everything is merely learned by rote. In this way, if I examine myself, I can feel that intellection isn't the mechanical outcome of a pedagogic procedure, but originates solely in my will to lend attention, in my exertion alone, in my refusal to be distracted or to hurry and, ultimately, in the whole of my mind, to the radical exclusion of all external actors. And this is precisely Descartes's initial intuition: he understood better than anyone that the tiniest move in thought involves the whole of thought, an autonomous thought that posits itself, in each of its acts, in its full and absolute independence.

But, as we have seen, this experience of *autonomy* doesn't coincide with the experience of *productivity*. This is because thought has to have *something* to understand, objective relationships between essences, structures, a sequence: in short, a pre-established order of relationships. Thus, as the price to be paid for freedom of intellection, the path to be travelled is as rigorous as can be:

Since there is only one truth in any matter, whoever discovers it knows as much about it as can be known. For instance, a child who has been taught arithmetic and does an addition according to the rules may be assured that he has discovered all that the human mind can discover as regards the sum he is considering. Indeed, the method of following the proper order and exactly enumerating all conditions of the problem comprises everything that gives the rules of arithmetic their certainty.[1]

Everything is established in advance: the object to be discovered and the method. The child who applies his freedom to doing an addition sum by the rules doesn't enrich the universe with a new truth; he merely recommences an operation that a thousand others have performed before him and that he will never be able to take farther than they have. The attitude of the mathematician is, then, a rather striking paradox and his mind might be said to be like that of a man who, having set off down a very narrow path, where each of his steps and the very posture of his body were rigorously conditioned by the nature of the

ground and the necessities of the walking, was imbued, nonetheless, with the unshakable conviction
that he was accomplishing all these acts freely. In
short, if we start out from mathematical intellection,
how shall we reconcile the fixed, necessary nature of
essences with freedom of judgement? The problem
is even more difficult, given that, in Descartes's day,
the order of mathematical truths was regarded by all
right-thinking people as a product of divine will. And
since there was no way round that order, Spinoza preferred to sacrifice human subjectivity to it: he would
show truth developing and asserting itself under its
own impulsion *through* those incomplete individualities
that are the finite modes. Faced with the order of
essences, subjectivity can only be the mere freedom
to adhere to the truth (the way certain moral philosophers argue that one's only *right* is to do one's *duty*) or
else it is confused thinking, a mutilated truth, the
subjective character of which can be dispelled by
development and clarification. In the latter case,
man disappears and no difference remains between
thought and truth: the true is the totality of the system
of ideas. If one wants to rescue man, all that remains—since he cannot *produce* any ideas, but merely

contemplate them—is to endow him with a simple negative power, the power to say 'no' to everything that isn't the truth. And so, in the guise of a unitary doctrine, we find two rather different theories of freedom in Descartes, depending on whether he is looking at his power to understand and to judge or simply wishing to rescue man's autonomy in its confrontation with the rigorous system of ideas.

His spontaneous reaction is to assert man's responsibility towards the truth. Truth is a human affair, since I must affirm it for it to exist. Before I pass *judgement*, which is the adherence of my will and a free commitment of my being, there exist only neutral, floating ideas that are neither true nor false. Hence man is the creature through whom truth appears in the world: his task is to commit himself totally, so that the natural order of existents may become an order of truths. He must think the world, will his thought, and transform the order of being into a system of ideas. In this, from the *Meditations* onwards, he emerges as that 'ontico-ontological' being of which Heidegger will later speak. Descartes begins, then, by bestowing total intellectual responsibility upon us. Every moment, he feels the freedom of his thought in regard to the sequence of essences. And he feels his loneliness too. Heidegger has said, No one can die for me. But before him, Descartes said, No one can understand for me. In the end, you have to say yes or no—and decide what is true, alone and for the entire universe. Now, this adherence is a metaphysical, absolute act. Commitment isn't relative; we aren't speaking of an approximation that can be revisited. But just as, for Kant, the moral individual acts as legislator of the community of ends, Descartes, as scientist, decides on the laws of the world, for the 'yes' that one has eventually to pronounce before the reign of truth can come about demands the commitment of an infinite power that is given all at once: there is no way of saying 'slightly' yes or 'slightly' no. And man's 'yes' is no different from God's:

> It is only the will, or freedom of choice, which I experience within me to be so great that the idea of any greater faculty is beyond my grasp; so much so that it is above all in virtue of the will that I understand myself to bear in some way the image and likeness of God. For although God's will is incomparably greater than mine, both in virtue of the

knowledge and power that accompany it and make it more firm and efficacious, and also in virtue of its object, . . . nevertheless it does not seem any greater than mine when considered as will in the essential and strict sense.[2]

This complete freedom, precisely because it isn't a matter of degrees, clearly belongs equally to every human being. Or rather—since freedom isn't a quality among others—it is clear that every human being *is* freedom. And the famous assertion that good sense is the most widely shared thing in the world doesn't simply mean that every man has in his mind the same germs of thought, the same innate ideas, but 'goes to show that the power of judging well and distinguishing truth from falsehood, is naturally equal in all men.'[3]

A human being cannot be more of a human being than others, because freedom is similarly infinite in each one. In this sense, no one has shown the link between the spirit of science and that of democracy better than Descartes, since universal suffrage couldn't be based on anything other than this universal capacity for saying yes or no. And we can, no doubt, find many differences between human beings: one will have a sharper memory, another a broader imagination; one will grasp things more quickly and another will compass a wider field of truth. But these qualities aren't constitutive of the notion of Man: we have to see them simply as chance bodily attributes. And what alone characterizes us as human creatures is the use we freely make of these gifts. It matters little how quickly we have understood, since understanding, however it comes to us, must be total for everyone or not exist at all. If Alcibiades and the slave understand the same truth, then they are entirely alike in understanding it. Similarly, a man's situation and powers cannot increase or limit his freedom. Here, following the Stoics, Descartes made a crucial distinction between freedom and power. To be free isn't, in any way, to be able to do what one wishes, but to wish to do what one is able to:

> There is nothing that is entirely within our power except our thoughts; this is, at least, the case if one takes the word 'thought' as I do for all the operations of the soul, so that not only meditation and willing, but even the functions of seeing, hearing, determining to perform one movement rather than another

etc., inasmuch as they depend on it, are thoughts... I did not mean by this that external things are not at all in our power, but only that they are so insofar as they may follow from our thoughts, and not *absolutely* or *entirely,* because there are other powers outside of ourselves which can prevent the effects of our intentions.[4]

Thus, with variable and limited power, man has total freedom. We glimpse here the *negative* aspect of freedom. For, ultimately, if I do not have the power for a particular action, I must abstain from desiring to perform it: 'to try always to conquer myself rather than fortune; to change my desires rather than the order of the world'.[5] In short, to practise *epoche* in the field of morality. Freedom, nevertheless, in this initial conception, has a certain 'efficacity'. It is a positive, constructive freedom. It probably cannot change the quality of the movement that is in the world, but it can modify the direction of that movement:

The soul has its principal seat in the little gland in the middle of the brain, whence it radiates into all the rest of the body by the mediation of spirits, nerves, and even blood

... And the whole action of the soul consists in this: merely by willing something, it makes the little gland to which it is closely joined move in the way required to produce the effect corresponding to this volition.[6]

It is this 'efficacity', this constructiveness of human freedom that we find at the origin of the *Discourse on the Method*. For, ultimately, the Method is *invented*: '[C]ertain paths that I have happened to follow ever since my youth have led me to considerations and maxims out of which I have *formed* a method . . .'[7] Better still, each rule of the Method (except the first) is a maxim of action or invention. Doesn't the analysis prescribed by the second rule call for a free and creative judgement that produces schemas and conceives hypothetical divisions that it will verify shortly afterwards? And mustn't the order advocated in the third rule be sought and prefigured amid disorder before one submits to it? The proof is that if it doesn't actually exist, it will be invented: 'establishing an order in thought even when the objects had no natural priority one to another'.[8] And don't the enumerations of the fourth precept presuppose a power of generalization and classification specific to the human mind? In a word, the rules of the Method are on the level of Kantian schematism; they represent, all in all, very general directives for free, creative judgement. And wasn't Descartes the first, while Bacon was teaching the English to follow experimental findings, to call on physicists to precede their experiments with hypotheses? In this way, we discover first in his works a magnificent humanistic affirmation of creative freedom, which constructs the truth one piece at a time; which at every moment anticipates and prefigures the real relations between essences by producing hypotheses and schemas; which—equal for God and for man, equal in all men, absolute and infinite—forces us to assume that fearful task that is supremely *ours*: to cause a truth to exist in the world, to make the world true; and which disposes us to live with *generosity*, 'a sentiment that everyone has of his own free will, combined with the resolve never to be lacking in it'.

But the pre-established order intervenes here immediately. For a philosopher like Kant, the human mind constitutes truth; for Descartes, it merely discovers it, since God has established all the relationships that pertain between essences once and for all. Moreover, whatever path the mathematician has chosen to solve his problem, he cannot doubt the result once it has been arrived at. The man of action, contemplating his undertaking, can say: this is mine. But not the man of science. As soon as he discovers it, the truth becomes foreign to him: it belongs to everyone and to no one. He can merely register it and, if he sees the relations that make it up clearly, he doesn't even have the scope to doubt it: seized by an inner illumination that drives his entire being onward, he can only lend his adherence to the theorem that has been discovered and, hence, to the order of the world. The judgements '2 and 2 make 4' or 'I think, therefore I am' are of value only insofar as I affirm them, but I cannot help but affirm them. If I say that I don't exist, I am not even creating a fiction; I am simply bringing together words whose meanings destroy each other, just as they would if I spoke of square circles or three-sided cubes. The Cartesian will is forced into affirmation:

> For example, during these past few days I have been asking whether anything in the world exists, and I have realized that from the very fact of my raising this question it follows quite evidently that I exist. I could not but judge that something which I under-

stood so clearly was true; but this was not because I was compelled so to judge by any external force, but because a great light in the intellect was followed by a great inclination in the will . . .[9]

Descartes clearly persists in terming this irresistible adherence to what is obviously the case 'free', but this is because he lends a totally different sense to the word 'freedom' here. Adherence is free because it isn't given under any constraint external to ourselves; in other words, it isn't caused by a movement of the body or by psychological impulsion: we are not on the terrain of the passions of the soul. But if the *soul* remains independent of the body in the process of assenting to evidence, and if, in terms of the definitions in the *Treatise on the Passions*, we may call the affirmation of clearly and distinctly conceived relations an action of the thinking substance taken in its totality, then if we consider the will in relation to the understanding, these terms no longer have any meaning. For a moment ago we termed the possibility for the will itself to determine whether it said 'yes' or 'no' to the ideas conceived by the understanding 'freedom'; this meant, to put it another way, that the die was never

511

cast, the future never predictable. Whereas now, with regard to cases of obvious fact, the relation of the understanding to the will is conceived as a rigorous law, in which the clarity and distinctness of the idea play the role of determining factor where affirmation is concerned. In short, Descartes is much closer here to Spinoza and Leibniz, who define the freedom of a being by the development of its essence independently of any external action, although the moments of that development follow one upon the other with rigorous necessity. It is at this point that he goes so far as to deny the freedom of 'indifference' or, rather, to make it the lowest degree of freedom:

> For in order to be free, there is no need for me to be capable of going in each of two directions [*indifférent*]; on the contrary, the more I incline in one direction—either because I clearly understand that reasons of truth and goodness point that way, or because of a divinely produced disposition of my inmost thoughts—the freer is my choice.[10]

The second term of the alternative—'because of a divinely produced disposition of my inmost thoughts'—concerns faith in the strict sense of the term. Here, as the understanding cannot provide sufficient reason for the act of faith, the entire will is shot through with an inner, supernatural light named grace. We may perhaps be scandalized to see this autonomous, infinite freedom suddenly *affected* by divine grace and *disposed* to affirm what it does not see clearly. But is there ultimately any great difference between natural light and this supernatural light that is grace? In the latter case, it is absolutely certain that it is God who does the affirming, employing the intermediary of our will. But is this not also true in the former case? If ideas have being, they do so insofar as they come from God. Clarity and distinctness are merely the signs of the inner cohesion and absolute density of being of the idea. And if I am irresistibly inclined to affirm the idea, I am so precisely insofar as it weighs on me with all its being and absolute positivity. It is this pure, dense, flawless, full being that asserts itself within me by its own influence. Thus, since God is the source of all being and all positivity, a true judgment, which is positivity and fullness of existence, necessarily has its source not in me, who am nothing, but in Him. And we shouldn't see this theory merely as an effort to reconcile a rationalist metaphysics with

Christian theology: it expresses, in the vocabulary of the day, the awareness the scientist has always had of being pure nothingness, a mere beholder of the stubborn, eternal consistency and infinite gravity of the truth he contemplates. Admittedly, three years later in 1644 Descartes came back to the question, this time conceding the freedom of indifference:

> We are so conscious of the freedom and indifference which are in us, that there is nothing which we understand more clearly; so that the omnipotence of God should not keep us from believing it.[11]

But this is a mere precaution: the enormous success of the *Augustinus* had made him anxious and he didn't want to risk being condemned at the Sorbonne.[12] We should, rather, point out that this new conception of freedom without free will now extended to all areas of his thinking. Does he not, indeed, say to Mersenne:

> You reject what I say, namely that it is enough to judge well to act well; and yet it seems to me that the ordinary doctrine of the Schoolmen is that *Voluntas non fertur in malum, nisi quatenus ei sub aliqua ratione boni repraesentatur ab*

intellectu. [13] Hence the saying, *omnis peccans est ignorans*; with the result that, so long as the understanding never represented something to the will as good which was not, the will could not fail in its choosing.[14]

The argument is now complete: the clear vision of the Good entails the act in the same way as the distinct vision of the True entails assent. For the Good and the True are one and the same thing: namely, Being. And if Descartes can say that we are never so free as when we do Good, he is here substituting a definition of freedom by the *value* of acts—the freest act being the best, the most in keeping with the universal order—for a definition in terms of autonomy. And this accords with the logic of his doctrine: if we don't invent *our own* Good, if the Good has an *a priori*, independent existence, how could we see it and not do it?

Yet in the search for the True, as in the pursuit of Good, we find a genuine human autonomy. But only insofar as the human being is nothing. It is by his nothingness, and inasmuch as he has dealings with Nothingness, Evil and Error that man escapes God, for God, who is infinite fullness of being, cannot either conceive or govern nothingness. He has put the

positive in me: he is the author responsible for everything in me that *is*. But by my finitude and limitedness,
by my shadow side, I turn away from Him. If I retain
a freedom of indifference, I do so in relation to what
I do not know or what I know poorly, in relation to
truncated, mutilated or confused ideas. To all these
nothings, I can, as a nothing myself, say *no*: I *am able
not to* decide to act or affirm. Since the order of truths
exists outside me, what will define me as autonomy
isn't creative invention, but refusal. It is by refusing
until we can refuse no longer that we are free. Thus
methodical doubt becomes the very model of the free
act: '*Nihilominus . . . hanc in nobis libertatem esse experimur,
ut semper ab iis credendis, quae non plane certa sunt et
explorata possimus abstinere.*'[15] And elsewhere: '*Mens quae
propria libertate utens supponit ea omnia non existere, de
quarum existentia vel minimum potest dubitare.*'[16]

The reader will recognize something like a fore-
shadowing of Hegelian negativity in this power to
escape, to disengage oneself and to withdraw. All
propositions asserting something outside of our
thought are tinged with doubt; in other words, I can
bracket out all existents and I am exercising my freedom to the full when I, myself an empty nothingness,

void everything that exists. Doubt is a breaking of contact with being; through it man has the permanent possibility of extricating himself from the existing universe and suddenly contemplating it from on high as a pure succession of phantasms. It is, in this sense, the most magnificent affirmation of the reign of the human: the hypothesis of the Evil Genius shows clearly that man can escape all deceptions and traps; there is an order of truth because man is free; and even if that order didn't exist, it would be sufficient that man was free for there never to be a reign of error. This is because man, being this pure negation, this pure suspension of judgement, may, so long as he remains motionless, like someone holding his breath, withdraw at any moment from a false, fake nature; he can even withdraw from all that is nature within him: from his memory, imagination and body. He can withdraw from time itself and take refuge in the eternity of the moment: nothing reveals better than this that man isn't a 'natural' being. But at the point when he achieves this unparalleled independence, against the omnipotence of the Evil Genius, and even against God, he catches himself being pure nothingness: over against the *being* that is entirely bracketed out, all that remains is a mere *no* that has neither body nor memory, knowledge nor *personhood*. And it is this translucent rejection of everything that is itself attained in the *cogito*, as is shown by the following passage: '*Dubito ergo sum, vel, quod idem est. Cogito ergo sum.*'[17] Even though this doctrine takes its inspiration from the Stoic *epoche*, no one before Descartes had put the emphasis on the link between free will and negativity; no one had shown that freedom in no sense comes from man insofar as he is a fullness of existence among other fullnesses in a flawless world, but insofar as he *is not*, insofar as he is finite and limited. But this freedom cannot in any way be creative, since it is *nothing*. It doesn't possess the power to produce an idea, since an idea is a reality; in other words, an idea possesses a certain *being* that I cannot impart to it. Moreover, Descartes will himself limit its scope, since in his view, when being finally appears— absolute, prefect, infinitely infinite being—we cannot refuse it our adherence. We see at this point that he hasn't taken his theory of negativity to its limit, 'since truth consists in *being* and falsehood in *non-being* only'.[18] The power of refusal that is in man consists solely in rejecting the false—in short, in saying no to non-being. If we can withhold our assent from the works of the Evil Genius, this is not in any sense insofar as they *are* (i.e. insofar as, true or false, they have at least, inasmuch as they *are* our representations, a minimum of being) but insofar as they *are not*—that is to say, insofar as they refer mendaciously to objects that don't exist. If we can withdraw from the world, we can do so not inasmuch as it exists in its full, lofty majesty as an absolute affirmation, but inasmuch as it appears to us confusedly by way of our senses and we conceive it imperfectly through a number of ideas whose foundations are beyond our grasp. Thus Descartes is perpetually wavering between the identification of freedom with the negativity or negation of being—which can be described as the freedom of indifference—and the conception of free will as mere negation of the negation. In a word, he failed to conceive negativity as productive.

A strange freedom. It breaks down, ultimately, into two phases: in the first, it is negative and this represents an autonomy, but it boils down merely to refusing to assent to error or to confused thought; in the second phase, it changes meaning and is a positive adherence, but the will loses its autonomy at that point

519

and the great clarity that is in the understanding penetrates and determines the will. Is this really Descartes's intention and does the theory he constructed really correspond to the initial sense this proud, independent man had of his free will? It does not seem so. First, whether he is going back over the history of his thinking, as in the *Discourse on the Method* or encountering himself as an unshakable fact on the path of his doubt, this individualist, whose very person plays such a role in his philosophy, conceived a disembodying, de-individualizing freedom. For, if we are to believe him, the thinking subject is initially *nothing* but pure negation; that nothingness, that little quivering of air that alone escapes the enterprise of doubting and is *nothing other* than doubt itself; and when it moves out of that nothingness, it does so to become pure assumption of being. There isn't much difference between the Cartesian scientist, who is ultimately the mere *vision* of eternal truths, and the Platonic philosopher, dead to his body and dead to his life, who is nothing but the contemplation of Forms and in the end equates himself with science itself. But *the man* in Descartes had other ambitions: he viewed his life as an enterprise; he wanted science to be *done* and to be done by him, but his freedom didn't allow him to 'do' it. His wish was that people would cultivate their passions, provided they made good use of them: he glimpsed, so to speak, the paradoxical truth that there are *free* passions. Above all he prized true generosity, which he defined in the following terms:

> I believe that true Generosity, which makes a man esteem himself as highly as he can legitimately esteem himself, consists only in this: partly in his understanding that there is nothing which truly belongs to him but this free control of his volitions, and no reason why he ought to be praised or blamed except that he uses it well or badly; and partly in his feeling within himself a firm and constant resolution to use it well, that is, never to lack the volition to undertake and execute all the things he judges to be best—which is to follow virtue perfectly.[19]

Yet this freedom he invented, which can hold back desires only until the clear sight of the Good determines the resolutions of the will, cannot bear out this proud sense of being the true author of his acts and the continual initiator of free undertakings, any more than it can give him the means of inventing operational schemes in accordance with the general rules of the Method. This is because Descartes, dogmatic scientist and good Christian that he is, allows himself to be crushed by the pre-established order of eternal verities and the eternal system of values created by God. If he doesn't invent his own Good, if he doesn't construct Science, man is free in name alone. And Cartesian freedom here is like Christian freedom, which is a false freedom: Cartesian man and Christian man are both free for Evil, not for Good; they are free for Error, not for Truth. By way of the natural and supernatural light he dispenses to them, God leads them by the hand towards Knowledge and Virtue, which He has chosen for them; they simply have to let themselves be led; the entire merit in their ascension is His. But, inasmuch as they are nothingness, they escape His grasp; they are free to let go his hand along the way and plunge into the world of sin and non-being. On the other hand, of course, they can always choose to keep themselves from intellectual and moral Evil: keep and preserve themselves, suspend their judgement, suppress their desires and halt their actions in time. All that is asked of them, ultimately, isn't to thwart God's intentions. But, in the end, Error and Evil are forms of non-being: man doesn't even have the freedom to produce anything on that terrain. If he persists in his vice and his prejudices, what he creates will be a *nothing*; the universal order will not even be troubled by their obstinacy. 'The worst,' says Claudel, 'is not always certain.' In a doctrine that confuses being and perception, the only field of human initiative is the 'bastard' terrain Plato speaks of that is 'glimpsed only in dreams', the frontier between being and non-being.

However, since Descartes notifies us that God's freedom is no more entire than that of man and that the one is in the image of the other, we have a new means of investigation available to us for determining more exactly the exigencies within himself that philosophical postulates didn't enable him to satisfy. If he conceived divine freedom as very similar to his own, then it is of his own freedom, as he would have conceived it without the fetters of Catholicism and dogmatism, that he speaks when he describes God's freedom. There is an obvious phenomenon of sublimation and transposition in this. Now, Descartes's God is the freest of the Gods forged by human thought; he is the only creative God. In fact, he is subject neither to principles—even the principle of identity—nor to a sovereign Good that he would merely be bringing about. He didn't merely create existents according to rules that might be said to have imposed themselves on his will, but he created both beings and their essences, the world and the world's laws, individuals and first principles.

> Mathematical truths, which you call 'eternal', were established by God, and depend on him entirely, like all other created beings. In truth, it would be speaking of God like a Jupiter or Saturn, making him subject to Styx and the Fates, to say that these truths are independent of him. . . . [I]t is God who set up these laws in nature, as a king sets up laws in his kingdom.[20]

As for the eternal truths, I say once more that they are true or possible only because God knows them as true or possible; they are not, contrariwise, known to God as true as though they were true independently of him. And if men properly understood the sense of their words, they could never say without blasphemy that the truth about something is antecedent to God's knowledge of it; for in God knowing and willing are but one thing; so that from the very fact of his willing something, He knows it, and for this reason alone is such a thing true. We must not say, then, that if God did not exist, nevertheless these truths would be true.[21]

> [Y]ou ask what made it necessary for God to create these truths. What I say is that God was just as much free to make it untrue that all straight lines drawn from centre to circumference are equal, as he was not to create the world. And certainly these truths are not necessarily conjoined with God's essence any more than other creatures are.[22]

> Moreover that God wished some truths to be necessary does not mean that he necessarily wished them; for it is one thing to wish them to be necessary and quite another to wish it necessarily or to be the necessity of wishing it.[23]

The meaning of the Cartesian doctrine reveals itself here. Descartes understood perfectly that the concept of freedom included the demand for absolute autonomy, that a free act was an absolutely new product, the germ of which couldn't be contained in an antecedent state of the world, and that consequently freedom and creation were one and the same. God's freedom, though similar to man's, loses the negative aspect it had within its human shell; it is pure productivity; it is the extra-temporal, eternal act by which God brings a world, a 'Good', and eternal Truths into being. Henceforth, the root of all Reason is to be found in the depths of the free act; it is freedom that is the foundation of the true; the rigorous necessity that appears in the order of truths is itself subtended by the absolute contingency of a creative free will, and this dogmatic rationalist might, like Goethe, say not 'In the beginning was the Word', but 'In the beginning was the Deed.' As for the difficulty of maintaining freedom in the face of truth, he glimpsed a solution in a conception of creation that was simultaneously an intellection, as though the thing created by free decree stood, so to speak, before the freedom that keeps it in being and, in the same process, yielded itself up for comprehension. In God, will and intuition are one; the divine consciousness is both constitutive and contemplative. And, similarly, God invented Good. His perfection does not incline him to decide what is best; rather, what he has decided is, by the very effect of his deciding it, absolutely good. An absolute freedom that invents Reason and Good and has no other limits than itself and being true to itself—this is, in the end, the divine prerogative so far as Descartes is concerned. On the other hand, there is no more in this freedom than in human freedom, and he is aware, in describing the free will of his God, of merely having developed the implicit content of the idea of freedom. This is why, all things considered, human freedom isn't limited by an order of freedoms and values that might be said to offer themselves up for our assent as eternal *things*, as necessary structures of being. It is the divine will that has laid down these values and truths; it is that will that sustains them: our freedom is bounded by divine freedom only. The world is merely the creation of a freedom that preserves it indefinitely; truth is nothing unless it is willed by this infinite divine power, and unless it is taken up and confirmed by human freedom. The free man stands alone over against an absolutely free God; freedom is the ground of being, its secret dimension; in this rigorous system, it is, in the end, the profound meaning and true face of necessity.

So Descartes, in his description of divine freedom, eventually returns to, and clarifies, his initial intuition of his own freedom, which, as he said, 'is
known without proof and merely by our experience
of it'.[24] It is of little consequence to us that he was
forced by his times—and also by his starting point—
to reduce human free will to a merely negative power
to deny itself, until finally it yields and abandons itself
to divine solicitude; it is of little consequence to us
that he hypostasized in God this original, *constituent*
freedom, the infinite existence of which he grasped
by way of the *cogito* itself: the fact remains that a formidable power of divine and human affirmation runs
through his universe and sustains it. It would take two
crisis-ridden centuries—a crisis of Faith and a crisis
of Science—for humanity to take back this creative
freedom that Descartes vested in God, and for us at
last to surmise the truth, which is the essential basis
of humanism, that man is the being whose emergence
causes a world to exist. But we shall not criticize
Descartes for having vested in God what properly belongs to us; we shall, rather, admire him for having,
in an authoritarian age, laid the groundwork for
democracy, for having fully followed through the

exigencies of the idea of *autonomy* and for having understood, long before the Heidegger of *Vom Wesen des Grundes*, that the sole ground of being was freedom.[25]

Notes

1   René Descartes, 'Discourse on the Method', Part II, in *Philosophical Writings* (Elizabeth Anscombe and Peter Thomas Geach trans.) (London: Nelson's/The Open University, 1970), p. 22 (translation modified).

2   René Descartes, 'Fourth Meditation', in *Meditations on First Philosophy* (John Cottingham ed. and trans.) (Cambridge: Cambridge University Press, 1996), p. 40.

3   Descartes, 'Discourse on the Method', Part I, in *Philosophical Writings*, p. 7.

4   René Descartes, 'A***' (March 1638), in *Oeuvres et lettres* (Paris: Gallimard/NRF, 1953), pp. 1001–02.

5   Descartes, 'Discourse on the Method', Part III, in *Philosophical Writings*, p. 26.

6   René Descartes, *The Passions of the Soul* (Stephen H. Voss trans.) (Indianapolis: Hackett Publishing Company, 1989), pp. 37, 41.

7   René Descartes, 'Discourse on the Method', Part
    I, in *Philosophical Writings*, p. 8. The emphasis is
    Sartre's. [Trans.]

8   Ibid., p. 21.

9   Descartes, 'Fourth Meditation', in *Meditations on
    First Philosophy*, p. 41.

10 Ibid., p. 40 (translation modified).

11 René Descartes, *Principles of Philosophy* (Dordrecht:
    Kluwer Academic Publishers, 1984), p. 19 (trans-
    lation modified; Sartre is quoting from the French
    translation with additions and corrections by
    Descartes himself, whereas the Kluwer edition is
    based on the original Latin text [Trans.]).

12 The reference is the posthumously published *mag-
    num opus* of the Bishop of Ypres, Cornelius Otto
    Jansen, entitled *Augustinus, seu doctrina S. Augustini
    de humanae naturae sanitate, aegritudine, medicina,
    adversus Pelagianos et Massilienses* (Leuven/Louvain,
    1640). [Trans.]

13 The will does not incline towards evil, except in-
    sofar as that evil is represented by the understand-
    ing as being in some way good. [Trans.]

14 René Descartes, 'A Mersenne' (27 april 1637?), in
    Oeuvres et lettres, p. 963.

15 'We nonetheless experience in ourselves a freedom such that we can always abstain from believing those things which are not absolutely certain and established.' From René Descartes, *Principles of Philosophy*, Part 1, Section 6 (Dordrecht: Kluwer, 1991), p. 4.

16 'The mind uses its own freedom and supposes the non-existence of all the things about whose existence it can have even the slightest doubt.' From René Descartes, 'Synopsis of the following six meditations', in *Meditations on First Philosophy*, p. 9. See also René Descartes, 'Abrégé des Six Méditations suivantes', in *Oeuvres et lettres*, p. 262. [Trans.]

17 'I doubt, therefore I am or, which is the same thing, I think, therefore I am.' See René Descartes, 'La Recherche de la vérité par la lumière naturelle', in ibid., p. 898. [Trans.]

18 Letter to Clerselier, 23 April 1649.

19 Descartes, *The Passions of the Soul*, p. 104.

20 René Descartes, 'Descartes to Mersenne, 15 April 1630', in *Philosophical Writings*, p. 259.

21 René Descartes, 'Descartes to Mersenne, 6 May 1630', in ibid., pp. 260–1.

22 René Descartes, 'Descartes to Mersenne, 27 May 1630, in ibid., p. 262. The date of this letter is misprinted in the English source. [Trans.]

23 René Descartes, 'Au Père Mesland' (2 May 1644?), in *Oeuvres et lettres*, p. 1167.

24 These lines provide the heading of Section 39 of Part 1 of Descartes's *Principles of Philosophy*, which was published originally in Latin at Amsterdam in 1644 and translated into French in 1647. See Descartes, *Oeuvres et Lettres*, p. 588. [Trans.]

25 Simone Pétrement takes me to task in *Critique* for having overlooked 'freedom against oneself' in this article. The fact is that she isn't, herself, familiar with the dialectic of freedom. Freedom against *oneself* does, of course, exist. And the self is *nature* from the standpoint of the freedom that wishes to change it. But for it to be 'self', it must first be freedom. Nature is, otherwise, mere exteriority and hence radical negation of the person. Even *helpless confusion* [*le désarroi*]—in other words, the inner imitation of exteriority—and even *alienation* presuppose freedom.